To my wonderful wife,

Betty Wheeler Jeffcoat

*who has sacrificed much
that I may preach the gospel,
who is a devoted companion,
and dedicated mother in every sense
to our three daughters,
who wields a Christian influence
in public life and in private life,
who is committed to
the doctrine of Jesus Christ,
and without whose encouragement
this effort would have been more difficult,
this book is affectionately dedicated.*

The Bible and "Social" Drinking

William Dawson Jeffcoat

Publishing Designs, Inc.
Huntsville, Alabama

Publishing Designs, Inc.
P.O. Box 3241
Huntsville, Alabama 35810

All biblical references in this book are from the American
Standard Version unless otherwise indicated.

Library of Congress Cataloging-in-Publication Data

Jeffcoat, William Dawson, 1929-
The Bible and social drinking / William Dawson Jeffcoat.
p. cm.
Includes bibliographical references and index.
ISBN 0-929540-54-9 (alk. paper)
1. Drinking of alcoholic beverages—Religious aspects. 2.
Temperance—Biblical teaching. I. Title.
HV5180.J44 2006
361.8'32292—dc22
2005034093

Printed in the United States

TABLE OF CONTENTS

PART ONE
NEGATIVE ARGUMENTATION
OF THE PROBLEM

PART TWO
AFFIRMATIVE ARGUMENTATION
OF THE PROBLEM

PREFACE

Because of the multiple complex and contradictory theories within the ranks of modern society relative to ethyl alcohol, and "social" drinking in particular, virtually any discussion will arouse emotions and evoke heated disagreements. Yet the issue is of such profound significance that it must be removed from the realm of emotion and propaganda and viewed from a realistic and factual level.

This book has been designed with this purpose in mind. Not all persons, however, will agree with the views expressed. The only consideration asked, therefore, is that persons examine the arguments which have been advanced, in the light of biblical precepts and principles, and govern themselves accordingly.

ACKNOWLEGMENT

The writer gratefully acknowledges his indebtedness to brother Thomas B. Warren for his sound advice and wise counsel in suggesting the form which this book should follow. If there are any mistakes in the material, however, the writer accepts complete responsibility for the same.

This book was originally undertaken as a guided research project, and was presented in May 1978 to brother Warren in Harding Graduate School of Religion in Memphis, Tennessee, as a requirement in Philosophy of Religion and Apologetics. Since the culmination of that work, however, the writer has considerably expanded the material to that of the present length.

"Wine is a mocker,
strong drink a brawler;
and whosoever erreth thereby is not wise."

(Proverbs 20:1)

PRELIMINARY CONSIDERATIONS

Statement of the Problem

The problem to be discussed in this book is whether or not the Bible, the word of God, sanctions "social" drinking or "moderate" non-medicinal consumption of alcoholic beverages.[1] This subject has evoked frequent discussions and differences of opinion through the years. The view is held by many persons that such activities constitute matters of mere personal preference. It is claimed that it is neither enjoined nor prohibited in the Bible and that, therefore, it is without inherent moral quality and may be innocently engaged in without fear of wrongdoing.

The theory has been advanced that Jesus made and imbibed alcoholic beverages. His enemies have insisted upon it, that they might reflect disgrace upon His character and discredit upon His cause. Those who imbibe such beverages have affirmed it, that, under the protection of Jesus' example, they might escape condemnation. Some of His most sincere and conscientious advocates have felt themselves compelled to admit the charge, and, without pleading His practice as a rule to follow, have attempted His defense. Others, many of whom perhaps are no less sincere or conscientious, have claimed that no defense is necessary, but that Jesus' example as a "moderate" imbiber may be imitated.

The charge that the Bible sanctions such views is false. In the purview of this book evidence shall be introduced to refute the claims and establish

---

1. Such terms as "social" drinking, "moderate," and "moderation," are placed within quotation marks because the writer views them as inappropriate in regard to the issue.

the fact that the imbibing of ethyl alcohol as a beverage in any form and to any degree is sinful. Often such abstention is referred to as total abstinence. It should be observed however that the adjective "total" in the phrase "total abstinence" is a superfluous term. Since abstinence or abstention involves doing without, giving up or refraining, to so do is to act entirely, wholly, completely or totally.

Importance of the Problem

Laws of God

The problem is important because the consumption of alcoholic beverages is contrary to the laws of God, which are revealed in the Bible. Although the modern world is rapidly casting aside all restraints and rejecting the righteous principles of God, the Bible provides ample proof that His laws cannot be rejected without punishment. Acts are morally right if they are in agreement with the laws of God, and they are morally wrong if they are contrary to or inconsistent with His laws. God imposes certain moral restrictions on all accountable person, and, in order to be righteous, they must obey His laws. The laws of God, which inhibit, also protect humanity, and without rational thinking there can be no respect for such laws. Persons under the influence of alcoholic beverages render themselves incapable of rational thinking. The significance of the problem therefore can be seen from the fact that such persons render themselves incapable of having respect for the laws of God. Although they violated His laws in taking the first drink, they continue to so do in willfully rendering themselves incapable of having respect for His laws.

Effects Upon Society

The problem is important because of its effects upon society. The true import may be discerned by a careful analysis of the physical, social, and economic problems of extreme proportions which have resulted from the consumption of alcoholic beverages. Although such consumption has caused multiple problems in the United Sates since its beginning, there have been notable proliferations in the last half century. Formerly, most imbibing took place in saloons or taverns and not in the home. Imbibing in any form and to any degree before the general public was uncommon. With the aid of skillful and subtle advertising by the alcoholic beverage industry, however, this has changed. In fact, our ultra-permissive society has largely accepted "social" drinking as a normal way of life. The 1974 Gallup survey of adults in the United States, eighteen and older, indicates that 68 percent imbibe alcoholic beverages.[1] This represents an increase of 6 percent from their previous survey in 1969.

In 1974, Dr. Morris E. Chafetz, chairman of a government task force investigating alcohol and health, stated, "Most Americans drink. Drinking is learned mostly at home or from adolescent peers. Being a drinker, rather than an abstainer, is thus an American norm."[2]

Definitions and Classifications of the Problem

Definitions

Alcohol

The physiologically active ingredient of intoxicating beverages is, of course, alcohol. Although a large quantity of industrial alcohol is now manufactured synthetically from various petroleum products, that which is in all alcoholic beverages is made by fermentation of sugar with yeast.

The term is derived from an Arabic word, *kuhl* or *kuhol,* which is indicative of a fine powder. In early usage the term was often descriptive of that which was used as a cosmetic for darkening the eyelids. Later the term came to mean "essence." A physician and alchemist from Switzerland, Paracelsus,[3] used the term to refer to the essence of wine, or *alcool vini.* The Latin term *vini,* for wine, was dropped in the early nineteenth century with the term being used to designate wine spirits.

There are numerous misconceptions relative to the agents and effect of alcoholic beverages. The term "alcohol" is applied by chemists to a group of liquids which contain the elements carbon, hydrogen, and oxygen combined in a way which differentiates them from other substances containing these same elements. There are many kinds of alcohol

---

1. "The Rising Number of Drinkers," *Washington Post,* 10 June 1974, p. B2.
2. *Second Special Report to the U.S. Congress on Alcohol and Health,* by Morris E. Chafetz, Chairman (Washington, D.C.: Government Printing Office, 1974), p. 1.
3. A.D. 1493–1541.

including amyl, butyl, ethyl, methyl, and propyl, some of which are classified by various types.[1] Ethyl alcohol, the main agent in alcoholic beverages, is often referred to as grain alcohol or ethanol.

Methyl alcohol or methanol, most frequently referred to as wood alcohol, and which is used as a solvent and in automotive antifreeze, is also used. As a violent poison, it has often led to blindness or death when used as an ingredient in illicit liquor.[2]

The federal government classifies ethyl alcohol as a drug,[3] and Dr. Frank Overton refers to it as a "narcotic drug."[4] Scientists classify drugs as (1) sedatives, (2) analgesics, and (3) anesthetics. Ethyl alcohol can act as a sedative in small amounts, and as an analgesic in even smaller quantities, with its most characteristic effect being that of an anesthetic.[5]

In defining ethyl alcohol and its action, Raymond G. McCarthy states,

> Alcohol is classified pharmacologically as an anesthetic. The predominant characteristic of an anesthetic is a progressive descending depression of the central nervous system. In varying dosages, alcohol may act as an analgesic, a soporific, as anesthetic, a narcotic, or a hypnotic.[6]

It is the main drug affect of this most active element which leads persons to imbibe such beverages.[7] According to a leading authority, persons do not drink in order to produce an impairment in cortical

1. There are eight types of amyl alcohol, four types of butyl alcohol or butanol, and two types of propyl alcohol.

2. *Encyclopaedia Britannica,* 1959 ed., s.v. "Methyl Alcohol," by Donald Guyer Zink, p. 362.

3. *Alcohol: Some Questions and Answers* (Washington, D.C.: Government Printing Office, 1981), p. 3.

4. Frank Overton, *Applied Physiology Including the Effects of Alcohol and Narcotics* (New York: American Book Co., n.d.), p. 140.

5. John S. Sinacore, *Health, a Quality of Life,* 2nd ed. (New York: Macmillan Co., 1974), p. 323.

6. Raymond Gerald McCarthy, ed. *Drinking and Intoxication* (Glencoe, Illinois: Free Press, 1959), p. 26.

7. Raymond Gerald McCarthy and Edgar M. Douglass, *Alcohol and Social Responsibility: A New Educational Approach* (New York: Thomas Y. Crowell Co., 1949), p. 88

function or to reduce their critical faculty; they drink in order to feel differently.[1]

Although ethyl alcohol is the chief agent in producing intoxication, persons do not imbibe pure ethyl alcohol. It is always consumed, however, as an agent in wine, brewed beverages, or distilled spirits. The other elements which are present in, or added to, alcoholic beverages contribute only flavor, aroma, and color to a major degree. The effects of impurities or other contents are of far less importance than the effects of ethyl alcohol which is always present.

Poison

The dominant action of ethyl alcohol when brought into contact with the tissues of the human body is similar to that of other substances which because of their power to injure are referred to as poisons. *Poison* is defined as "a substance that through its chemical action usually kills, injures, or impairs an organism; something destructive or harmful."[2] Professor of Chemistry, W. Lee Lewis said,

> Toxic means poison, and to intoxicate means to poison. An intoxi-
> cating drink is a poisonous drink. Therefore, when a man is (or
> was) intoxicated he is (or was) poisoned. Not all persons die who
> are poisoned as it depends upon the extent of the intoxication.
> Some poisons are instantly fatal, others slower, and still others
> only cumulatively so.[3]

According to Drs. W. H. Willcox and John Glaister, poisons may be classified in various ways, involving their chemical composition, their action on the body, and their physical characters. Included among these

---

1. P. Schilder, *Psychoanalysis, Man and Society* (New York: Norton, 1951), n.p., quoted in Edith S. Lisansky, "The Psychological Effects of Alcohol," in *Alcohol Education for Classroom and Community*, ed. Raymond Gerald McCarthy (New York: McGraw-Hill Book Co., 1964), p. 116.

2. "Poison," in *Webster's New Collegiate Dictionary*, ed. Henry Bosley Woolf (Springfield, Mass.: G. and C. Merriam Co., 1973), p. 888.

3. Emma L. Benedict Transeau, *Effects of Alcoholic Drinks* (Boston: Scientific Temperance Federation, 1938), p. 3.

are irritant poisons, gaseous poisons, corrosive poisons, and systemic poisons, the latter of which includes alcohol.[1]

Drs. Maurice Victor and Raymond D. Adams have stated that distilled spirits contain enanthic ethers, which give the flavor but have no important pharmacologic properties, and impurities such as amyl alcohol (fusel oil) and acetaldehyde, which act like alcohol but are more toxic.[2] Professor John J. Abel, after an exhaustive study of all the reported impurities found in alcoholic beverages at the time of his investigation summarized his results by stating, "Ethyl alcohol alone is poisonous enough to account for all of the evils of alcoholism."[3]

Classifications

For a better understanding of alcoholic beverages it is necessary to know the forms in which ethyl alcohol is used. Such beverages are usually classified according to the materials from which they are made and the processes by which they are prepared. The two basic classes are (1) fermented and (2) distilled.

Fermented

Most of the alcohol employed today is made by the process of fermentation. Alcohol by this means results only when some fruit, vegetable, cereal, or grain juice spoils, decays, or rots. Alcohol can never be produced when the substance is in a wholesome condition. Scientists have discovered that fruit or vegetable juices which contain sugar, or

---

1. *Encyclopaedia Britannica,* 1959 ed., s.v. "Poison," by William Henry Wilcox and John Glaister, pp. 119–20. Dr. Wilcox was lecturer on Chemical Pathology and on Forensic Medicine in St. Mary's Hospital in London, England, for thirty-five years. Dr. Glaister is Regius Professor of Forensic Medicine, in the University of Glasgow, in Glasgow, Scotland.

2. Maurice Victor and Raymond D. Adams, "Alcohol," in *Harrison's Principles of Internal Medicine,* eds. Maxwell M. Wintrobe et al. (New York: McGraw-Hill Book Co., 1970), p. 668. Dr. Victor is Professor of Neurology, Western Reserve University School of Medicine; Chief, Neurology Service, Cleveland Metropolitan General Hospital. Dr. Adams is Bullard Professor of Neuropathology, Harvard Medical School; Chief of Neurology Service and Neuropathologist, Massachusetts General Hospital.

3. Emma L. Benedict Transeau, p. 17, quoting John J. Abel, *Physiological Aspects of the Liquor Problem,* vol. 2.

starch which changes to sugar when exposed to the air at a temperature of from forty-five degrees to seventy-five degrees Fahrenheit, practically always results in alcoholic fermentation.[1] Such fermentation is referred to as vinous fermentation.

Other kinds of fermentation or decomposition are caused by other germs; for example, sour milk is lactic acid fermentation; vinegar is acetic acid fermentation; mold on bread or cheese indicates a kind of putrefaction called fermentation.

The fermented beverages are subdivided according to the material used, into two principal kinds: (1) Those obtained from plant and fruit juices, the chief of which are wine and cider, and (2) those obtained from grain, the chief of which are beer and ale. As the grains have to be put through a process of malting before a fermentable liquid can be obtained, the resulting beverages are referred to as malt liquors.

Beverages from Plant and Fruit Juices

Vinous liquors or wines are made by the fermentation of the sugar in fruits, which produces alcohol and carbonic gas. Therefore the amount of alcohol produced by vinous fermentation depends chiefly upon the amount of sugar in the liquid allowed to ferment. The fresh juice of ripe grapes, for example, contains 15 to 30 percent sugar, which is made up or composed of about equal parts of glucose and fructose. If enough is present, the alcoholic strength may reach 12 to 14 percent. Wines stronger than 12 or 14 percent have been fortified by the addition of distilled liquors. In this regard, Wayne E. Oates stated,

> The maximum amount of alcohol content is not much over 13 percent through the process of fermentation. However, wines may be "fortified" and thus contain more alcohol.[2]

Such additions increase the alcohol content of some wines, such as sherry, up to the level of 20 percent, and others to as much as 23 percent. It is

---

1. The starting material, which varies, may be molasses or starchy materials such as corn, wheat, or potato mashes. Since starch is not attacked directly by yeast it is necessary first to convert the starch to sugar by cooking under pressure, followed by the use of enzymes, which break down proteins and starches. Yeast is added after which fermentation takes place.

2. Wayne E. Oates, *Alcohol In and Out of the Church* (Nashville: Broadman Press, 1966), p. 1.

quite correct to observe that champagne, for instance, is more intoxicating than numerous other wines.

Although wine by comparison is not as potent as is straight whiskey, it is certainly not as innocuous as some persons suppose. In fact, common table wine is approximately two to three times as potent as beer, while fortified wine is much stronger. In comparison, it represents virtually half as much ethyl alcohol as the same quantity of straight whiskey.

Cider is made by the same process. The term is also applied to un-fermented juice, but when so used it is usually referred to as sweet cider. Often the term "hard cider" is employed for fermented juice, which is intoxicating. Wild yeast cells, which are in the air or which were on the surface of apples before they were crushed, act on the sugar of the juice by turning it into alcohol and carbonic gas. Alcohol thus formed is the same kind of alcohol as that in wine or other intoxicating beverages. The percentage of alcohol content depends upon the amount of sugar in the juice. If the process of fermentation is allowed to reach its limit, the cider will finally contain from 8 to 10 percent alcohol. The alcohol in hard cider has the same power to impair mental functions, to weaken self-control, and to lead to an increasing desire for more as has the alcohol in wine, beer, or whiskey.

Beverages from Grain

The presence of alcohol in beer and other malt liquors is also because of yeast, but the cultivated yeast used in brewing belongs to a slightly different species from that of the wild yeasts which produce wine and cider. Malt liquors are made by extracting starch from grains and vegetables, and malting them to change the starch to sugar, which is then fermented. The proportion of alcohol in fermented malt liquors varies from 3.5 percent in light beer to 9 percent in strong ale. There are excep-tions however. A beer known as E-K-U 28 was imported into the United States from West Germany in 1980. Purported to be the strongest beer in the world, with an alcoholic content of 13.2 percent, persons have been known to have passed out after the consumption of three bottles.[1]

Although ethyl alcohol is the principal intoxicating agent in beer, it is not the only one. Beer, in fact, contains a major property that is not found in various other alcoholic beverages. Hops, which are used in the

1. "Parade," *Nashville, The Tennessean,* 11 October 1981, p. 7.

brewing process, and which are derived from the same plant family as marijuana, have a part. The active agent in hops is a fine powder called lupulin, which dulls the senses in small does and causes stupor or coma in larger amounts. In this sense it operates as a narcotic which is a medical term for any substance or class of drugs which induce sleep and stupor and relieve pain; opiates, anesthetics, and others are included. Some pharmacologists include barbiturates, although they do not relieve pain. From a legal viewpoint, opium, its alkaloids and derivatives are included; the cocoa leaf and its principal derivative, cocaine, and the plant *cannabis sativa* L., otherwise known as "marijuana."[1]

A narcotic is also scientifically defined as

> a substance which when swallowed, inhaled, or injected into the system induces drowsiness, sleep, stupefaction, or insensibility, according to its strength and the amount taken.[2]

Pathologically speaking, narcosis is, "the production of a narcotic state; the operation or effects of narcotics upon the system; a state of insensibility."[3] Former Associate Biochemist, in the United States Department of Agriculture, Frank Rabak, indicates that lupulin, "a sticky, yellowish, granular powder," is from the standpoint of brewing,

> the most important substance because it contains the resins and volatile oil which imparts the characteristic bitter taste and aroma to beer.[4]

It is additionally said that from a botanical standpoint, lupulin is "the resinous yellow powder found under the scales of the calyx of the hop," while chemically speaking, it is "the bitter principle obtained from this powder."[5] Two lupulic acids, humulone and lupulone, come from lupulin. One of these, humulone, has virtually the same chemical formula as cannabinol, the active principle of marijuana. A. H. Wright, Emeritus

1. Helen H. Nowlis, *Drugs on the College Campus* (Garden City, New York: Anchor Books, 1969), p. 127. See also *Family Health Guide and Medical Encyclopedia*, 1970 ed., s.v. "Narcotic," p. 742.
2. "Narcotic," in *Oxford Universal Dictionary on Historical Principles*, 3rd ed., C. T. Onions (Oxford: Clarendon Press, 1944), p. 1309.
3. Ibid., "Narcosis," p. 1309.
4. *Encyclopaedia Britannica*, 1959 ed., s.v. "Hop," by Frank Rabak, pp. 734–35.
5. "Lupulin," in *Oxford Universal Dictionary on Historical Principles*, p. 1178.

Professor of Agronomy in the University of Wisconsin, indicates that cannabinol is a narcotic.[1] Geraniol, a toxic chemical substance which comes from the hop oil in lupulin, is used chiefly in perfumes and soap.[2] In his work in regard to the effect of additives, Dr. Frank Overton also states that beer usually contains one or more chemical additives not only injurious but actually poisonous to the body.[3] These include sodium hydrosulphite which is extensively employed in the dyeing of vat colors; gum arabic, a natural resin which is produced from sticky secretions from trees, and is used in the manufacture of adhesives;[4] papain or papayotin, from the milky juice of papaya fruit, and an enzyme which greatly resembles pepsin in its digestive action,[5] along with cobalt and tannic acid.

Although some persons feel that beer is a relatively harmless beverage, it is a well known fact that persons who drink beer compose a large percentage of alcoholics in various hospitals and clinics. It is equally true that all alcoholic beverages have primarily the same effects on the human body, with the only important difference being the amount of alcohol they contain. Any two beverages containing the same quantity of alcohol will produce virtually the same effect.

Distilled

The distillation of liquor increases alcohol content. Distillation is the process by which one part of a liquid is separated from another part, or one liquid is separated from another. The separation is caused by boiling and condensing the resulting vapor. Alcohol which is mixed with water will turn to vapor more rapidly than will the water because alcohol boils at a lower temperature than does water. When the vapor is again condensed, the liquid will contain a larger proportion of alcohol than the liquid in the container. It is possible to separate some of the water from most alcohol by the process of distillation, although propyl alcohol

---

1. *Encyclopaedia Britannica,* 1959 ed., s.v. "Hemp," by A. H. Wright, p. 422.

2. "Geraniol," in *Webster's New Collegiate Dictionary,* p. 482. See also *Encyclopaedia Britannica,* 1959 ed., s.v. "Perfumes," by William A. Poucher, p. 505.

3. Frank Overton, p. 43.

4. *Encyclopaedia Britannica,* 1959 ed., s.v. "Resins," by Edward L. Kropa, p. 210A.

5. Ibid., s.v. "Papaya," by William Popenoe, p. 229.

which occurs in fusel oil, an agent in distilled liquors, cannot be separated from water by distillation.[1]

Whiskey, rum, brandy, and gin are so made, and usually carry an alcohol content of 47 to 54 percent. Whiskey is made from distilled malt liquors; rum is made from fermented molasses or sugar cane juice; brandy is made by distillation from fermented fruit juices; gin is made from roots and herbs which have been treated with alcohol.

In regard to ruin, the type of the compound formed by the reaction between acid and alcohol and other secondary components differ according to the numerous modifications and the method of manufacture. Raw materials may vary from fresh cane juice, to molasses, to even the soured scum and washings, as well as the residue remaining in the still from a prior distillation. According to a noted English chemist, John George Noel Gaskin, "rums may contain from 43 percent to 79 percent by volume of ethyl alcohol at importation."[2]

There is thus a great difference between alcoholic beverages of the twentieth century and wines of the first century. Modern alcoholic beverages are far more potent than were the wines of the first century. In fact, not all wines of the first century were intoxicating, and those which were had not been fortified by additional alcohol.

Limitations and Presuppositions of the Problem

Limitations

The writer does not propose to explicate in this book every aspect of "social" drinking, including every refutation which might be advanced. It shall be limited to the introduction and elucidation of prime negative and affirmative arguments.

The word "social" in connection with drinking is used in the sense of imbibing non-medicinally light or small amounts of mind-altering or intoxicating alcoholic drinks as beverages. Thus, fermented wine for medicinal purposes or for the Lord's Supper is not under consideration.[3]

---

1. Ibid., s.v. "Propyl Alcohols," p. 591.

2. Ibid., s.v. "Rum," by John George Noel Gaskin, p. 635.

3. Excellent statements relative to wine in the Lord's supper were written by Henry Leo Boles, "The Kind of Wine in the Lord's Supper," *Gospel Advocate* 110 (17 October 1968): 664; J. W. Roberts, "What Kind of Element in the Cup on the Lord's Day, Fermented or Unfermented?" *Firm Foundation* 81 (18 August 1964):524, 532; and Guy N. Woods, *Questions and Answers Open Forum Freed-Hardeman College Lectures* (Nashville: Williams Printing Co., 1976), p. 362.

Although the writer neither believes that the Bible condemns its use nor requires such, neither is included in the term "beverage."

Presuppositions

Presuppositions in this book include the views that (1) God exists as a rational being, and is infinite in all His attributes; (2) God created man in His image, exhibited an interest in man, and revealed His will to man; (3) man, who is lost because of sin, and as a rational being, is held accountable to the will of God; (4) God's will is truth without which man cannot be saved; (5) God's will is revealed in the Bible, which is inspired of God, essential, complete, inerrant, perpetually relevant, all-sufficient, and authoritative; (6) God will allow no additions to the Bible, no subtractions from it, and no modifications or perversions of it; (7) God authorizes through the Bible by direct statement, approved account of action, and by implication; (8) God has made it possible to ascertain that which is authorized by the Bible; (9) God has decreed a final judgment of man, with the Bible forming the basis of that judgment; and, (10) those who obey God will be saved in heaven, and those who disobey God will be lost in hell.

Methodology of the Problem

In the remainder of this book it will be shown that it is contrary to the will of God to imbibe ethyl alcohol as a beverage in any form and to any degree. The material will be presented in two parts. Part One, comprising negative argumentation of the problem, will consist of theories in favor of "social" drinking, followed by their refutation. Part Two, dealing with affirmative argumentation of the problem, will consist of arguments in opposition to "social" drinking, followed by Concluding Observations.

Part One will consist of two chapters involving major negative arguments and miscellaneous negative arguments. Part Two will contain two chapters discussing major affirmative arguments and miscellaneous affirmative arguments. Concluding Observations will contain graphic illustrations of the harmful effect of "social" drinking, and a plea for Christian concern for the will of God in this respect.

PART ONE

NEGATIVE ARGUMENTATION OF THE PROBLEM

1

Major Negative Arguments

Definition of Wine Argument

This argument[1] involves the claim that in biblical times the term "wine," without exception, indicated a fermented and thus intoxicating liquid.[2] By virtue of this view, it is further claimed that several passages in the Bible sanction "social" drinking. Such reasoning is without merit, as shall be proved by the presentation of external and internal evidence.

External Evidence

External evidence, which is defined as evidence gathered from outside the Bible, comes from both Roman and Greek writers of antiquity. These

---

1. It should be observed that the term "argument" logically described, involves a coherent reason or series of reasons given in proof or rebuttal of something. It refers to the basic unit of reasoning and is defined as a unit of discourse in which beliefs are supported by *reasons*. It therefore simply involves the action of *proving* something to indeed be the case, or true. In an argument the proposition or propositions that form the evidence for the inference are called the premise or premises, and the proposition to which the inference is made is called the conclusion. The person who presents the argument must be claiming that if certain things (the premises) are true, then, something else, (the conclusion) should be also true, and, he must be claiming that the premises are indeed true. There is an actual argument *when* and *only when* both these claims are present. In the framework of logic the law of rationality requires that persons draw *only* such conclusions as may be warranted by the *evidence*. On the contrary, an assertion is merely a statement with *no evidence* presented from which a conclusion may be warranted.

2. "Wine," in *People's Bible Encyclopedia*, ed. Charles Randall Barnes (New York: Eaton and Maine, 1900), pp. 1176–77; Horace Bumstead, "The Biblical Sanction for Wine," *Bibliotheca Sacra* 38 (January 1881):115.

include Aristotle, Athenaeus, and Pliny, each of whom testify to the fact that unfermented wine existed in antiquity.[1]

In an attempt to break the force of such evidence, the objection is made that it is only in a comparative sense, and not in an absolute sense, that the testimony of such writers as to the unintoxicating nature of various wines should be accepted.

It should be noted, however, that the much more potent fortified wines and distilled spirits of the twentieth century were unknown until relatively modern times.[2] The objection therefore is without validity.

The Greek term *oinos,* which is rendered "wine," has been employed by ancient secular writers in several ways. (1) Anacreon, who wrote in 500 B.C., said, "Only males tread the grapes, setting free the wine *(oinos)."* (2) Varro spoke of "gathering wine." (3) Cato referred to "hanging wine," or grapes on the vine. (4) Columella spoke of "unintoxicating wine." (5) Celsus said, "Gather the berries of the myrtle, and from them express wine." (6) Ovid said, "And scarce can the grapes contain the wine they have within." (7) Ibycus stated, "And newborn clusters teem with wine, beneath the shadowy foliage of the vine."[3] It can be seen, therefore, that during this early period, juice in the grape was referred to as wine. In fact, the Hebrew term *yayin* and the Greek term *oinos* were, as Professor Sir Richard Jebb said of *oinos,* general terms in those early days.

Internal Evidence

Internal evidence, which is defined as evidence gathered from inside the Bible, may be supplied in three ways. The Bible discriminates (1) by the contrasting ways in which it refers to wine, (2) by the terms which are employed to designate wine, and (3) by various descriptive phrases which are used.[4]

Contrasts

In one class of passages wine is commended, and in another class it is condemned, in each ease in the strongest and most unmistakable language.

---

1. Aristotle, *Meteorologica* 4.9; Athenaeus, *Deipnosophistae* 1. 27; 5199; Pliny, *Natural History* 14.11.
2. For the history of distillation see pp. 156–158.
3. Ferrar Fenton, "The Bible and Wine," in *Paul's Letters to Timothy and Titus,* ed. Don De Welt (Joplin, Missouri: College Press, 1961), p. 327.
4. All biblical references in this book are from the American Standard Version unless otherwise indicated.

It is contrasted as (1) a blessing and cursing,[1] (2) sanctioned and condemned,[2] (3) that which cheereth and is a mocker,[3] (4) an emblem of spiritual blessing and of divine wrath,[4] and (5) that which is allowed and interdicted.[5]

The natural inference is, therefore, that two distinct or different substances are designated by these totally diverse characterizations.

Terms

There are twenty-four or more distinct terms in the Bible, characterized by twenty-eight renderings, which either directly or indirectly have reference to wine.[6]

Old Testament

The Old Testament employs nineteen or more of these terms, with twenty-seven renderings.[7] The definition and classification of each term will be discussed with special emphasis being given to the three most prominent terms: *yayin, tirosh,* and *shekar.*

Yayin. The term is employed 136 times, with four renderings. It is rendered "wine" 132 times, "wineskins" two times, and "wine cellars" and "banqueting" one time each.

Yayin is the first and most frequently used word for wine in the Old Testament, appearing in the earliest and in the latest history, from the time of Noah[8] to that of Nehemiah.[9] It is a generic term for "all sorts of wine,"[10] new or old, unfermented or fermented. Although usually fermented, *yayin* was not always intoxicating, and in most instances in

---

1. Ps. 104:15; Hab. 2:15.

2. Jn. 2:1–11; Prov. 4:17.

3. Judg. 9:13; Prov. 20:1.

4. Is. 55:1; Ps. 60:3.

5. Deut. 7:13; Prov. 23:29–32.

6. For a complete listing of each term, see Appendix A, Table One, pp. 196–199.

7. Friedrich Heinrich Wilhelm Gesenius, *Hebrew and Chaldee Lexicon of the Old Testament Scriptures,* trans. Samuel Prideau Tregelles (np., 1857; reprint ed., Grand Rapids: Wm. B. Eerdmans Publishing Co., 1957), pp. 347, 847, 863.

8. Gen. 9:21.

9. Neh. 13:15.

10. Neh. 5:18.

which it was used as a beverage, no doubt was but slightly alcoholic in content.[1]

The term occurs twenty-one times in connection with *shekar*. Its root was probably *yavan* or *yanah,* the primary idea of both being that of turbidness, or boiling up, which is characteristic of grape juice as it passes into the vat.[2]

In some instances *yayin* specifies the blood of the grape which has been freshly expressed.[3] By a natural extension of meaning, it gradually came to designate wine in all its subsequent stages, and even applied retrospectively to wine still confined in the cluster.[4]

In Numbers 6:4 *yayin* refers to the vine. In Deuteronomy 28:39 it is ranked among things to be sucked, gathered, or eaten. In Isaiah 16:10 it is used for the grapes to be trodden, while in Isaiah 55:1 it likely signifies thick grape syrup or honey.[5] In Proverbs 9:2–5 *yayin* refers to a boiled wine, or syrup, the thickness of which rendered it necessary to mix with water before consumption.[6] In several instances in the Septuagint,[7] *yayin* is rendered *gleukos.*[8] Denoting what the Greeks specified as *gleukos* or sweet wine, the term is employed by Flavius Josephus in referring to the grape juice expressed into Pharaoh's cup, in Genesis 40:11.[9] In reference to the contents of Pharaoh's cup, the highly respected biblical commentator, Adam Clarke, stated,

---

1. "Wine," in *Unger's Bible Dictionary*, ed. Merrill Frederick Unger (Chicago: Moody Press, 1957), p. 1168; and "Wine," in *Fausset's Bible Dictionary,* ed. Andrew Robert Fausset (Grand Rapids: Zondervan Publishing House, 1975), p. 722.

2. Frederick R. Lees, "Wine," in *Popular and Critical Bible Encyclopedia and Scriptural Dictionary,* ed. Samuel Fallows (Chicago: Howard Severance Co., 1914), 3:1724.

3. Gen. 49:11.

4. Jer. 40:10.

5. cf. Is. 7:22.

6. Frederick R. Lees, "Wine," in *Popular and Critical Bible Encyclopedia and Scriptural Dictionary,* 3:1725.

7. It is thought that the Septuagint, which is the Greek translation of the Hebrew Old Testament, was completed by some 70 or 72 scholars at Alexandria, Egypt, between 284–247 B.C. Most of the Septuagint, some of which was cited by Christ on occasion, has been preserved in copies of the original.

8. G. Abbott-Smith, *A Manual Greek Lexicon of the New Testament* (New York: Charles Scribner's Sons, 1921), p. 93.

9. Frederick R. Lees, "Wine," in *Popular and Critical Bible Encyclopedia and Scriptural Dictionary,* 3:1725.

From this we find that wine anciently was the mere expressed juice of the grape, without fermentation. The *saky,* or cup-bearer, took the bunch, pressed the juice into the cup, and instantly delivered it into the hands of his master. This was anciently the *yayin* of the Hebrews, the *oinos* of the Greeks, and the *mustum* of the ancient Latins.[1]

Yayin is also connected with the Latin term *vinum* as well as with *oinos,* in which sense it is usually rendered in the Septuagint. From the foregoing description, therefore, it is observed that *yayin* does not always denote a fermented liquid with resulting intoxicating properties.

Tirosh. The term is employed thirty-eight times, with two renderings. It is rendered "new wine" thirty-six times and "vintage" two times.

Derived from the verb *yarash,* it means "to seize, or inherit, thus to possess."[2] It is used of the vine, the fruit of the vineyard in its natural condition, as a possession. It is found "in the cluster," [3] gathered,[4] put into "store-houses," [5] trodden,[6] and that which shall "overflow" from the vats.[7] It is spoken of as being poured out or drunk in only one instance.[8] It is referred to as the most general term for vintage fruit or the produce of the field or what would most likely be known today as the orchard.[9] Three words are employed in the Septuagint in regard to *tirosh,* namely, *oinos, rox,* and *methusma.*

In thirty instances *tirosh* is mentioned in connection with corn or *dagan;* in twenty-one instances it occurs with oil or *yitzhar.* Thus, the three terms form a triad of blessings: corn-fruit or the produce of the

1. Adam Clarke, *Genesis to Deuteronomy,* A Commentary and Critical Notes, vol. 1 (New York: T. Mason and G. Lane, 1837; reprint ed. New York: Abingdon Press, n.d.), p. 231.

2. Frederick R. Lees, "Wine," in *A Cyclopedia of Biblical Literature,* ed. John Kitto (Edinburgh: Adam and Charles Black, n.d.), 2:953.

3. Is. 65:8.

4. Deut. 11:14.

5. 2 Chron. 32:28.

6. Mic. 6:15.

7. Joel 2:24; Prov. 3:10.

8. Is. 62:9.

9. "Wine," in *Fausset's Bible Dictionary,* p. 722; and Frederick R. Lees, "Wine," in *Popular and Critical Bible Encyclopedia and Scriptural Dictionary,* 3:1726.

field, vineyard, and orchard. A Hebrew parallelism, which illustrates the position that *tirosh* was used for grapes in their natural state, is found in Micah 6:15.

Thou shalt sow, but shalt not reap; thou shalt tread the olives, but shalt not anoint thee with oil; and the vintage, but shalt not drink the wine.

"Vintage" and "wine" in the text come from *tirosh* and *yayin* respectively. It may be seen, therefore, that *tirosh* was the natural source of *yayin,* as the olive was of the oil.

The term is constantly connected with the mention of conditions affecting the natural growth, such as drought[1] and dew.[2] It has a proleptical application to the juice while still in the grape, and by another figure to the grapes in the press.[3]

Tirosh is however a comprehensive term, applying both to the freshly expressed, unfermented juice of the grape, or *must,*[4] and also to a light kind of wine which was made in antiquity by checking the process of fermentation before it had run its full course.[5] In discussing the term in Isaiah 24:7, Albert Barnes stated that it denotes properly *must,* or wine that is newly expressed, and thus unfermented.[6] It may be observed that other expositors hold the same view.[7] That it also included the

---

1. Is. 24:7; Joel 1:10.

2. Gen. 27:28; Deut. 33:28.

3. Archibald Robert Stirling Kennedy, "Wine and Strong Drink," in *Encyclopaedia Biblica,* eds. Thomas Kelly Cheyne and John Sutherland Black (London: Adam and Charles Black, 1903), 4:5307.

4. *Merith,* which corresponds etymologically in Syraic, is defined as new wine, or *must,* as it comes from the press.

5. *Must* was often used at once, being drunk fresh. To preserve in a sweet state, it was placed in an air-tight *amphora,* and deposited in a cool place, where it would keep for a whole year or more. It was also preserved by being boiled until it became a kind of jelly.

6. Albert Barnes, I*saiah,* Notes on the Old Testament, vol. 1 (Edinburgh: Gall and Inglis, 1945; reprint ed. Grand Rapids: Baker Book House, 1950), p. 391.

7. "Wine," in *Unger's Bible Dictionary,* p. 1168; Burton Scott Easton, "Wine," in *International Standard Bible Encyclopedia,* ed. James Orr (Grand Rapids: Wm. B. Eerdmans Publishing Co., 1939), 5:3086; and G. Coleman Luck, "Wine," in *Wycliffe Bible Dictionary,* eds. Charles F. Pfeiffer, Howard Frederic Vos, and John Rea (Chicago: Moody Press, 1975), 2:1812.

expressed juice is certain, for tithe was levied on *tirosh*;[1] but tithe, as follows from Deuteronomy 14:26, was levied not on the raw fruit, but on what came from *yekeb,* the area of the vat from which the juice came. In Joel 2:24 and Proverbs 3:10 *tirosh* is described as filling the vats. Unless it was the custom to leave the juice in the vat for the purpose of fermentation, it would denote the unfermented juice of the grape.

Tirosh, or *must,* which was intended for intoxicating purposes, was allowed to ferment by being exposed to the open air in large earthenware vessels, or *dolia,* for nine days; but light wines were made by the *dolia* being closed and fermentation checked after five days or so.[2]

In certain passages *tirosh* clearly denotes the product of fermentation. Its application in this respect, however, was apparently limited to new wine, either while still in the fermenting stage or during the next few months while the maturing process was still incomplete.[3]

Often Hosea 4:11 has been adduced in evidence that *tirosh* was of great intoxicating character. "Whoredom and wine and new wine take away the understanding." In the text, "wine" comes from *yayin* and "new wine" from *tirosh.* It is argued that *"tirosh* appears as the climax of engrossing influences, in immediate connection with *yayin."*[4]

In reply, it should be observed that in a climax the last term must be the strongest or highest in degree. In this instance, if it is a climax, *tirosh,* or new wine, must be more potent than *yayin,* but *tirosh* in the other thirty-seven passages where it occurs cannot be proved to be of strong character. *Yayin,* on the other hand, is in many passages clearly an intoxicating wine. The passage under consideration therefore contains no such climax as regards the degree of the intoxicating power.

A careful investigation of the context will reveal that the people of Israel had apostatized from God and committed idolatry, which in the Bible is called whoredom, and is so attended by licentiousness and sensuality in the use of intoxicating beverages. *Tirosh,* however, as has been shown, does not always mean wine, but vine-fruit or grapes in

1. Deut. 12:17; 14:23.
2. Samuel Rolles Driver, *The Books of Joel and Amos,* Cambridge Bible for Schools and Colleges (Cambridge: University Press, 1898), pp. 79–80.
3. Archibald Robert Stirling Kennedy, "Wine and Strong Drink," in *Encyclopaedia Biblica,* 4:5307.
4. "Wine," in *Unger's Bible Dictionary,* p. 1168.

clusters, and therefore by a figure of speech, vineyards, possessions, and riches, all of which took away their hearts from God.[1]

The children of Israel had apostatized from God in three ways. (1) They followed strange gods, instead of the true God; (2) their best affections consisted in sensual pleasure, instead of being fixed upon God; (3) their estimate of good was limited to earthly things, represented by *tirosh,* the natural fruit of the vineyard.

Three things are said to take away the understanding. As whoredom is not the same as *yayin,* so *yayin* is not the same as *tirosh.* As physical intoxication is not an essential characteristic of whoredom, neither is it of *tirosh,* in particular when *yayin* is adequate for intoxication. There is no point in using *yayin* and *tirosh* in the passage if both mean intoxicating wine. The passage would then read, "Whoredom and *yayin* (intoxicating wine) and *tirosh* (intoxicating wine) take away the understanding." Such statement would be tautologous. The three terms are symbolical.[2] Thus it can be seen that *tirosh* is a general term denoting the natural product, freshly expressed juice, and new wine of light alcoholic properties.[3]

Shekar. The term is employed twenty-two times, with one rendering, "strong drink."

It is represented twelve times by *sikera* and one time by *oinos* in the Septuagint, both of which are generic. As *yayin* is the generic term for the liquid of *tirosh,* so *shekar* is the generic term for the liquid of *yitzhar*[4] or of any other fruit than the grape, such as dates, pomegranates, barley, or millet. Archibald Kennedy stated that the etymology warrants the inference that *shekar* is to be regarded as a comprehensive designation for every kind of intoxicating beverage from whatever source it may be derived.[5]

---

1 P. Anstadt, "Communion Wine," *The Quarterly Review of the Evangelical Lutheran Church* 16 (January 1886):9.

2. William Patton, *Bible Wines: The Laws of Fermentation and Wines of the Ancients* (New York: New York Temperance Association, 1874; reprint ed. Fort Worth: Star Bible and Tract Corporation, 1976), p. 59.

3. For a further discussion of *tirosh,* see "Tirosh," *Gospel Advocate* 31 (24 July 1889):472–73.

4. In Deuteronomy 14:26, *shekar* answers to the *yitzhar* of verse 23, as *yayin* answers to *tirosh* in the same verse.

5. Archibald Robert Stirling Kennedy, "Wine and Strong Drink," in *Encyclopaedia Biblica,* 4:5309.

On the contrary, Moses Stuart indicates that it no doubt denoted sweet juices of all kinds originally but in distinction from *yayin* came to be applied to juices of fruits other than grapes, and that by virtue of the saccharine principle, it may become alcoholic, but can be kept and used in an *unfermented state.*[1] On this point, Frederick R. Lees says, *"Shekar* signifies 'sweet drink' expressed from fruits other than the grape, and drunk in an unfermented or fermented state."[2]

Although a variety of intoxicating beverages made from several fruits were known in antiquity, the translation of *shekar* to "strong drink" is unfortunate because it suggests the idea of distilled liquors which were not known at that time. [3]

Asis. The term is employed five times, with two renderings. It is rendered "sweet wine" four times and "juice" one time.

It is apparently a poetical synonym of *tirosh,* denoting primarily the freshly expressed juice of the grape or other fruit.[4] It is derived from *asas* signifying "to tread," and therefore refers to the method by which the juice was expressed from the grape. Thus, it would very properly refer to new wine which had recently been expressed. It conveys the idea of that which is sweet and pure,[5] and is probably the same as "the sweet" of Nehemiah 8:10, where it is referred to as *mamtaqqim.* If fermented at all, its alcoholic properties would no doubt be slight.

Shemarim. The term is employed five times, with three renderings. It is rendered "lees" two times, and "wines on the lees" and "dregs" one time each.

Derived from the verb *shamar,* "to preserve," it signifies the thicker or sedimentary part of the mixture which has not been perfectly com-

1. William Patton, p. 57, citing Moses Stuart in Stuart's letter to Eliphalet Nott, New York, p. 15. Emphasis mine, WDJ.

2. Frederick R. Lees and Dawson Burns, *Temperance Bible Commentary* (London: n.p., 1870), p. 418.

3. Burton Scott Easton, "Wine," in *International Standard Bible Encyclopedia,* 5:3086; William Patton, p. 57, citing Moses Stuart in Stuart's letter to Eliphalet Nott, New York, p. 14.

4. Archibald Robert Stirling Kennedy, "Wine and Strong Drink," in *Encyclopaedia Biblica,* 4:5308.

5. Frederick R. Lees, "Wine," in *A Cyclopaedia of Biblical Literature,* 2:952.

bined with the rest. In Isaiah 25:6 where it occurs twice, it is rendered "wine on the lees," but the literal meaning is "a feast of fat things, a feast of preserved things," and the natural inference is that of "preserves."[1]

Sobe. The term is employed three times, with two renderings. It is rendered "drink" two times and "wine" one time.

From *sabah,* "to drink to satiation," it likely denotes a rich boiled wine, such as would quickly surfeit. In Isaiah 1:22 the illusion to mixing with water favors the idea of a boiled wine.[2] Related to the Latin *sapa,* *"must* boiled down,"[3] *sobe* likely has reference to any kind of intoxicating beverage.

Chemer. The term is employed two times with one rendering: "wine." No doubt used in a generic sense, it is like a poetic substitute of *yayin,* with which it is almost identical in meaning.

Chamar. The term is employed six times with one rendering: "wine." Closely related to *chemar,* it denotes the action of foaming or agitating. It is descriptive of the appearance of freshly expressed grape juice, or of juice in the process of fermentation. The compilers of the Talmud considered *chamar* as a sweet wine.[4]

Mesek, Mimsak, and Mezeg. Mesek, which is employed one time, is rendered "mixture." *Mimsak* is employed two times with two renderings: "mixed wine" and "mingled wine." *Mezeg,* which is employed one time, is rendered "mingled wine."

The three terms, which are closely related, occur in a verbal form in several passages.[5] Wine which is compounded from some other ingredient is signified, but whether drugged or diluted is not indicated. No definite conclusion can thus be drawn as to the quality of wine, or as to the

1. P. Anstadt, *The Quarterly Review,* p. 11.
2. Ibid., pp. 7–8.
3. "Wine," in *Fausset's Bible Dictionary,* p. 723.
4. Frederick R. Lees, "Wine," in *Popular and Critical Bible Encyclopedia and Scriptural Dictionary,* 3:1725. The Talmud, which consisted of Jewish civil and canonical law, comprised 63 volumes, WDJ.
5. Prov. 9:2, 5; Ps. 102:9; Is. 5:22; 9:14.

nature of the substance introduced, whether spices or water.[1] That the latter is often the case is evidenced by the fact that the Septuagint in these and other passages render the term *kerannumi,* which denotes a weakening of wines by dilution.[2]

Fermented wine was used in ancient times as a medicine as well as a beverage. As a beverage, however, it was thought of as a mixed drink. Plutarch, for instance, says, "We call a mixture 'wine,' although the larger of the component parts is water."[3] On the contrary, wine was mixed with drugs, as is stated by Everett Ferguson.

> The mixing of wine with drugs was common in the Near East and explains why "mixed" in such passages as Psalm 75:8 and Proverbs 23:29 (cf. Song of Solomon 8:2) means a stronger drink, contrary to classical usage.[4]

Usually a writer simply referred to a mixture of water and wine as "wine." The term for unmixed wine,[5] was used to indicate that the beverage was not a mixture of water and wine. In the Talmud, which contains the oral traditions of Judaism from about 200 B.C. to A.D. 200, there are several tractates in which the mixture of water and wine is discussed.[6] At times the ratio would be one-to-one and even lower, but it should be noted that such a mixture was referred to as "strong wine." The ratio of water to wine no doubt varied, for Homer referred to a ratio of twenty parts water to one part wine,[7] while Pliny mentioned a ratio of eight parts water to one part wine.[8]

---

1. William Latham Bevan, "Wine," in *Smith's Dictionary of the Bible,* ed. Horatio Balch Hackett (Boston: Houghton, Mifflin and Co., 1890), 4:3542.

2. Joseph Henry Thayer, *Greek-English Lexicon of the New Testament* (New York: American Book Co., 1889; reprint ed., Grand Rapids: Zondervan Publishing House, 1962), p. 344; "Mingle," in *An Expository Dictionary of New Testament Words,* ed. William Edwyn Vine (Old Tappan, New Jersey: Fleming H. Revell Co., 1940), 3:71–72.

3. Plutarch, *Moralia* 140f.

4. Everett Ferguson, "Wine as a Table-Drink in the Ancient World," *Restoration Quarterly* 13 (1970):151.

5. *Akratesteron.*

6. cf. Shabbath 77a; Pesahim 108b.

7. Homer, *Odyssey* 9. 108; cf. *Natural History* 14. 6.

8. Pliny, *Natural History* 14. 6.

In antiquity wine was usually stored in large pointed jugs called *amphorae*. When it was to be used it was poured from these containers into large bowls called *kraters*, and then mixed with water. From these bowls, cups or *kylixes* were then filled. It is important to observe that before wine was drunk it was mixed with water. The *kylixes* were filled not from the *amphorae* but from the *kraters*.

The Greeks of the Classical Period looked upon the drinking of unmixed wine as a Scythian or barbarian custom.[1] If the consumption of such wine was objectionable in ancient times, surely the imbibing of modern distilled beverages, which are much stronger, should not be considered as any less objectionable today.

Dam-anabim. The term, which is employed one time, is rendered "blood of grapes." As it is used in Genesis 49:11, it conveys the idea of simple expressed grape juice.

Dam-enab. The term, which is employed one time, is rendered "blood of the grape." The singular of *dam-anabim,* as employed in Deuteronomy 32:14, it is also indicative of unfermented grape juice.

Mishrath-anabim. The term, which is employed one time, is rendered "juice of grapes." It is derived from the verb *sharah,* meaning to "loosen, or macerate." As used in Numbers 6:3, it denotes the unfermented juice of grapes.

Ashishah. The term is employed four times, with three renderings. It is rendered "cake of raisins" two times, and "cakes of raisins" and "raisins" one time each. In no instance does it denote a liquid.

Anabim. The term, which is employed only one time, is rendered "cakes of raisins." Its literal meaning is "grapes."

Chomets. The term, which is employed six times, is rendered "vinegar."

A weak wine, which has entered the acetic stage of fermentation, it was used by those engaged in the labors of the field to soften and render more palatable the dry bread which formed the food of the reapers.[2] It

1. Athenaeus, *Deipnosophistae* 10. 427b.
2. cf. Ruth 2:14.

was also used as a beverage, likely mixed with water, in which case it resembled the *posca* of the Romans, which was not intoxicating in nature.[1]

Yekeb. The term is employed eleven times, with two renderings. It is rendered "winepress" eight times, and "winepresses" three times. It is descriptive of the lower vat, while *gath* denotes the upper portion of the press.[2]

Mamtaqqim. The term is employed two times with two renderings, "sweet" and "most sweet." From *mahthaq*, it denotes the thick, sweet wines, devoid of intoxicating properties, which needed to be greatly diluted because of their thickness.

This completes the list of Hebrew terms which either directly or indirectly have reference to wine. It has been observed that twelve terms are either rendered "wine" or contain the term in their employment.

New Testament

The New Testament employs five terms with six renderings. The terms with their definitions and classifications follow.

Oinos. The term, which is employed thirty-four times, is rendered "wine."

It is a generic term, characterizing both fermented and unfermented wine.[3] One writer refers to it as a "neutral word," which denotes both winefat and fermented juice.[4] It likely has a common etymological origin with *yayin* in the Old Testament, which carries the same basic meaning, and is employed in the Septuagint to denote both *yayin* and *tirosh.* Equivalent to the generic Latin term *vinum, oinos* is used eight times in connection with the adjective *neos,* denoting that which is new. Two

---

1. "Wine," in *Cyclopaedia of Biblical, Theological and Ecclesiastical Literature,* eds. John McClintock and James Strong (New York: Harper and Brothers, Publishers, 1849), 10:1013.

2. "Wine," in *Fausset's Bible Dictionary,* p. 723.

3. Henry Leo Boles, "The Kind of Wine in the Lord's Supper," *Gospel Advocate* 110 (17 October 1968):664.

4. J. W. Roberts, "What Kind of Element in the Cup on the Lord's Day, Fermented or Unfermented?" *Firm Foundation* 81 (18 August 1964):524.

times "new" should be supplied. It is connected two times with the adjective *kalon,* designating that which is good. In thirteen instances it is undefined. The remaining times, it is used figuratively in the book of Revelation.

Gleukos. The term, which is employed one time, is rendered "new wine." The equivalent of the Hebrew term *tirosh,*[1] it was no doubt produced from the purest juice of the grape, which flowed spontaneously from the grape before the treading began. Kept in such fashion to preserve its sweetness, it could not be new wine in the proper sense of the term, for several months likely had passed between the vintage and the feast of Pentecost, during which time it is referred to. It could have applied, as *mustum* was by the Romans, to wine that had been preserved for about a year in an unfermented state, which view has been expressed by various scholars.[2]

If the precautions designed to keep wine in an unfermented state were neglected it would ferment, as was likely the case at times with *gleukos,* which was not an aged wine. Perhaps such a species is referred to in Acts 2:13.

Sikera. The term, which is employed one time, is rendered "strong drink." Occurring in Luke 1:15, and as a literal rendering of the Hebrew *shekar,* it is no doubt used generically for all kinds of beverages from other fruits than grapes.

Oxos. The term, which is employed six times, is rendered "vinegar." Used in connection with the crucifixion of Jesus, and equivalent to the Hebrew *chomets,* it denotes a thin sour wine which had completed acetous fermentation.

Gennema tas ampelou. The phrase, which is employed three times, is rendered "fruit of the vine." It is used in connection with the institution of the Lord's supper.[3]

---

1. Joseph Henry Thayer, *Greek-English Lexicon of the New Testament,* pp. 118, 442.
2. "Wine," in *Cyclopaedia of Biblical, Theological, and Ecclesiastical Literature,* 10:1014.
3. Henry Leo Boles, p. 664.

This completes the list of Greek terms which either directly or indirectly have reference to wine. It has been observed that three terms are either rendered "wine" or contain the word in their employment.

Summary

A summary of the results of the investigation of the terms for wine in the Bible reveals the following: (1) There are nine terms in the Old Testament and three in the New Testament which are rendered "wine" either singly or in connection with some other term. (2) There are ten additional terms in the Old Testament and two in the New Testament which refer to the juice or products of the grape or of other fruits. (3) There are a total of twenty-four terms in the Bible which are applied to products of the grape or of other fruits. (4) Of the twenty-four terms, four have no reference whatever to the juice of the grape or to the juice of any fruit. *Ashishah* denotes a cake of raisins; *anabim* denotes cakes of raisins; *shemarim* denotes the thicker part of wine or preserves; and *yekeb* denotes the winepress. (5) Of the remaining twenty terms and phrases which do refer to the juices of fruits, three Hebrew terms, *yayin, shekar,* and *chemar,* and three Greek terms, *oinos, gleukos,* and *sikera* are generic. (6) One Hebrew term, *chomets,* and one Greek term, *oxos,* denote a wine that has entered the acetic stage of fermentation. (7) Three Hebrew terms, *mesek, mimsak,* and *mezeg,* denote a wine either fermented or unfermented, which has been drugged or diluted. (8) Five Hebrew terms, *tirosh, dam-anabim, dam-enab, mishrath-anabim,* and *mamtaqqim,* denote some form of grape or other juice. (9) With the exception of one Hebrew term, *sobe,* there is no term in the Bible that must indicate an intoxicating beverage. (10) On the other hand, there are eight terms, *shemarim, dam-anabim, dam-enab, mishrath-anabim, ashishah, anabim, yekeb,* and *mamtaqqim,* which signify an unfermented article. (11) Ten other terms, *yayin, tirosh, shekar, asis, chemar, chamar, mesek, mimsak, mezeg,* and *oinos,* the most important and most frequently employed, allow persons to determine by considering the context or circumstances, whether an intoxicating beverage is intended. Persons should not assume that such is the case without examining the facts.

After having examined at length the terms which represent wine in the Bible, it has been proved that the assumption that the term always designates that which is alcoholic in nature is false.

Regarding this, the scholarly H. Leo Boles states,

> The translators of the Bible into English have repeatedly recognized the fact that the unfermented juice of the grape, as it is squeezed from the grapes and trodden from the grapes and as it flows from the press, is wine.[1]

Concerning the two wines of the Bible, unfermented and fermented, the question is often asked: If this is the case why is the Bible not more explicit in reference to wine in order that there could be no mistake about it? One may as well ask why the Bible refers to the four corners of the earth, if the earth is round, or why does the Bible not directly condemn gambling and dancing, if they are wrong. The obvious answer is that the Bible is not a treatise on astronomy, gambling, dancing, or wine making. It sets forth general principles for the instruction, guidance, and well being of humanity.

Descriptive Phrases

There are several descriptive phrases in the Bible which denote unfermented characteristics. Reference is made to (1) the vine and the tree,[2] (2) the first-fruits, which are first ripe,[3] (3) the cluster of the grape,[4] (4) the grape that is gathered,[5] (5) grapes dried up in the pod,[6] (6) the pure blood of the grape,[7] and (7) the juice which is pressed from the grape into the cup.[8]

In reference to the latter passage, Flavius Josephus, a Jewish historian of the first century, used the Hebrew term *yayin* for descriptive purposes.

---

1. Henry Leo Boles, "The Wines of the Bible," *Gospel Advocate* 75 (23 February 1933):178.
2. Num. 6:4; Judg. 9:13.
3. Num. 18:12; Neh. 10:37.
4. Is. 65:8.
5. Jer. 40:10; Is. 62:9.
6. Is. 16:10; Joel 2:24.
7. Gen. 49:11; Deut. 32:14.
8. Gen. 40:11.

No Prevention Argument

Some persons claim that methods of preserving grape juice and various other juices in a condition free from fermentation were unknown in antiquity.[1] Others claim that the only degree to which fermentation can be preserved is that of the state of vinegar, which is the final stage of fermentation.

From these claims, it is further stated that since this is the case, unintoxicating wine could not have existed. Regarding the second claim, it should be observed that when wine reached the acetic stage of fermentation, in which stage it became vinegar, it was unintoxicating. In a later section, this principle shall be discussed at length. In the course of the present argument, evidence shall be presented to refute the first claim and establish the fact that methods of preserving sweet or unfermented juices did indeed exist. At this point it is essential to consider various properties which are involved in the process of fermen-tation.

Essential Properties

Grape juice, the prime agent, contains two leading elements: sugar and gluten. Chemical elements in sugar are carbon, hydrogen, and oxygen; gluten is composed of carbon, hydrogen, oxygen, and nitrogen. Nitrogen, an unstable element, constantly seeks union with other elements. In so doing, it hastens the decay of vital organisms and tends to the formation of new substances. The decay of the gluten in grape juice affords the necessary conditions for the reception and growth of yeast germs.[2] In the presence of yeast the sugar is gradually converted into alcohol, while carbonic acid escapes from the liquid.[3] There were several

---

1. Thomas George Dunning, *Alcohol and the Christian Ethic* (Wallington, Great Britain: Religious Education Press, Ltd., pp. 32–33.

2. Louis Pasteur determined through experiments that yeast which induces the fermentation that makes alcohol in grape juice, comes to life outside grapes, rather than spontaneously from within. The yeast microbes, which come from the air, do not penetrate the protective skin of the grape. See Paul De Kruif, *Microbe Hunters* (New York: Harcourt, Brace and Co., n.d.), pp. 93–99.

3. Albion Roy King, *Basic Information on Alcohol* (Washington, D.C.: Narcotics Education, Inc., 1964), pp. 22–23.

methods in antiquity by which this process could be prevented and the grape juice kept or preserved fresh and unfermented.

Gluten Separation

The gluten could be separated from the other elements. Gluten, enclosed in minute cells, is located in the lining of the skin and in the envelope of the seed. By careful manipulation the flowing juice in which the sugar is concentrated may be released without disturbing the fermentable pulp. Persons in antiquity understood this principle and applied it in practice. They were familiar with a drink which they called *protropum*. Pliny indicated that it was a "sweet wine drawn off before treading the grapes."[1] Such a liquid, slowly coming spontaneously from the grape, and composed or made up almost entirely of the sweet portion of the grape, could not have been quick to ferment.

It has been argued, however, that "Pliny expressly tells us that it was allowed to ferment."[2] Although this is true, it does not mean that fermentation was essential to *protropum*—it was called that before anything was said about its undergoing that process—but that *protropum* could ferment, after which it was known by another name.

The value of the careful handling of the grapes to prevent the escape of the gluten is indicated by several items in the directions and descriptions of Roman writers of wines. They frequently insisted that the grapes should be trodden by foot, rather than crushed by a heavy beam.[3]

The juice, which was obtained by careful pressure before the grapes had been fully trodden, was preserved in its unfermented state.[4] When the gluten had been expressed with the sweet juice, it was still possible to bring about a separation. The fermentable pulp could be strained out by means of filters. Pliny stated, "Wines are most beneficial when all

---

1. Pliny, *Natural History* 14. 9.
2. Dunlop Moore, "The Bible Wine Question," *Presbyterian Review* 2 (January 1881):104.
3. Columella, *De Re Rustica* 12. 37.
4. Columella, *De Re Rustica* 12. 41; See also William Ramsay, "Vinum," in *Smith's Dictionary of Greek and Roman Antiquities*, ed. William Smith (London: Walton and Maberly, 1849), p. 1201.

their potency has been overcome by the strainer."[1] Pliny, in this instance, referred to the use of the filter to destroy the strength of wine in which fermentation had already begun. It does not follow, however, that because it was used for that purpose it was applied to no other. The filter was employed to separate the gluten or fermentable substance, as well as to strain out the pulp. On this point, William Ramsay indicates that the strength of wine was destroyed by the filter in order that persons might drink more.[2] Plutarch, after referring to the process of filtration in the same terminology as Pliny, indicates that the process was often repeated until the intoxicating strength was withdrawn.[3]

It is certain, therefore, that wines of antiquity were filtered in order to deprive them of their intoxicating properties. However, that was not the only method by which fermentation could be prevented.

Moisture Removal

There were methods by which moisture could be removed from grapes. Fermentable subjects will not ferment except in the presence of water, and unless they are kept by means of water in contact with that which is fermented.[4]

There were two ways in which water was removed. Grapes could be dried before the skin was broken. Preserved in that condition, even after a considerable period of time, they afforded the ingredient for an unfermented beverage, after they had been soaked in water. Columella and Varro each describe this type of wine,[5] which was the Roman *passum,* so called because the grapes were spread out in order to dry.

It has been argued from Columella,[6] however, that it was fermented.[7] In this case, however, as in that of *protropum,* already mentioned, the statement merely indicates the fact that *passum* was sometimes allowed to ferment, and not that fermentation was essential to its being *passum.*

---

1. Pliny, *Natural History* 23. 24.
2. William Ramsay, "Vinum," in *Smith's Dictionary of Greek and Roman Antiquities,* p. 1203.
3. Plutarch, *Symposiacs* 8. 7.
4. Leon C. Field, *Oinos: A Discussion of the Bible Wine Question* (New York: Phillips and Hunt, 1883), p. 25.
5. Columella, *De Re Rustica* 12. 39; Varro Ap. Non. 551. 27.
6. Columella, *De Re Rustica* 12. 39.
7. Dunlop Moore, p. 105.

On the contrary, Columella spoke of *passum* in such fashion as to indicate that it was *passum* immediately before any fermentation could have taken place.[1]

The second way by which water could be removed was by boiling the grapes. By this most common and successful method, water was evaporated and fermentation was prevented. Varro, Columella, and Pliny describe the boiled wines of the Romans and give them different names according to the extent to which evaporation was carried. Not only were such wines used as honey and to give body to lighter wines, but they were diluted and often served as common beverages.

In connection with this method, it should be observed that since grape juice boils at 212 degrees Fahrenheit and ethyl alcohol evaporates at 172 degrees Fahrenheit, it is evident that if there were any alcohol in a liquid, boiling would expel it.

Air Exclusion

In order to prevent fermentation, air may be excluded from the juice. Research conducted by Louis Pasteur has established the fact that germs from yeast are introduced by air into fermentable liquids. Although persons in antiquity did not understand the theory, they were acquainted with the fact. It was their custom to line earthen containers with pitch, and after having filled them with fresh juice, seal[2] them, and either sink them in water or bury them in the ground. Cato, Columella, Pliny, and Plutarch, each testify to this fact.[3] In fact, Columella said of the juice preserved in such manner, "It will thus remain sweet for a whole year."[4]

Reduced Temperature

Fermentation may be prevented by keeping the grape juice at a temperature below 40 degrees Fahrenheit. Vinous fermentation is possible only at a temperature between 40 and 113 degrees Fahrenheit.

---

1. Columella, *De Re Rustica* 12. 39.

2. Wax and other stable substances were used for sealing purposes, WDJ.

3. Cato, *De Re Rustica* 120; Columella, *De Re Rustica* 12, 29; Pliny, *Natural History* 14. 11; Plutarch Q. N. 26.

4. Columella, *De Re Rustica* 12. 29.

Above the latter point the acetous supplants the vinous process; below the former point the ferment is inoperative.

Pliny, in reference to the Greek *gleukos*, stated, "As soon as the *must* is taken from the vat and put into casks, they plunge the casks in water till midwinter passes and regular cold weather sets in."[1]

By such a combination, therefore, of the last two methods, the exclusion of air and the reducing of temperature, grape juice was kept fresh.

Sulphur Fumigation

Sulphur fumigation was another method by which fermentation was prevented. Oxygen was absorbed by this method and the action of the nitrogenous element in the gluten was arrested. In reference to this method Frederick R. Lees stated,

> When the Mishna forbids smoked wines from being used in offerings (Menachoth, VIII, 6, et. comment), it has chiefly reference to the Roman practice of fumigating them with sulphur, the vapor which absorbed the oxygen, and thus arrested the fermentation.[2]

Summary

The methods which have been presented clearly indicate the theory that vinous fermentation could not have been prevented is false. Not only these writers, but many others can be cited to testify to the fact that persons in antiquity possessed methods of preserving wines sweet throughout the year.[3] If wines were alcoholic they would preserve themselves. The peculiarity was in preserving them sweet since the juice loses its sweetness when, by fermentation, the sugar is converted into alcohol. Thus, to preserve wines sweet throughout the year meant

---

1. Pliny, *Natural History* 14. 11.
2. Frederick R. Lees, "Wine," in *A Cyclopaedia of Biblical Literature,* 2:956.
3. cf. Mrs. T. P. Holman, "Wines of the Bible and of the Ancients," *Gospel Advocate* 27 (27 May 1885):326; "Communion Wine," *Gospel Advocate* 31 (24 July 1889):473; Emmet Russell, "Wine," in *Zondervan Pictorial Bible Dictionary,* ed. Merrill C. Tenney (Grand Rapids: Zondervan Publishing House, 1963), p. 895; J. W. Roberts, p. 524; Albion Roy King, pp. 22–23; and William Patton, pp. 25–53.

that they were preserved unfermented and, thus, were not considered as intoxicating.[1]

That there was an intoxicating wine in antiquity is not denied. The Bible and early secular writers, however, are clear in their denunciation of such wine. The object in this section has been to indicate that there was, as well, a wine which did not intoxicate. By surveying the issue in this light, the harmony in otherwise seemingly conflicting passages in the Bible can be seen.

Cana Argument

The Claim

It is commonly claimed that Jesus made intoxicating wine when He performed His first miracle in Cana of Galilee.[2] From this claim, it is inferred that the use of intoxicating beverages are permissible today. W. J. Wiltenburg expresses the view as follows: "At the very least the story of Cana's wedding feast indirectly approves the use of alcoholic beverages."[3] The same can be seen from the following statement of Herschel H. Hobbs:

> There is no point in debating whether or not this was real wine. The Greek word *oinos* normally denotes the fermented juice of the grape. The ruler's appraisal of it in verse 10 suggests that it was wine of the best quality.[4]

The claim is also voiced by James Burton Coffman in the following words:

---

1. Although the writer does not subscribe to the view that fermented grape juice is *not* permissible in the Lord's supper, those who do, and yet at the same time hold the view that grape juice could not be kept without fermenting in the first century, cannot logically explain how unfermented juice could continually be supplied in that period. This is particularly significant since the vintage season was between June and September, depending on the type of grapes, climatic conditions, and the location of the vineyard.

2. Jn. 2:1–11.

3. W. J. Wiltenburg, "The Bible and the Attitudes of Ministers on Drinking," *Pastoral Psychology* 9 (April 1958):39.

4. Herschel H. Hobbs, *An Exposition of the Gospel of John* (Grand Rapids: Baker Book House, 1968), p. 64.

Also, the opinion of the ruler of the feast that the wine Jesus made was superior in quality to that they had drunk earlier, supports the conclusion that it was not merely pure grape juice.[1]

Although Coffman correctly states that such wine was far less potent than modern intoxicating beverages, he, along with the others, assumes the very point to be proved. It may be also observed in this connection that frequently those who are opposed to "social" drinking hold the view that Jesus made intoxicating wine at Cana. Such a view, however, is illogical and untenable in light of the context under consideration.

Nature of the Miracle

It should be noted that Jesus turned water to wine. There is a process by which nature can do the same. When this process is followed, an intoxicating beverage *can*, not *must*, be the result. If the process of nature has just reached the stage of being ripe in the pod of the grape, the liquid is not intoxicating. Jesus, however, passed over every step through which moisture must pass, according to the laws of nature, to be an intoxicant. Grape juice becomes intoxicating during the natural process in the following manner: (1) Moisture from the earth enters the roots of the grape vine. (2) It travels in the form of sap through the vine into the branches. (3) From there it travels into the pod of the grape where it goes through a maturing and ripening stage. (4) The juice is extracted and allowed to ferment.

The generic term *oinos* is used to describe that which Jesus made. The fact is stated that the water had "now become *(gegenemenon)* wine." The expression thus seems to indicate the transformation of the water into the pure juice of the grape in the same manner in which it takes place every year within the cluster of the vine, but differentiated from that by the miraculous rapidity of the process.[2] In regard to *oinos*,

---

1. James Burton Coffman, *Commentary on John* (Austin: Firm Foundation Publishing House, 1974), pp. 61–62.

2. R. C. Trench quotes both Augustine and Chrysostom, who express the view that Jesus made wine in the same way in which it occurred every year, by speeding up the process. Richard Chenevix Trench, *Notes on the Miracles of Our Lord*, 15th ed. (London: Kegan Paul, Trench, Trubner and Co., 1895), pp. 114–15. H. Olshausen and Daniel D. Whedon hold the same view, as does J. W. McGarvey. John William McGarvey and Philip Y. Pendleton, *The Fourfold Gospel* (Cincinnati: Standard Publishing Foundation, n.d.), p. 118.

A. B. Rich states, "It simply designates a vinous beverage, but gives no clue to its nature. This must be determined by reference to the context, if at all."[1]

The word for "taste" in verse 9 is *geuo*, meaning "to taste, try the flavor, enjoy, experience, or to take nourishment."[2] The verdict of the ruler of the feast was pronounced upon tasting the wine. Flavor would have been immediately evident, but not toxic effects. Scientists have determined that it is in the process of fermentation that alcoholic content develops. When Jesus turned water to wine, however, He passed over the natural process.

The claim based on the miracle at Cana presupposes at least three theories, namely (1) unfermented grape juice was never known as wine in the first century, (2) there was no way by which vinous fermentation could be prevented, and (3) the phrase "drunk freely" *(methuo)* always denotes intoxication. Since the first two theories have already been discussed, in the course of this argument thorough consideration and proof will be advanced to demonstrate the falsity of the third theory.

Self-Contradictory Theory

In answer to the theory that the phrase "drunk freely" always denotes intoxication or drunkenness, it should be noted that there is absolutely nothing in the passage to indicate that the Son of God sanctioned in the least respect the consumption of intoxicating wine as a beverage!

Often persons who attempt to justify "social" drinking condemn drunkenness and cite such texts as 1 Peter 4:3 and Ephesians 5:18 as proof. Those who hold the view that, according to John 2:1–11, Jesus sanctioned "social" drinking but not drunkenness, subscribe to an illogical and self-contradictory theory. All doctrines which are self-contradictory are false. That under consideration is self-contradictory for the following reasons: (1) It is affirmed that excess is wrong, and that drunkenness constitutes excess. (2) Endorsement is given to the view that "drunk freely" always means to "get drunk or become intoxicated." (3) If such

---

1. A. B. Rich, "Do the Scriptures Prohibit the Use of Alcoholic Beverages?" *Bibliotheca Sacra* 37 (July 1880): 403.

2. George Allen Turner, *The Gospel According to John* (Grand Rapids: Wm. B. Eerdmans Publishing Co., n.d.), p. 80.

were true in this instance, it follows that Jesus supplied a large quantity[1] of intoxicating wine to persons who were already drunk. In light of the position that Jesus contributed to increased drunkenness by supplying intoxicating wine to a crowd of persons who were already drunk, the following dilemma must be faced.

Dilemma

Either (1) such advocates must affirm that Jesus was not guilty of sin (in which case they would be affirming that it is not sinful to contribute to drunkenness) or (2) they must affirm that Jesus was guilty of sin (in which case they place themselves in contradiction to such passages as Hebrews 4:15 and 1 Peter 2:22–24). In either case, they are committed to false doctrine. Since this is the case, it is clear that their affirmation is false. The argument may be stated in a deductive form as follows:

(1) If Jesus supplied intoxicating wine to the wedding guests at Cana, then He contributed to their intoxication; and if intoxication is sinful, then Jesus sinned.

(2) Either Jesus did not contribute to their intoxication or He did not sin.

(3) Either Jesus did not supply intoxicating wine to the wedding guests at Cana, or intoxication is not sinful.[2]

If the argument is valid and the propositions are true, the conclusion must be true. The argument *is* stated in valid form, as can be proved by the use of truth tables. The first proposition is true based on the fact that intoxication is a matter of degree or a state of "becoming softened." If "drunk freely" in John 2:10 means "become intoxicated," as some persons affirm, then those under consideration were intoxicated. Since additional wine was not supplied until they had "drunk freely," it follows that Jesus did contribute to intoxication if He supplied intoxicating wine.

The second proposition is true based on such passages as Habakkuk 2:15 and Proverbs 23:31–32. Since, therefore, the argument is valid and the propositions are true, the conclusion must be true. There is absolutely

---

1. About 160 gallons.
2. By destructive dilemma.

nothing in the context of John 2:1–11 to indicate that Jesus sanctioned the imbibing of intoxicating beverages. Persons who accept the previously defined definition of "drunk freely" must face the dilemma. In an effort to escape the force of the argument, various replies are voiced.

Replies

First, it is replied that the persons under consideration were not intoxicated. It should be seen, however, that if "drunk freely" means intoxicated, the statement of the ruler of the feast indicates that they were intoxicated. According to such reasoning, the ruler said, "Every man at the beginning doth set forth intoxicating wine; and when men have gotten drunk, then that which is less potent." If this were the practice of every man under such conditions, the persons under consideration were drunk, because they had reached the point where additional wine was being supplied. According to the theory, therefore, the people had already used their best wine, which had brought them to a state of intoxication, not knowing that Jesus would provide an even more potent supply. In order to be consistent, persons who hold this view must take the position that these persons were drunk, because they had reached the point where additional wine was being supplied. The only difference in that situation, according to such reasoning, was that an even more intoxicating wine was provided at the end, and that by Jesus Christ! If this definition of "drunk freely" were true, according to the ruler of the feast the latter wine was not provided until the persons were drunk. Notice the following: (1) At what point was additional wine supplied? (2) It was supplied after men had "drunk freely," which, according to the theory, means intoxicated. (3) Jesus supplied additional wine. (4) According to the theory, therefore, these persons were already drunk! When persons accept a proposition, logically they must accept the conclusion that necessarily follows. Those who do otherwise act in an inconsistent manner.[1]

Second, persons may reply by stating, "It is not true." Such a reply, however, does not adequately answer the argument. By such fashion

---

1. See the writer's articles, "Christian, Abstain from Social Drinking!" *The Spiritual Sword* 4 (January 1973):20–23; and "The Case against Social Drinking," *Gospel Advocate* 119 (3 February 1977):65, 71–72.

any argument may be answered or passed over regardless of how conclusive the proof may be.

Third, it may be replied that those who are not linguistic scholars should not discuss the issue. In reference to this, it should be observed that if this were true, it would follow that persons must be authorities in every discipline, including Hebrew, Greek, archaeology, geography, logic, and all other Bible related studies before discussing any Bible topic. Since no person on earth is an authority in every Bible related discipline, no person could speak or otherwise defend the truth. It does not follow that because persons do not know everything, they do not know anything. All persons know some things, although no persons on earth know everything.

Fourth, it may be replied that Jesus did not have in mind "social" drinking when He performed the miracle at Cana and, therefore, since the passage does not apply, it should not be used to promote abstinence. Although it is no doubt true that Jesus did not have in mind "social" drinking at the time, by the same kind of reasoning, Ephesians 5:19 and Colossians 3:16 could not be employed to denounce mechanical instrumental music in Christian worship. Also it should be remembered that it is the advocates of "social" drinking who use the passage to defend their practice. Any passage that is used to attempt support of a false position may be reviewed in defense of truth!

Fifth, it may be replied that since John 2:1–11 is in a first-century setting, it does not apply today. In answer, it may be said that if the passage has only a first-century application because it is in a first-century setting, the same principle would follow with all New Testament passages. It would follow, therefore, since the entire New Testament is in a first-century setting, no New Testament passage would have application today.

Sixth, it may be replied that logic has no place in such matters. In answer, it should be observed that logic is simply the science of correct reasoning. All persons who understand Bible teaching in regard to this matter, or any other Bible matter, have had to correctly employ principles of logic even if they do not realize that fact. Although persons should not subscribe to every view of David Hume, he did correctly hold that no one ever turns against reasoning until reasoning turns against him.

Key Phrase

The key phrase to be considered in the theory is "drunk freely," or "well drunk" as it is rendered in the King James Version. The claim, as has been previously advanced, is that it always denotes intoxication.

In answer, it should be observed that in every one of forty-three versions or translations of the Bible, with eighteen renderings, each of which the writer of this book has consulted, quantity rather than quality is stressed. Predominant renderings are "drunk freely," used eighteen times, and "well drunk," used in seven instances. Each of four standard translations employs either "drunk freely" or "well drunk," and each of five Roman Catholic versions consulted indicate quantity.[1]

Methuo

The term *methuo* is to be understood in the generic sense of being repleated, satiated, or saturated, and not in the restricted and emphatic sense of intoxication. It is a term which conveys or expresses the idea of being drenched with moisture.[2] That it does not always mean intoxication was recognized by John Wycliffe six centuries ago, when he rendered the expression, "whanne men ben fullid."[3] On this point Thomas Summers states, "Drunk freely suggests the idea of *drunk largely.*"[4] Lexicographers are agreed that the root *methe,* or *methu,* signifies excessive drinking without reference to the kind of liquid used. The verbs *methuo* and *methusko* retain this primary meaning of fullness. In dealing with another text which concerns the same term, S. T. Bloomfield states,

> *Methuein,* from *methu* (probably derived from the Northern word *med* or *meth),* signifies to moisten; and *methuesthai,* "to be mois-tened with liquor," and, in a figurative sense (like the Latin *madere vino),* "to be filled with wine." In Classical use it generally, but not always, implies intoxication. In the Hellenistic writers, however,

---

1. For an expanded list of renderings, see Appendix A, Table Two, pp. 200–02. It should be observed that Roman Catholics approve of so-called moderate drinking, WDJ.
2. Henry George Liddell and Robert Scott, *A Greek-English Lexicon* (Oxford: Clarendon Press, 1940), p. 1091; George Ricker Berry, *Classic Greek Dictionary* (Chicago: Follett Publishing Co., 1962), p. 430.
3. See Appendix A, Table Two, p. 201.
4. Thomas Osmond Summers, *Commentary on the Gospels,* vol. 1 (Nashville: A. H. Redford, 1872), p. 31.

as Josephus, Philo, and the LXX, it seldom denotes more than "drinking freely," and the hilarity consequent; which is probably the sense here.[1]

Various commentators and lexicographers, along with Anstadt, view the term as meaning *"well wined,* after they had drank wine, as much as they wished, till they were satisfied with wine, whether it was much or little."[2] In the Septuagint, *methuo* is repeatedly used in its primary sense of being "filled up." In Psalm 23:5,[3] *methuskon* is used in the expression, "thy cup runneth over." In Song of Solomon 5:1, *methusthete* denotes those who "drink abundantly." In Jeremiah 31:14, *methuso* is employed in connection with "I will satiate the soul of the priests."[4] That the wedding guests were not drunk may be seen from the following words of A. T. Robertson:

> When men have drunk freely *(hotan methusthosin).* Indefinite temporal clause with *hotan* and first aorist passive subjunctive of *methusko.* The verb does not mean that these guests are now drunk.[5]

On the same point Henry Alford says,

> The saying of the ruler of the feast is a general one, not applicable to the company then present. We may be sure that the Lord would not have sanctioned nor ministered to actual drunkenness. Only those who can conceive this will find any difficulty here.[6]

Statement of the Ruler

The statement of the ruler of the feast is important to the basic issue. To deny that the wine which Jesus made was intoxicating raises the question as to why the statement was recorded in the Bible.

---

1. Samuel Thomas Bloomfield, *Greek New Testament with English Notes* (London: Longman, Brown, Green and Longmans, 1855), p. 532.
2. P. Anstadt, *The Quarterly Review,* p. 29.
3. In the Septuagint, the text is Psalm 22:5.
4. In the Septuagint, the text is Jeremiah 38:14. "Satiate," which means to satisfy fully, is also included in the Septuagint translation of Genesis 42:34; Psalm 36:8; 75:5, 10; and Proverbs 5:19.
5. Archibald Thomas Robertson, *Word Pictures of the New Testament,* vol. 5 (Nashville: Broadman Press, 1932), pp. 36–37.
6. Henry Alford, *The Greek Testament,* vol. 1 (London: Rivingtons, 1861), p. 707.

In reply, it may be said that it was because of the unusual circumstances surrounding the serving of the wine. Their best wine and that which proved to be of poorer flavor, had been depleted. Jesus then provided a wine which even surpassed their best wine in flavor. The unique feature was that this wine was provided at the end. In order to justify "social" drinking based on John 2:1–11, it must be proved that the wine under consideration was alcoholic in content. Of the Lord's miracle at Cana, R. C. Foster states,

> If Jesus made intoxicating wine here, then this is the only time He ever used His power to furnish to man that which is destructive of his nature and powers. Why, then, gratuitously accuse Jesus of this when it is not even hinted in the record? The Greek word *oinos* (wine) does not necessarily mean intoxicating wine. The wine of the miracle had a delightful flavor which excelled anything the ruler had experienced, judging by his emphatic comment.[1]

Good Wine

Frequently the theory is advanced that "good wine" in the context denotes intoxicating wine. The phrase no doubt has to do with the taste or flavor of the wine rather than with its potency, as has already been indicated. It should be noted that the adjective used in verse 10 to describe the wine made by Jesus is not *agathos*, good, simply, but *kalos*. The term was applied by the Greeks to everything so distinguished in form, excellence, goodness, usefulness, and eminence, as to be pleasing. At times, the term had to do with that which was beautiful to look at, shapely, or magnificent. At other times, it indicated that which was good, excellent in nature and characteristics and, therefore, well adapted to its end or superior to other kinds.[2] Obviously in verse 10, it was used in this sense.

It has been established beyond fair contradiction that it was a very common thing to preserve wine in an unfermented state in antiquity, and that when thus preserved, it was regarded as of a higher and better

---

1. R. C. Foster, *Studies in the Life of Christ*, vol. 1 (Cincinnati: F. L. Rowe, Publisher, n.d.), p. 139.

2. Joseph Henry Thayer, *Greek-English Lexicon of the New Testament*, p. 322.

quality than any other. Wine which was drawn off before pressing was called "free run" and was considered as better than pressed wine. Pliny, Plutarch, and Horace, each mention that the best wine was that which was harmless or innocent. Pliny indicated that *good wine* was that which was destitute of spirit. The phrase, therefore, does not mean that it was stronger. Great misunderstanding has developed from imposing upon the ancient Greek text and ancient Jewish habits of food and drink, entirely the modern and northern European conception that the term "wine" always indicated an intoxicating beverage. Among the ancient Orientals and Romans, such an idea was not universally attached to wine. In fact, according to various Roman Classical writers, their best wines were not fermented.

Common Beverage

The common beverage of the Romans was grape juice, which they mixed with water, both hot and cold, and often with spices. Ferrar Fenton cites Valerius Maximus and Aulus Gellius as indicating that fermented wine was rare in early Roman times.[1] Fresh grape juice or *mustum* was boiled until it became thick, after which it was stored to be eaten with bread or mixed with water to make an unfermented beverage. To give variety of flavor, herbs and spices were often boiled in the juice during its preparation. Such was the superior wine of antiquity, the sweetest and nicest flavored, and not the most intoxicating as some persons have indicated.

Many of the wines of antiquity which were alcoholic were intoxicating only to a small degree. They contained, even diluted, but four or five percent alcohol. They usually were taken only when largely diluted with water.[2]

The family at Cana were likely poor people, and therefore could not afford to procure the best and costliest wine for their wedding feast, but used that which was inexpensive, and usually drunk by poor people. It is, therefore, not necessary to suppose that the wine which Jesus made was better than that which the bridegroom had provided, because it

---

1. Ferrar Fenton, "The Bible and Wine," in *Paul's Letters to Timothy and Titus,* p. 312.
2. William Smith, "Wine," in *A Dictionary of the Bible,* eds. Francis Nathan and M. A. Peloubet (Chicago: John C. Winston Co., 1884), p. 747.

was more intoxicating, but it was better because it was intrinsically of a superior quality. It was sweeter, more aromatic and pleasant to the taste, like the first free flow from the vat during the treading of the grapes. Such wine, not fermented, and that which all the guests could drink with complete safety, was the *good* wine.[1]

Quality

The quality of wine depends on a number of circumstances. (1) The period in which grapes ripen is significant. Immanuel Benzinger states,

> The time when grapes ripen varies with local conditions: in the district of Tiberius and in the valley of the Jordan, some kinds are ripe in June; in the coast plain, the vintage season occurs about the middle of August; in the mountainous country, during September.[2]

(2) The climate in which the grapes were grown is an important factor. Palestine was particularly known for good wines. (3) The quality of wine depends upon the kinds of grapes that are used. Some grapes contain more sugar than others while others contain more gluten. Wine will partake of the quality of the grapes from which it is pressed. (4) There is a difference in the quality of wine grown in different years in the same area. A warm climate will produce a sweeter and better flavored wine than a cold and moist climate. (5) There is a difference, even from the same kind of grapes, depending on the manner in which they are processed. If grapes are not fully ripe or green grapes are mixed with ripe grapes, the resulting wine will be acrid and sour. (6) The juice which flows out during the treading, without pressure, is considered the best. It is sweeter and much more finely flavored than that which flows from heavy pressure. The first flow from the vat, therefore, was considered the very best wine.[3]

---

1. P. Anstadt, *The Quarterly Review,* pp. 30–31.

2. Immanuel Benzinger, "Wine, Hebrew," in *New Schaff-Herzog Encyclopedia of Religious Knowledge,* ed. Samuel Macauley Jackson (Grand Rapids: Baker Book House, 1957), 12:382; See also "Wine," in *International Standard Bible Encyclopedia,* 5:3086; and "Vines," in *A Dictionary of the Bible,* ed. James Hastings (Edinburgh: T. and T. Clark, 1899), 2:32.

3. P. Anstadt, *The Quarterly Review,* p. 30.

Object of the Miracle

The declared object of the miracle was to manifest the "glory" of Jesus.[1] It was not to place the sanction of His divine approval upon the marriage relation, nor was it for the purpose of contributing to the pleasure of a festive gathering, although both were incidentally accomplished.

The nature of Jesus was such that (1) He "went about doing good,"[2] (2) He was "holy, harmless, and undefiled,"[3] and (3) He came "to succor them that are tempted."[4] Shame, sorrow, and strife would not have been caused by such a character as Jesus Christ. Such a manifestation would have been diabolic, detrimental, and destructive to mankind.

In manifesting His glory, Jesus demonstrated His identity with God: "He made the water wine."[5]

His example should not be pleaded by the makers, sellers, or imbibers of wine to justify the use of modern intoxicating beverages of whatever kind, even at a wedding. The view has no weight unless it can first be proved that the contents of the "six waterpots" were alcoholic and, second, that the wine He created was as potent as modern fortified wines.

Those who hold the view that all wine was intoxicating in the first century present the character of Jesus Christ in an immoral light at the marriage of Cana. They must assume that the bridegroom had provided, as he thought, a sufficient quantity of intoxicating wine, but before the feast was ended, the guests had consumed it all and, as a consequence, were drunk. Then the Lord, instead of reproving them for their indulgence as every faithful servant of the Lord would do, made a large quantity of stronger or still more intoxicating wine for their use on the same occasion. Think of such an event! A faithful servant of the Lord in the present day would not be at ease if he were at a wedding where intoxicating wine was flowing freely. And if he could not prevent it, he would leave as soon as possible. On the other hand, what would be thought of a Christian who not only approved of such drinking by guests

---

1. Jn. 2:11.
2. Acts 10:38.
3. Heb. 7:26.
4. Heb. 2:18.
5. Jn. 4:46.

at a wedding, but after they had consumed all that had been provided, on his own accord would provide a large amount of an even more intoxicating beverage to be consumed by the same guests.

All faithful servants of the Lord know that such an act would be disgraceful to the cause of Christ! Christians could have no respect for such a person. Yet, this is precisely what those who hold the view that all wine was intoxicating in the first century must assume the Lord did!

Those who believe in the divine nature and sinless character of the Son of God pity those who have no better Christ than this! Christians have a Christ for whom no apology is necessary, and for whose acts they must not blush with shame, but whose example is worthy of supreme imitation and highest admiration in all ages, by all nations, to the end of time!

2

MISCELLANEOUS NEGATIVE ARGUMENTS

Scriptural Injunction Argument

The view is quite commonly expressed that since the New Testament does not explicitly command individuals to abstain from the consumption of alcoholic beverages, the practice is not absolutely forbidden by the New Testament. In fact, one who so advocates has been quoted by Albert Hill as follows:

> Christ's disciple does not abstain from alcoholic beverages because of scriptural injunction. Nowhere does the Bible say that it is morally wrong to drink an alcoholic beverage. It does teach that it is a sin to drink to excess or to become intoxicated.[1]

The argument constitutes a basic misunderstanding which is prevalent to a great extent in the religious world today. The implication is that any act forbidden must be specifically enjoined by a scriptural injunction. Such reasoning is erroneous because no positive prohibition is given for many activities which are sinful. The New Testament does not explicitly state that it is sinful to use mechanical instrumental music in Christian worship or to sprinkle infants as a religious practice. Neither does the New Testament explicitly state that it is sinful to gamble or use heroin; yet, true Christians know that such activities are sinful. The fallacy of such reasoning may be observed in the following statement: "Since the New Testament does not command persons to abstain from using heroin, its use must not be absolutely forbidden." Although the New Testament does

---

1. Albert Hill, "Moderate Drinking," *Gospel Defender* 8 (March 1967):1

not explicitly state that its use is sinful, persons are not justified in assuming that its use is permissible. This is true because its use is forbidden by implicit statements in the New Testament. Various principles and specific instructions in the New Testament, which concern evils that result from the use of things, prohibit not only the use of heroin but the imbibing of all kinds of intoxicating beverages as well.

In reference to the significance of implicit statements it has been said,

> Everything the Bible teaches, it teaches either (1) explicitly, or (2) implicitly. And, whatever it teaches implicitly is just as true, factual, binding, or authoritative as is that which is taught explicitly. When geometry sets forth *explicitly* the axiom that "the whole of anything is the sum of its parts," then geometry sets forth *implicitly* that the whole of anything is larger than any of its parts, and that the part of anything is smaller than the whole to which it relates. And, that which is here taught *implicitly* is just as true as is that which is taught *explicitly*.[1]

Principles involved in implicit teaching will be dealt with to a greater degree later in the book.[2]

Ephesians 5:18

Often efforts are made to justify the light intake or consumption of alcoholic beverages based on the King James Version rendering of Paul: "And be not drunk with wine, wherein is excess . . ."[3] The claim is advanced that since Paul places emphasis and condemnation on "excess," the imbibing of alcoholic beverages in lesser quantities is permissible.[4]

The conclusion is not warranted, however, for "excess" has reference to results, not quantity.[5] The term, *asotia,* from which the expression comes, is rendered "riot" in Titus 1:6 and 1 Peter 4:4 and, as an adverb, is rendered "riotous" in Luke 15:13. It is also rendered "riot" in the American Standard

---

1. Roy Clifton Deaver, "Establishing Bible Authority," *Harding Graduate School of Religion Lectures* (Nashville: Gospel Advocate Co., 1971), p. 221.

2. See "Implicit Authority Argument," pp. 129–37.

3. Eph. 5:18 (KJV).

4. Horace Bumstead, "The Biblical Sanction for Wine," *Bibliotheca Sacra* (January 1881):89.

5. Samuel Thomas Bloomfield, *Greek New Testament with English Notes,* p. 403.

Version of the alleged proof text. As employed, the term has reference to an incorrigible, abandoned, and dissolute life.[1] Because of such effects, therefore, persons should not imbibe alcoholic beverages to any degree.

Luke 21:34

Efforts have been made to justify "social" drinking from the statement of Jesus, "But take heed to yourselves lest haply your hearts be overcharged with surfeiting, and drunkenness, and cares of this life . . ."[2]

It is claimed that if Jesus had intended for persons to practice abstinence, He would not have thought it sufficient to admonish His disciples to guard against being overcome by drunkenness. It is also claimed that the Bible would not contain so many condemnations of the "excessive" use of alcoholic beverages if it did not, at the same time, sanction their "moderate" use.[3] Such a position however cannot be sustained.

Evil Practices Denounced

By the prohibition of any practice Jesus denounced everything which leads to it or partakes of its spirit. By condemning a class of sins in their more aggravated form, He condemned them in all their degrees. In denouncing drunkenness, therefore, He denounced "social" drinking, which is but a stage of drunkenness. The absurdity of the interpretation which wrests from such passages the sanction for "social" drinking is exposed by applying the same principle to other passages in the Bible, as may be seen from the following examples.

Parallel Examples

It would be just as reasonable to construe the injunction "be not overmuch wicked . . ."[4] to mean that wickedness is acceptable so long as

---

1. Joseph Henry Thayer, *Greek-English Lexicon of the New Testament*, p. 82; David Martyn Lloyd-Jones, *Life in the Spirit* (Grand Rapids: Baker Book House, 1974), p. 14.

2. Lk. 21:34. "Overcharged" is from *barunthosin*, literally, "weighed down." "Surfeiting," from *kraipale*, denotes giddiness.

3. The same construction is placed on Romans 13:13; 1 Corinthians 5:11; 6:10; and Galatians 5:21.

4. Eccles. 7:17.

persons do not multiply it. By the same reasoning, it could clearly be stated that "wherefore putting away all filthiness and overflowing of wickedness . . ."[1] means that wickedness is sanctioned so long as it is not excessive. Furthermore, the statement that unbelievers "think it strange that ye run not with them into the same excess of riot . . ."[2] could be construed to mean that indulgence in minor irregularities is permissible. In immediate connection with one of the phrases most often or commonly cited in defense of "social" drinking, namely, "not given to much wine . . . ," is another biblical qualification of deacons, ". . . not greedy of filthy lucre."[3] The kind of reasoning which would allow "social" drinking, based on the preceding passages, along with this passage, would also allow dishonesty or deceit in business to a lesser degree, based on this passage.

The Teaching of Jesus

It is clear that the greater part of the teaching of Jesus is of a general nature. He made no attempt to cover every ramification of every possible course of action by particular precepts. There were many evil practices of His own day which He did not expressly forbid.

Jesus did not speak directly against slave-holding or polygamy. There is little doubt, however, that the whole tendency of His attitude, example, and teaching was to condemn and eliminate such practices. He did not attempt to provide specifically against evils which might arise for the first time in future ages. Had Jesus forbidden by name the use of various fermented beverages which were known in His day, it would likely have been thought of as sanction to use distilled beverages, which were not known until many centuries later. Although He did not expressly forbid many things, He did enunciate laws of personal duty which cover these and every other form of sinful indulgence. Thus, for the whole sphere of human behavior, He has established comprehensive principles which are suited for every conceivable circumstance and need. The principles of Jesus are universal in their character and adaptations, and no

---

1. Jas. 1:21.
2. 1 Pet. 4:4.
3. 1 Tim. 3:8.

contingency of the future can exhaust their significance or exceed their application.

Commendation Argument

It is charged that Jesus commended intoxicating wine based on His allusions to wine in three parallel passages, Matthew 9:17, Mark 2:22, and Luke 5:37–39. The passage in Luke shall be examined since it contains an important addition not found in either Matthew or Mark. The passage is as follows:

> And no man putteth new wine into old wine-skins; else the new wine will burst the skins, and itself will be spilled, and the skins will perish. But new wine must be put into fresh wine-skins. And no man having drunk old wine desireth new, for he saith, The old is good.

There are a number of extremely interesting things to observe in connection with this important statement.

New Wine

It is only in this passage, and those parallel with it, that *oinos neos,* or new wine, occurs in the New Testament. Persons have commonly held the view that the phrase denotes wine recently expressed, but already in a state of active fermentation. Such wine, it is stated, could not safely be put into a leather bottle which had become old and weak since the chemical forces would rapidly rend the fabric. On the other hand, it is claimed that when the skin was new and strong, it could withstand the strain of fermentation, or, being elastic, could stretch and still remain whole.

No skin, however, could remain whole if fermentation should get ⸴nder full headway. The carbonic acid gas generated by the process would rupture a new skin almost as rapidly as an old one. Elihu recognized this principle when he stated, "Behold, my breast is as wine which hath no vent; like new wine-skins it is ready to burst."[1]

But if "new wine" is not wine in the act of fermentation, it can no more be wine which has completed that process because, if the

---

1. Job 32:19.

fermentation were complete, old skins would be as serviceable as new ones. The conclusion, therefore, would seem to be inevitable that if it were neither a wine in active fermentation nor one fully fermented, it must have been unfermented.

Preservation of Unfermented Juice

Fermentation would not necessarily take place within the skin. It has already been noted that in antiquity there were at least five methods by which fermentation could be prevented.

Grape juice could have been carefully expressed, filtered, and boiled in order that any impurity might be expelled. Then it could with complete safety have been put into a bottle, which could have been so prepared as to entirely exclude air. No other precaution would have been necessary. It was with this end in view that a new skin was always selected, one that was neither cracked nor ripped. A new skin would also keep the new wine perfectly sweet. An old skin would almost inevitably have some of the sour remains of a former vintage adhering to it. Thus, when the fresh grape juice was poured in, fermentation would necessarily follow. It was for this same reason that Columella, in describing the common process of preserving unfermented wine, placed equal stress on its being put into a new *amphora*.[1]

Any one of these processes of removing the gluten, evaporating the moisture, preventing the access of air, or reducing the temperature, would have resulted in the preservation of wine in an unfermented state. On the other hand, if it had been thought best, any two or all of the methods might have been combined. This being the case, therefore, another proof is furnished for the generic character of *oinos*.

Luke 5:39

Though it is not included in the accounts of Matthew and Mark, verse 39 is an integral part of the narrative since it contains, if anything does, Jesus' outspoken commendation of intoxicating wine: "And no man having drunk old wine desireth new; for he saith, The old is good." The first question which arises concerns whether the term "new wine" has

---

1. Columella, *De Re Rustica* 12. 41.

the same signification in this verse as in the two preceding verses. Although it cannot be maintained that *oinos neos* always denotes a wine which is free from fermentation, the Septuagint rendering of Job 32:19 being an example, there can be no doubt that it does in the present instance. Neither can there be any question that it is used in this sense in the Septuagint rendering of Isaiah 49:26. In this text, the Hebrew *asis* is rendered *oinos neos,* which in the American Standard Version is translated "sweet wine." In the passage under consideration the implication is that it has the same signification as in the passage preceding. Used consecutively, and without any intimation of a change of meaning, it may be concluded that it has undergone none. The "new wine" of verse 39 is the "new wine" of verse 39, and the "old wine" of verse 39 is the "new wine" fermented and strengthened by age. The verse therefore says, "And no man having drunk old [fermented] wine desireth new; (that of the last vintage and unfermented) for he saith, The old is good."

The expression, "The old [wine] is good" (better than the new wine), is not Jesus' judgment as to the better wine. He is simply stating a general verdict, and in no way gives commendation of it. Of this idea, A. B. Rich stated, "This was not the judgment of Christ respecting the superiority of old, fermented wines, but of drunkards, whose habit it had been to drink them."[1] It is not the universal judgment of men, nor does it make plain that wine, either fermented or partially fermented, was not a favorite drink among the Jews. It simply states that one who has acquired a taste for old wine does not care for the new. It is said that the effect of imbibing alcoholic beverages is to create a desire for such beverages which grows with indulgence. The longer, therefore, that it is gratified, the stronger must be the beverage which will satisfy its craving. A simple unintoxicating wine therefore would have no value for one accustomed to intoxicating wine.

In rebuttal it is argued that the Lord did not state, "No drunkard having drunk old wine," but "no man *(oudeis)."*[2] *Oudeis,* however, is not always or necessarily universal in its application. That the Greek term is at times or occasionally so employed in the New Testament is quite evident from John 3:32. "No man *(oudeis)* receiveth his testimony," (KJV)

---

1. A. B. Rich, p. 404.
2. Dunlop Moore, p. 91.

John said, speaking of Jesus. But he immediately added in verse 33, "He that hath received his testimony . . . ," (KJV) showing that the negative was not used in an absolute sense. If it had been the desire or intent to make an unqualified statement in Luke 5:39, the separate forms *oude eis* would have been used, as they are in such passages as Romans 3:10 and 1 Corinthians 6:5.

It has been objected that Jesus "does not speak of those whose habit it had been to drink old, fermented wines; for He uses the aorist participle *pion*, which does not mark a habit."[1]

Such is the case, but on the other hand it does not deny a habit either. The briefest act of drinking may be viewed as going on, and thus be expressed by the present; so the most extended act of drinking may be viewed simply as brought to pass, and thus be expressed by the aorist. The passage therefore could be rendered, "No man, after he has begun to drink old wine, desireth new." The text does not indicate that such persons will never desire the new.

The American Standard Version omits *eutheos* (straightway), but the very idea of the parable is concentrated in this verb. All the known facts in the case warrant its retention. Habits and tastes change gradually, but here there is a strong implication that a slight experience will work a transformation of prejudice, and the old wine give place to the new. Although the King James Version describes it as "better," there is no objective comparison whatever between the old and the new wine. It is merely the opinion of the individual who is quite satisfied with what he has. It is good enough for him.[2]

There is no basis therefore for the claim that Jesus commended intoxicating wine according to the present context.

Luke 7:31–35

The theory has been advanced that according to the context of Luke 7:31–35, the Lord was a winebibber and therefore commended the imbibing of alcoholic beverages.

---

1. Ibid.

2. Relative to wineskins and wines, a similar view is expressed by Mrs. T. P. Holman, "Wines of the Ancients and of the Bible," *Gospel Advocate* 27 (3 June 1885):342.

In the passage, however, there is not the slightest encouragement for the use of such beverages. The whole force of the reproof of Jesus to the men of His day lay in the falsehood of the statements of His and John's critics. The charge against John, the Nazarite,[1] was a lie, and the libel against Jesus was also a lie, both invented by malicious adversaries because the two teachers denounced the hypocrisy and vices of that day and of all future days.

If the first claim, on the authority of His enemies, is believed, the second and the third must be accepted, for the authority is the same.[2] Jesus, who lived under the law of Moses, did not violate any law or principle of the law during His earthly life. There are, however, several vital teachings in the Old Testament which would have been violated had Jesus imbibed intoxicating beverages.

Winston defines the English term "winebibber," as applying to a drunkard.[3] The scholarly *Oxford Universal Dictionary* renders the term, "a tippler, a drunkard."[4] The Greek term *oinopotes* is used only in this connection in the New Testament. The Septuagint employed it to render the Old Testament Hebrew term *sovai-yayin*, or, "soakers of wine."[5] It is also found in Classic Greek.[6]

It has been said that it was Jesus Himself who acquainted men with the charge by stating that His drinking wine brought on Him a railing accusation of the men of His generation.[7]

It should be observed, however, that Jesus did not say that he drank *intoxicating* wine. There is therefore no ground for the charge that He was a winebibber! It is true that the Lord attempted no explicit denial of the charge or allegation, but neither did He deny that John had a demon, or that He was Himself also a glutton and "a friend of publicans and sinners," who, in addition to being carnal, were devoted to indulgence of passions or appetites.

---

1. An alternate spelling is "Nazirite."
2. William Patton, p. 81.
3. "Winebibber," in *The Winston Dictionary* (Philadelphia: John C. Winston Co., 1954), p. 1143.
4. "Wine," in *The Oxford Universal Dictionary on Historical Principles*, p. 2433.
5. Prov. 23:20.
6. Anacreon 72; Polybius 20. 8.
7. Dunlop Moore, p. 88.

A question can be raised as to why the Lord made no denial of these charges. Perhaps it was because He knew that none was called for. The Lord's enemies knew that they were false. Although they knew that He was not a winebibber, they fully intended to destroy His influence as a moral teacher and religious leader. They had determined that they could accomplish this most effectively by attacking His character. Jesus was aware of the fact that those who knew Him needed no denial, and that those who hated Him would accept none.

The fact that the Lord's enemies put gluttony, sensuality, and wine-bibbing on a par proves the estimation in which winebibbing was held. Although considered a disgrace in that day, as it is by all righteous thinking persons today, on the ground of several unscrupulous slanders, persons are asked to believe that Jesus exposed Himself to that disgrace! It would be just as reasonable to regard Him "who did no sin" as a blasphemer because He was charged with that offense before the high court of Caiaphas.

Such slanderous charges had been made against Jesus on other occasion, when it was said, for instance, that He was a Samaritan and had a devil. The food and drink which Jesus consumed was not calculated, like alcoholic drinks of today, to engender an intemperate appetite and rob persons of their powers of reason and affection. Jesus dismissed the slander by the simple remark, "And wisdom is justified of all her children,"[1] which implies that His disciples were acquainted with His manner of life and could justify Him against the base slanders of His enemies.

Those who hold the view that Jesus consumed wine which John the Baptist refused, in attempting to justify their position, assume that John refused *only* intoxicating wine! They fail to recognize the fact that, in regard to grapes and grape products as concerns the Nazarite vow, Moses declared,

> He shall separate himself from wine and strong drink; he shall drink no vinegar of wine, or vinegar of strong drink, neither shall he drink any juice of grapes, nor eat fresh grapes or dried. All the days of his separation shall he eat nothing that is made of the grapevine, from the kernels even to the husk.[2]

---

1. Lk. 7:35.
2. Num. 6:3–4.

It may be seen, therefore, that Nazarites were to abstain, not only from intoxicating wine, but from all products of the vine, from the kernel or grape stone to the husk. This requirement would, of course, include unfermented and, thus, unintoxicating grape juice or wine. Since it is the case, according to the law of the Nazarites, that John would have refused unfermented grape juice or wine also, those who allege that Jesus imbibed intoxicating wine as a beverage, so do without validity. Since John, in being true to the law, would have refused both intoxicating and unintoxicating wine, it cannot be proved that because Luke 7:34 states, "The Son of man is come eating and drinking," the Lord imbibed intoxicating wine, for He could have "come eating and drinking" unintoxicating wine!

Some persons think that it is unreasonable to believe that Jesus would have been accused on the basis of imbibing unintoxicating grape juice, and that the Pharisees were not so foolish as to make such an accusation. The writer denies that such belief is unreasonable! It should not be considered as unreasonable in view of the fact that often, even today, when persons are enraged, jealous, and filled with intense envy, they will go to any length to endeavor to sustain their case. When such persons do not have reasons, it is commonly said that one excuse is as good as another! That the Pharisees manifested such an attitude can readily be seen, not only from the context, but from the remainder of the book of Luke, along with the books of Matthew, Mark, and John. The Pharisees were indeed beside themselves with jealousy and envy, and they were highly enraged because Jesus had repeatedly stymied their slanderous interrogations at every point! The Lord had shown their teachings to be false and their thoughts and conduct to be filled with hypocrisy.

Those who attempt to use such passages to justify their evil practices, or to condone the activities of others, make indeed a serious charge against the sinless Son of God! There are those, however, who endeavor to escape the force of the argument by alleging that John was not a Nazarite. Existing evidence is not supportive of the allegation.[1] That John was given to austerity and the practice of ascetic customs cannot be successfully denied. Albert Barnes stated that John came "neither

---

1. Mt. 11:18–19; Lk. 1:15; 7:33–34.

eating nor drinking, abstaining as a Nazarite."[1] The scholarly J. W. McGarvey said, "John's life of Nazarite abstinence was wisely adapted to the special mission on which he was sent."[2] Arnold Ruegg states, "The angelic injunction that he should drink neither wine nor strong drink points to his taking the vows of a Nazarite."[3] Alfred Edersheim affirms that he was a "life-Nazarite, as Samson and Samuel of old had been."[4] Herbert Lockyer indicates that he was "a Nazarite from his birth."[5] The imitable H. Leo Boles declares, "John was a Nazarite (Luke 1:15), and had to live as he did."[6]

Those who insist that Jesus imbibed an intoxicating wine as a beverage must face that following argument which is stated in the form of a destructive dilemma.

(1) If Jesus imbibed intoxicating wine as a beverage, then He experienced a degree of drunkenness; and if drunkenness is sinful, then Jesus sinned.

(2) Either Jesus did not experience a degree of drunkenness, or He did not sin.

(3) Either Jesus did not imbibe intoxicating wine as a beverage, or drunkenness is not sinful.

If the argument is valid and the propositions are true, the conclusion must be true. The argument *is* stated in valid form as can be proved by the use of truth tables. The first proposition is true based on the fact that intoxication (drunkenness) is but a matter of degree or a state of "becoming softened" according to the meaning of the term *methusko.* Drunkenness is sinful as per such passages as Romans 13:13, 1 Corinthians 6:9–10, Galatians 5:19–21, and Ephesians 5:18. The second proposi-

1. Albert Barnes, *Matthew and Mark,* Notes on the New Testament, vol. 1, p. 121.

2. John William McGarvey, *Matthew and Mark,* The New Testament Commentary, vol. 1 (Delight, Arkansas: Gospel Light Publishing Co., n.d.), p. 100.

3. Arnold Ruegg, "John the Baptist," in *New Schaff-Herzog Encyclopedia of Religious Knowledge,* 6:207.

4. Alfred Edersheim, *The Life and Times of Jesus the Messiah,* vol. 1, p. 106.

5. Herbert Lockyer, *All the Men of the Bible* (Grand Rapids: Zondervan Publishing House, 1958), p. 196.

6. Henry Leo Boles, *A Commentary on the Gospel According to Matthew* (Nashville: Gospel Advocate Co., 1952), p. 247.

tion is true based on such passages as Proverbs 23:31–32. Since the argument is therefore valid and the propositions are true, the conclusion is irresistible! There is absolutely nothing in the New Testament to indicate that Jesus imbibed or approved the imbibing of such intoxicants as a beverage.

The Good Samaritan

The claim is advanced, based on the parable of the good Samaritan, that Jesus commended the use of wine. In the story, the Samaritan bound up the man's wounds, "pouring on them oil and wine *(oinos)*."[1]

It should be observed that the commendation implied in the passage is of the medicinal use of wine. Even then its application was external, not internal. Although wine for such use would likely have been fermented, the claim is unwarranted in light of the fact that it was not used as a beverage. Even if its use had been prescribed internally, as was the case with Timothy, it would not have been a mere beverage, but a medicine.

General Arguments

Noah and Lot

It has been affirmed that since good men such as Noah and Lot used wine as a beverage, such use is biblically acceptable today.

Although it is true that various Bible characters used wine, it is not true that God sanctioned their use of intoxicating wine as a beverage. It can be as logically reasoned that since various Bible characters practiced polygamy, such is biblically permissible today. Not only does the Bible not commend good men for drinking such wine as a beverage, it nowhere commends good men for doing any other wrong act.

Numbers 28:7

Efforts have been made to justify the consumption of alcoholic beverages based on Numbers 28:7. It is alleged that since "strong drink" was to be used as a drink-offering unto God, the consumption of such beverages is permissible today.

---

1. Lk. 10:34.

Even if it could be proved that the "strong drink" under consideration[1] was intoxicating, the claim would not be proved. From several passages in the Bible[2] as well as from the writing of Flavius Josephus,[3] it may be observed that a libation of wine was daily offered to God. Josephus stated that it was poured "on the burnt-offerings." Since the drink-offering was poured out and not drunk, the claim is false. Many expositors, including Matthew Henry, C. J. Elliott, and Robert Milligan, hold this view.[4]

In none of the allusions which the Old Testament makes to the use of wine for religious purposes, is a fermented article indicated,[5] and in its only reference to the use of wine at any of the religious feasts an unfermented wine is specified.[6] Alvah Hovey quotes J. M. Van Buren in reference to the King James Version rendering of Numbers 28:7 as follows:

> We have a true and proper presentation of Numbers 28:7 in the Septuagint Greek of the Old Testament, made 300 years before Christ, by learned Jewish scholars, while these offerings were made daily. They did not see "strong wine" in the text . . . They simply transferred the Hebrew word *shekar*, with a slight change for euphony, into *sikera*.[7]

---

1. *Shekar.*

2. Ex. 29:40; Lev. 23:13; Num. 15:1–16; 28:7–29.

3. Flavius Josephus, *Wars of the Jews* 5. 13.

4. Matthew Henry, *Genesis to Joshua,* Commentary on the Whole Bible, vol. 1 (New York: Fleming H. Revell Co., n.d.), n.p.; C. J. Elliott, *Numbers,* A Bible Commentary for English Readers, ed. Charles John Ellicott (New York: Cassell and Co., n.d.), p. 557; Robert Milligan, *Scheme of Redemption* (St. Louis: Bethany Press, reprint ed., 1962), p. 143.

5. Two terms are employed in the requirements and references concerning drink-offerings. They are the generic *yayin* (Ex. 29:40; Lev. 23:13; Num. 15:7; 28:14; Deut. 14:26; Hos. 9:4) and the generic *shekar* (Num. 28:7; Deut. 14:26). The first juice to reach the lower vat was called the *dema,* and formed the first-fruits of the vintage, to be presented to God (Ex. 22:29 KJV). It was no doubt a fresh and unfermented article, similar to the Latin *protropum.*

6. Neh. 8:10. The Feast of the Tabernacles is referred to, and the fact that it occurred during the grape harvest confirms the unfermented character of "sweet" *mamtaqqim.*

7. Alvah Hovey, "Shekhar and Leaven in Mosaic Offerings," *The Old Testament Student* 6 (September 1886):16.

Judges 9:13

The view has been expressed that since the Bible does not condemn wine which has cheering qualities,[1] and only fermented and, thus, intoxicating wine could possess such qualities, intoxicating wine should not be condemned, or viewed as unacceptable.

The phrase "new wine" in Judges 9:13, which comes from *tirosh,* could easily denote unfermented wine. In addition, the Bible does not teach that only wine possesses cheering qualities. Zechariah declared, "Corn shall make the young men cheerful, and new wine the maids."[2] In this passage, in which "new wine" is from the same term *tirosh,* there is a clear indication that corn possesses the same cheerful quality, although that it is unintoxicating is readily admitted. The statement is simply indicative of the effects of food upon hungry persons.

Matthew 15:11

The theory has been advanced that Jesus did not condemn the imbibing of intoxicating wine because He said, "Not that which entereth into the mouth defileth the man; but that which proceedeth out of the mouth, this defileth the man."[3]

In reply it may be noted that, based on such reasoning, the intake of any harmful substance would be permissible, including such powerful poisons as cyanide or strychnine, and such harmful drugs as opium or heroin. Surely it can be seen by any rational person that those who would advocate such are hard-pressed for an argument!

Matthew, Mark, and John

Jesus on the Cross

It is claimed by various advocates of "social" drinking that Jesus, shortly before His death, consumed intoxicating wine as a beverage, and that in so doing, He sanctioned its consumption as a beverage. The idea is that Jesus refused a wine which was drugged while He still had some purpose to serve, but when there was no further purpose to be

---

1. Judg. 9:13.
2. Zech. 9:17 (KJV).
3. Mt. 15:11.

served and the end was imminent, He allowed Himself the indulgence of such wine.

It is true that, while on the cross, Jesus was offered one beverage, wine mixed with a narcotic,[1] which He declined, and another drink which He accepted.[2] The aforementioned claim is false, however, for two reasons. (1) It is incorrect to state that the Lord had no further purpose to serve, and (2) it is also incorrect to state that the two drinks were alike. Although there was little difference in time, to account for these contrasted attitudes of the Lord, there was a significant difference in the drinks which were offered.

It may be seen from the record of Matthew that Jesus tasted wine mingled with gall. The fact that He did not reject this drink until he had tasted it indicated His willingness to accept any simple liquid to supply His needs. Had He imbibed the drugged wine, the Lord could not have spoken as He did on the cross and have made His death what it was. After a taste therefore, He refused more, and "the imperfect *ethele* reads as though He was repeatedly urged to drink and as repeatedly refused."[3]

An investigation of the following parallel passages from Matthew and Mark indicate that there was a difference in the drinks offered the Lord. (1) "They gave him wine to drink mingled with gall: and when he had tasted it, he would not drink."[4] (2) "And they offered him wine mingled with myrrh: but he received it not."[5]

Now, notice the difference when the second drink was offered. (1) "And straightway one of them ran, and took a sponge, and filled it with vinegar, and put it on a reed, and gave him to drink."[6] (2) "And one ran, and filling a sponge full of vinegar, put it on a reed, and gave him to drink, saying, Let be; let us see whether Elijah cometh to take him down."[7]

---

1. Mt. 27:34; Mk. 15:23.
2. Mt. 27:48; Mk. 15:36; Jn. 19:30.
3. R. C. H. Lenski, *The Interpretation of St. Matthew's Gospel* (Minneapolis: Augsburg Publishing House, 1943), p. 1106.
4. Mt. 27:34.
5. Mk. 15:23.
6. Mt. 27:48.
7. Mk. 15:37.

In the account of John, no doubt is left as to whether Jesus accepted the second offering, that which is described in Matthew 27:48 and Mark 15:37, for John said, "When Jesus therefore had received the vinegar, he said, It is finished: and he bowed his head, and gave up his spirit."[1]

The term which is rendered "wine" in these passages is translated from *oinon* or *oinos,* while the term "vinegar" is employed to express the meaning of *oxous* or *oxos.*

An effort may be made to destroy the writer's reasoning in the present argument by stating that all versions do not use the term "wine" *(oinos)* in Matthew 27:34. Although it is true that some versions employ different renderings, particularly in regard to this passage, it may be observed that the widely used Nestle Greek Text and Westcott-Hort Text each use the terms *oinon* or *oinos.*[2]

In reference to the drink of Matthew 27:34, Robertson states that it is *later* manuscripts which read "vinegar *(oxos)* instead of wine."[3] Henry Alford, A. B. Bruce, and J. P. Lange each indicate that the term *oinon* is employed in Matthew 27:34 in such important codices as the Vaticanus and Sinaiticus.[4] In addition, Edersheim states that "the best manuscripts read wine" in Matthew 27:34.[5] The scholarly John A. Broadus in speaking of the same verse, says, "The correct text in Matthew is clearly "wine."[6] W. E. Vine also declares, "In Matthew 27:34 the best texts have *oinos,* "wine."[7]

---

1. Jn. 19:30.

2. Alfred Marshall, *The Interlinear Greek-English New Testament: Nestle Greek Text with a Literal English Translation* (London: Samuel Bagster and Sons, Limited, 1958), pp. 130–131, 212–213, 452; Brooke Foss Westcott, Fenton John Anthony Hort, *The New Testament in the Original Greek* (New York: Macmillan Co., 1949), pp. 68, 111, 235. See also Richard Francis Weymouth, *The Resultant Greek Testament* (London: James Clarke and Co., 1905), pp. 81–82, 140, 298.

3. Archibald Thomas Robertson, *Word Pictures of the New Testament,* vol. 1, p. 231. Emphasis mine, WDJ.

4. Henry Afford, *Alford's Greek Testament,* vol. 1 (Grand Rapids: Guardian Press, n.d.), p. 292; Alexander Balmain Bruce, "The Synoptic Gospels," in *Expositor's Greek Testament,* ed. W. Robertson Nicoll (Grand Rapids: Wm. B. Eerdmans Publishing Co., 2976), 1:328; John Peter Lange, *Commentary on the Holy Scriptures: Matthew* (Grand Rapids: Zondervan Publishing House, n.d.), p. 519.

5. Alfred Edersheim, *The Life and Times of Jesus the Messiah,* vol. 2 (Grand Rapids: Wm. B. Eerdmans Publishing Co., 1962), p. 590.

6. John A. Broadus, *Commentary on the Gospel of Matthew* (Philadelphia: American Baptist Publication Society, 1886), p. 569

7. "Vinegar," in *An Expository Dictionary of New Testament Words,* ed. William Edwyn Vine (Old Tappan, New Jersey: Fleming H. Revell Co., 2940), 4:188.

The fact that there was a difference between the *oinos* mingled with gall which the Lord was formerly offered, and refused, and the *oxos* (vinegar) which He later accepted, destroys the theory of those who advance the view that Jesus accepted an intoxicating beverage, while on the cross.

A Roman Illustration

The ancient Romans were aware of the difference between *oinos* and *oxos*. The fact that the Roman government demanded extreme discipline in their soldiers, as well as the fact that they recognized the dangers involved in soldiers functioning under intoxicated conditions may be observed from the following.

Upon entering the Roman army, soldiers were administered an oath which was renewed annually.[1] Orders were demanding and discipline was rigid. The soldier "swore never to desert the standard, to be *absolutely obedient* to orders given him and to be willing to give up his life for the safety of the Emperor and the Empire"[2] In the Roman system of government, there were consuls who exercised kingly power known as the *imperium*. The consular *imperium* gave its holder absolute power over the lives of the soldiers in the field, and death was the penalty for the neglect of duty, disobedience, or cowardice.[3]

Oxos, which served as the beverage of the lower orders, especially slaves, was the "only refreshment allowed to soldiers while engaged in active service."[4] An example of this principle may be seen in the case of an early Roman army of some 65,000 well-disciplined men whose leader supplied a very large quantity of "vinegar and biscuits for the use of the soldiers," but who "prohibited the indulgence of wine."[5]

---

1. Edward Gibbon, *The History of the Decline and Fall of the Roman Empire,* vol. 1 (Philadelphia: Porter and Coates, n.d.), p. 53.
2. Dorothy Mills, *The Book of the Ancient Romans* (New York: G. P. Putnam's Sons, 1937), p. 417. Emphasis mine, WDJ.
3. E. R. Boak, *A History of Rome to 565 A.D.* (New York: Macmillan Co. 1955), pp. 66, 87.
4. David Smith, "Vinegar," in *Dictionary of Christ and the Gospels,* vol. 2, ed. James Hastings (Grand Rapids: Baker Book House, 1973), p. 803.
5. Edward Gibbon, vol. 2, p. 364.

Although they were not allowed to use intoxicants under such conditions, they were provided with *oxos,* which is translated *homec* in the Septuagint and *posca* in Latin. *Oxos,* which was also given to them with meals, as well as to common workers, was good for quenching thirst and for refreshment. With a strong degree of sourness, it was used as seasoning in the preparation of foods. The term is set in the light of Psalm 69:21 which speaks of the innocent sufferer being given vinegar to drink.[1]

Vinegar, Wine, and Fermentation

In regard to Matthew 27:48, in speaking of the Lord's actions, Albert Barnes states that the vinegar which Jesus drank "was not intended to stupefy Him or blunt His sense of pain, like the wine and myrrh."[2]

Adam Clarke quotes Michaelis as follows:

> Wine mixed with myrrh was given to malefactors at the place of execution, to intoxicate them, and make them less sensible to pain. Christ, therefore, with great propriety, refused the aid of such remedies. But if vinegar was offered him, which was taken merely to assuage thirst, there could be no reason for his rejecting it. Besides, he tasted it before he rejected it; and therefore he must have found it different from that which, if offered to him, he was ready to receive.[3]

It may be observed, therefore, that Michaelis viewed the Lord as rejecting wine mixed with myrrh but accepting vinegar which was altogether a different drink. Jesus was not inconsistent in accepting the *oxos* after having refused the drugged wine. He refused the narcotic, but accepted the refreshment.

There are three kinds of fermentation, namely, (1) vinous fermentation, which is accompanied by the formation of alcohol; (2) acetous fermentation, which is accompanied by the formation of vinegar; and

1. Hans Wolfgang Heidland, "Oxos," in *Theological Dictionary of the New Testament,* eds. Gerhard Kittel and Gerhard Friedrich (Grand Rapids: Wm. B. Eerdmans Publishing Co., 1967), 5:288–89. See also G. Abbott-Smith, *A Manual Greek Lexicon of the New Testament,* p. 319.
2. Albert Barnes, *Matthew and Mark,* p. 319.
3. Adam Clarke, *Matthew–Acts,* A Commentary and Critical Notes, vol. 5, p. 273.

(3) lactic fermentation, which induces the souring process in milk. Intoxication does not result from acetous or lactic fermentation.

Oxos is the equivalent of *chomets,* which comes from *chamets* which etymologically means "to be acid," and therefore involves acidity, or something pungent or sour to the taste. Before such wine became soured, it passed through acetous fermentation whereby an additional chemical change was effected.[1]

Of *chomets,* the equivalent of *oxos,* Alvah Hovey said it was "neither exhilarating nor intoxicating."[2] When vinous fermentation is not well regulated a fresh chemical change takes place and the wine is converted into vinegar *(oxos).* If the vinegar is exposed to air it loses its properties and becomes insipid, in which form it was called *vappa* by the Romans, who used the word figuratively for a worthless blockhead.[3]

Even if it could be proved that *oxos,* the drink which Jesus accepted, was an intoxicating article it would prove nothing about the Savior's principles of abstinence, or to our duty in this matter. It was taken under circumstances so utterly exceptional, the only possible analogy which in our own case would be a medicinal consideration, that no inference can be drawn from it concerning the present subject.[4]

Acts 2:13

Some persons have asserted that on Pentecost Peter indicated the apostles were accustomed to drunkenness, when he said, "for these are not drunken, as ye suppose; seeing it is but the third hour of the day.[5]

The claim is made that since Peter only gave as their reason for not being drunk the fact that it was "but the third hour of the day," they were given to drunkenness on occasion. It is further claimed that since such activity was permissible for them, it is also acceptable today.

---

1. E. W. Herndon, "Wine in the Lord 's Supper," *Christian Quarterly Review* 5 (July 1886):329.

2. Alvah Hovey, p. 16.

3. William Ramsay, "Vinum," in *Smith's Dictionary of Greek and Roman Antiquities,* p. 1204.

4. See Appendix B, Table Four, pp. 206-08, for a list of renderings from various versions of *oinon* and *oxos* in Matthew 27:34, 48, Mark 15:23, 36; and John 19:30.

5. Acts 2:15.

The claim is without validity, and the charge is false for the following reasons: (1) The fact that *a* reason is given for abstaining from a particular activity, does not necessarily indicate that there are not other reasons for abstaining. (2) Even if it could be proved that the apostles were given to drunkenness on occasion,[1] it would only prove that they were guilty of sin, for the Bible plainly condemns drunkenness.[2] (3) The charge[3] had been made without proof and, at best, was only an assumption.

"The third hour of the day" is equivalent to the present-day nine o'clock in the morning. At this time, on a festival day such as this, no Jew would have yet broken his fast until at least the fourth hour.[4] So established was this practice that the apostle Paul indicates that was not usual even for drunkards to become drunken in the day-time.[5]

1 Corinthians 6:19–20

The idea has been advanced that 1 Corinthians 6:19–20 should not be used relative to the view that if alcoholic beverages are harmful to the human body, this passage condemns their consumption. The theory is based on the fact that the context has reference to fornication, or defilement by sexual immorality.

First, it should be observed that the writer of this book espouses the view that the intake of alcoholic beverages is harmful to the human body. Conclusive proof for the truthfulness of this position is discussed later.[6]

Second, regarding the theory that the passage should not be used, it may be noted that although the passage does apply to "fornication," or defilement by sexual immorality, the *principle* involved is the same regarding *any* harmful properties or agents. The fact that "fornication" would be harmful in a way other than physical, although it is not beyond

---

1. The writer does not hold this view!
2. Hab. 2:15; Lk. 21:34; Rom. 13:13; 1 Cor. 6:9–10; Gal. 5:19–21; Eph. 5:18.
3. The charge of the Jews.
4. Richard Belward Rackham, *The Acts of the Apostles* (London: Methuen and Co., 1901), pp. 17, 27.
5. 1 Thess. 5:7.
6. The discussion is in Part Two under the heading, "Physical Effects Argument," pp. 115–30.

the realm of possibility for it to be harmful in a physical way, does not negate the truthfulness of the writer's view.

Those who would deny the position that the passage condemns the intake of any harmful properties or agents will be hard pressed to inform thinking persons on what basis they would question the intake of opium, heroin, or any other destructive elements. Given their view, the intake of any harmful property or agent which is not prohibited by specific scriptural injunction would be permissible.[1]

Galatians 2:4; 5:1

It is claimed that such passages as Galatians 2:4 and 5:1 teach that Christians are at liberty or have freedom in Christ, restraints against personal preferences may be removed, and therefore alcoholic beverages may be consumed.

It should be observed that the principle under consideration in the alleged proof-texts is liberty or freedom from the law of Moses. However, this in no way negates responsibility to the law of Christ. In fact, Christians, as "servants of Christ,"[2] are "servants of righteousness."[3] Although the law of Christ is "the law of liberty,"[4] personal responsibility for individual actions is no less binding, for persons are to be governed or ruled by this "law."[5] Activities which are characterized by Christian liberty do not allow freedom to be used "for an occasion to the flesh."[6] Peter expressed the same principle when he stated, ". . . not using our freedom for a cloak of wickedness, but as bondservants of God."[7]

Freedom therefore is not freedom from restraint, and liberty is not the license for persons to do as they please, but only the freedom to do what they ought to do. Although many persons contend for freedom from restraint, such persons are often numbered with those who are

---

1. This latter view is discussed in Part One under the heading, "Scriptural Injunction Argument," pp. 60–64.
2. Eph. 6:6; cf. 1 Cor. 6:19–20.
3. Rom. 6:16–18.
4. Jas. 1:25.
5. "Law" denotes a rule of action.
6. Gal. 5:13.
7. 1 Pet. 2:16.

enslaved to alcoholic beverages. Christian liberty or freedom does not at any time and under any circumstance give license to that which is sinful.

Colossians 2:16–17

The theory has been advanced on occasion, based on Paul's declaration in Colossians 2:16–17, "Let no man therefore judge you in meat, or in drink. . . ," that Christians should remain silent regarding those who desire to engage in "social" drinking. The claim is made that the passage is never used by those who attempt to defend the view that the consumption of alcoholic beverages to any degree is sinful.

Those who so advocate are correct regarding the fact that the passage is not used by those who promote abstinence for such a purpose, although they are incorrect relative to such efforts being merely an attempt. The passage is not employed for the simple reason that it has no bearing on the present issue.

In the context, reference is made to certain Gnostic ideas. The matter to which Paul referred[1] involved Gnostic asceticism or a large number of regulations about what could and what could not be eaten and drunk. In other words, there was a return to all the food laws of the Jews, with their list of things clean and unclean. Paul was simply warning the Colossian brethren not to adopt these ascetic practices. There is, no doubt, reference here to the distinctions which the Jews made on this subject, implying that an effort had been made by Jewish teachers to show them that the Mosaic laws were binding on all. These laws relative to eating and drinking were not mere matters of law, but formed significant parts of a rigid mystic asceticism.

In regard to Paul's reference to judging, since the Bible does teach that persons are to be judged by their fruits, it may be correctly concluded that only such judging as is not required by the actual conduct of persons is condemned. All judging based on insufficient premises or motivated by ill will is of course prohibited. The judgment under consideration in this passage therefore has reference to the imposing of one's *own* laws upon another, which, of course, are none other than opinions.

---

1. i.e., eating and drinking.

The term "judge" *(krineto)* in Colossians 2:16 comes from *krino* which means "to condemn."[1] The word is here used in the sense of pronouncing a sentence. While it is true that persons are not to "judge" in this sense,[2] it does not follow that persons are not to cite others to what the Bible teaches relative to a particular matter. Since the Bible condemns false doctrine, Christians must not do less! There is a vast difference between pronouncing sentence upon *principles* and pronouncing sentence upon *persons.* The Lord will deal with all unrighteous *persons* in the final day of reckoning.[3]

The Lord's church does not err when it pleads with persons to accept what the Bible teaches regarding the imbibing of alcoholic beverages. The Lord's people, who are the church, are required to "contend earnestly for the faith,"[4] and Paul refers to the church as "the pillar and ground of the truth."[5] The church or individual Christians, for that matter, most certainly do not err in condemning the actions of those who imbibe alcoholic beverages!

Although the Lord referred to another matter when He said "judge not according to appearance, but judge righteous judgment,"[6] the *principle* applies in this case. The church absolutely does have the *right* and, in fact, even the *obligation* to judge or make determination between that which is right or wrong predicated, of course, on the word of God! If Christians are not to do this, there is no way in which Christians can, with God's approval, defend the purity of the truth and the sanctity of the church of the Lord against any false position!

When the Scriptures are correctly exegeted regarding a particular subject and, therefore, evidence and facts are ascertained, faith will be the result. When evidence is properly gathered and reasoned about accurately, truth will always be forthcoming. Once this takes place, in regard to the biblical view of alcoholic beverages or any other issue, Christians *must* love, proclaim, and defend this truth to the very best of their ability in order to be loyal soldiers of the Christ!

---

1. Joseph Henry Thayer, *Greek-English Lexicon of the New Testament,* pp. 360–61.
2. i.e., condemn persons and pronounce sentence upon them.
3. cf. Jn. 12:48.
4. Jude 3.
5. 1 Tim. 3:15. The term "ground" conveys the idea of support.
6. Jn. 7:24.

Let it be observed, in concluding this area of discussion, that the issue is not one of *personalities,* but of *principles.* The Bible, in *indelible* terms, condemns the imbibing of alcoholic beverages! Those, therefore, who so imbibe, whether members of the church of the Lord or otherwise, *condemn themselves,* for they disobey biblical precepts and principles.

1 Timothy 3:3, 8; Titus 1:7; 2:3

Frequently the view is expressed that because Paul stated that bishops are to be "not given to wine," and deacons and aged women are to be "not given to much wine," deacons and aged women may imbibe "moderate" amounts of intoxicating wine. On the other hand, some persons hold the view that in each instance "moderate" amounts are permissible.

The Renderings

The phrases under consideration are rendered as follows in the King James Version: (1) In discussing the qualifications of bishops Paul says they must be "not given to wine."[1] (2) In discussing the qualifications of deacons Paul says they must be "not given to much wine."[2] (3) In discussing deportment for aged women Paul says they must be "not given to much wine."[3]

In the American Standard Version the phrase in (1) is rendered "no brawler." The rendering in (2) is identical in both versions, while (3) is rendered "nor enslaved to much wine" in the American Standard Version.

Bishops, Deacons, and Aged Women

As they pertain to the qualifications of bishops, "not given to wine" and "no brawler" come from the adjective *paroinos,* which literally denotes "tarrying at wine."[4] The term "brawler" thus conveys the detrimental consequences of such action.

---

1. 1 Tim. 3:3; Tit. 1:7.
2. 1 Tim. 3:8.
3. Tit. 2:3.
4. "Brawler," in *An Expository Dictionary,* 1:146.

Relative to the qualifications of deacons, "not given to much wine," *prosechontas*, from *prosecho*, conveys the idea of turning one's mind to, or attending to, and is used of giving oneself up to.[1]

Concerning aged women, the term *enslaved*, from *dedoulomenas*, is nearly synonymous with "given" from *prosechontas* in 1 Timothy 3:8, though a stronger term, and illustrated in John 8:34 and Romans 6:14.[2]

Antitheses

It may be seen in each of these instances that even light consumption of alcoholic beverages is forbidden. The term *me paroinon* in 1 Timothy 3:3 is placed in antithesis to *nephaleon* in verse from *nepho*, signifying to be free from the influence of intoxicants,[3] while *me paroinon* in Titus 1:7 is placed in antithesis in verse 8 to *sophron*, indicative of sober, sound mind, or self-control,[4] and *enkrate*, denoting the exercise of self-control.[5]

Since *nephaleon, sophron*, and *enkrate* signify abstinence from intoxicating beverages, it follows that *me paroinon* cannot, therefore, mean merely freedom from their excessive use. On the other hand, they probably carry their literal signification, "not near wine," and even forbid the presence of an elder at drinking parties.[6]

In Titus 2:3 *me oino pollo dedoulomenas*, literally rendered "not to wine much enslaved," is placed in antithesis to *sophron* in verse 5, which has already been defined.

In reference to *me oino pollo prosechontas* in 1 Timothy 3:8 the scholarly Guy N. Woods states,

---

1. "Give," in *An Expository Dictionary*, 2:150.
2. Samuel Thomas Bloomfield, p. 557; Donald Guthrie, *The Pastoral Epistles* (Grand Rapids: Wm. B. Eerdmans Publishing Co., 1957), p. 192.
3. "Sober," in *An Expository Dictionary*, 4:44; A. E. Humphrey said of the term "not indulging the desire of winebibbings, revellings, carousings," *The Epistles to Timothy and Titus* (Cambridge: University Press, 1901), p. 103; See also Homer Austin Kent, Jr., *The Pastoral Epistles* (Chicago: Moody Press, 1958), p. 131.
4. "Sober," in *An Expository Dictionary*, 4:44.
5. "Temperate," in *An Expository Dictionary*, 4:114.
6. Albert Barnes, *Thessalonians, Timothy, Titus and Philemon*, Notes on the New Testament, vol. 8, p. 144; Homer Austin Kent, Jr., p. 132.

Obviously, any man, elder, deacon, preacher, Bible school teacher, or other person in the church cannot set the proper example of Christian living who engages in the use, in any degree, of that which has been the occasion of so much sorrow, grief and ruin in the world. Temperance in the use of harmful things is *total* abstinence. There is no such thing as a proper moderate use of drugs, alcohol, and other harmful substances.[1]

According to 1 Timothy 3:11 women in general *(gunaikas)* must be abstinent *(nephaleous)*. In Titus 2:2 Paul directs "that the aged men be sober," *(nephalious)*, literally, abstinent.[2] He indicates, according to Titus 2:4–5, that the injunction to be "not given to much wine" was given the aged women in order that *(ina)* they might "teach the young women to be sober *(sophronizosin)* . . . discreet *(sophronas)* . . . chaste *(agnas)*."

Teaching by Example

The most successful form of teaching is that of example, and that which is less than abstinence will disqualify persons for the work of instructing others in the principles of Christian conduct. In fact, in reference to one of the passages under present consideration, aged women would be unable to properly influence young women under such circumstances.

Paul, after writing to Titus that elders must be *me paroinos,* and that aged women must be *me oino pollo dedoulomenas,* gives the reason for this and other requirements in the following words:

> For the grace of God hath appeared, bringing salvation to all men, instructing us, to the intent that *(ina)*, denying *(arnesamenoi)* ungodliness and worldly lusts *(tas kosmikas epithumias),* we should live soberly *(sophronos)* and righteously and godly in this present world.[3]

---

1. Guy N. Woods, "Elders and Deacons in the Church," *Adult Gospel Quarterly* 83 (9 October 1977):30–31.

2. *Nephalious* in Titus 2:2, the same term as that used in 1 Timothy 3:2, 11, means abstinence from wine, Homer Austin Kent, Jr., p. 227.

3. Tit. 2:11–12.

In the passage, *arnesamenoi* signifies to utterly refuse, forsake, renounce, and abstain from,[1] while *epithumias* denotes strong desire, which would include *epithumia oinou,* the lust for wine.

The view that some consumption is permissible, based on the term "much," is absurd and unwarranted in light of the overwhelming nature of the evidence regarding the context.[2]

The correct explanation of each of these passages can only be determined as the interpretation is in harmony with the other significant terms in the contexts. Those who would disprove the writer's argument and substantiate the previously mentioned views must therefore do so on the basis of each context.

It should also be noted by those who claim that it is permissible for deacons and aged women to imbibe *some* wine, and yet accept the fact that drunkenness is sinful, that, in order to be consistent, they must accept the false view that drunkenness is *not* but a matter of degree.[3]

1 Timothy 4:4

Among the statements perverted by advocates of "social" drinking, is the following: "For every creature of God is good, and nothing is to be rejected, if it be received with thanksgiving."[4]

It is asserted that alcohol is a good creature of God and, therefore, its consumption is sanctioned of God. It may be replied that not only is alcohol not a "creature of God," but it does not exist in nature. It does not exist ready formed in plants, but is a product of vinous fermentation. Left to themselves grapes will rot on the vine. Alcohol is no more a creature of God than is arsenic, cyanide, and carbolic acid. Alcohol is useful for various things, but not as a beverage. Injected into the body of dead persons it serves as a preservative, while often its consumption by living persons leads to death.

---

1. cf. Heb. 11:24; Mt. 16:24; 26:34.
2. Out of the contrast between "not given to wine," and "not given to much wine," there arose the tradition that elders must not use *any* wine and deacons must not use *much* wine. The interpretation however has no foundation. The best rendering of the Greek term is "not quarrelsome over wine," Homes Rolston, *Timothy and Titus,* Layman's Bible Commentary, vol. 23 (Richmond: John Knox Press, 1963), p. 78.
3. The fact that drunkenness is but a matter degree is discussed on pp. 98–115.
4. 1 Tim. 4:4.

1 Timothy 5:23

A view which perhaps has been advanced more often than any other in defense of "social" drinking is predicated on the advise of Paul to Timothy in 1 Timothy 5:23. The theory is that since Paul advised Timothy to "use a little wine," such consumption is therefore permissible today. It has been stated that this advice constitutes a source of great embarrassment to advocates of abstinence.[1]

In the first century persons often mixed wine with water which was unfit for consumption, for the purpose of purifying it. When Paul instructed Timothy, "Be no longer a drinker of water, but use a little wine for thy stomach's sake and thine often infirmities," he recommended it for medicinal purposes. There was a medical need in both cases. In fact, even prior to the first century, wine was used for the purpose of purifying water.[2] "Social" drinking, however, is altogether a different matter.

It should be noted in regard to Timothy that (1) he was evidently an abstainer for it took the authority of an apostle to convince him that he should use wine, even as a medicine, which indicates that up to that time he had not consumed even small amounts. (2) He was instructed to drink a *little* wine. (3) It was for his *physical infirmities*. (4) He was instructed to drink *wine*.

Concerning the matter, it has been questioned, "Why must persons believe Timothy was drunk when he took 'a little wine for his stomach's sake,' and that such was excused for medicinal purposes simply so a degree of drunkenness view would be correct?"

The question does not present the least problem. Alcohol, as a drug, is a type of anesthetic. In order to refute the facts in the case, one must first *deny* the scripturality of anesthetization by morphine, codeine, or other similar pharmaceutical agents under *medicinal* conditions! Timothy's state was not "excused" for medicinal purposes, but rather it was reasoned and divinely sanctioned by an inspired apostle!

It has been previously shown that there is a great difference between intoxicating wines of the first century and various intoxicating beverages

---

1. Everett Tilson, *Should Christians Drink?* (New York: Abingdon Press, 1957), pp. 24–25.
2. R. J. Forbes, *Studies in Ancient Technology*, vol. 1 (Leiden: E. J. Brill, 1955), pp. 173–75; Pliny, *Natural History* 31. 40.

of today, including wine. On the other hand, if this passage did sanction "social" consumption of the type of wine used in the first century, it would not include the imbibing of modern beer, whiskey, gin, vodka, brandy, or other alcoholic beverages in light quantity.

Albert Hill has pointed out that some persons argue from the passage that Paul did not instruct Timothy to use wine for medicinal purposes but, rather, for two purposes, namely, "for thy stomach's sake and thine often infirmities."[1]

It is true that medicine is not mentioned in the text, but the implication is clear. Observe the following renderings of the passage. (1) "For the good of your stomach and your recurring illness;"[2] (2) "do your stomach good and help you to get over your frequent spells of illness;"[3] (3) "for your digestion, for your frequent ailments;"[4] and (4) "to strengthen your stomach and relieve its frequent attacks."[5] A. T. Robertson states that this was "a sort of medical prescription for this case,"[6] and that "infirmities" *(astheneias)*, "thine often infirmities" *(tas puknas sou astheneias)* is indicative of weakness or lack of strength.[7] The imitable David Lipscomb indicates that the apostle Paul recommended its use only for Timothy's sickness.[8]

It is further argued that when Paul said, "for thy stomach's sake," he had in mind food. Although such an observation is hardly worthy of consideration, it may be noted that food is consumed for the sake of the entire body and not merely for the stomach. The writer is not aware of a single lexicographer or scholar who argues from the viewpoint of food.

Infinitesimal Amounts

The query has often been raised as to whether the imbibing of infinitesimal amounts of alcoholic beverages constitutes sin. Such so-called

---

1. Albert Hill, "Moderate Drinking (No. 2)" *Gospel Defender* 8 (April 1967):1.
2. *New Berkeley Version in Modern English.*
3. *Phillips Translation.*
4. *New English Bible.*
5. *Williams Translation.*
6. Archibald Thomas Robertson, *Word Pictures of the New Testament,* vol. 4, p. 589.
7. Ibid., p. 590. See also Ethelbert William Bullinger, *A Critical Lexicon and Concordance to the English and Greek New Testament* (London: Samuel Bagster and Sons, Limited, 1969), p. 412.
8. David Lipscomb, "Bible Wines," *Gospel Advocate* 27 (24 June 1885):386.

arguments of a pinhead or molecule nature are but diversionary, and are merely alleged arguments because they are but quibbles of the rankest form. Those who are willing to face the issue *know* that such is not worthy of serious consideration because liquor lovers or merely condoners, for that matter *know* that "social" drinking is not practiced in such fashion! Even if it were, it is not difficult to prove that drunkenness is but a matter of degree.

Alcoholic Beverages: Distilled and Fermented

It has been advocated that there is a considerable difference between ethyl alcohol and beverages containing it, and between distilled and fermented liquors. The only distinction which exists, however, is one of degree. Ethyl alcohol is always the same thing in whatever form or under whatever means it is used. It is ethyl alcohol which gives type to fermented, as well as to distilled liquors.

Some persons think that beer is not an intoxicating beverage because it contains but a small percent of alcohol in comparison with the percentages found in most other fermented beverages, and even much less than that which is found in distilled alcoholic beverages. Such is not the case, however, because persons usually consume more beer at one time or at brief intervals, while persons confine their consumption of whiskey or other strong drinks to one comparatively small portion, which is frequently diluted.

Alcohol and Covetousness

It is claimed that the "moderate" consumption of alcoholic beverages is parallel to the use of money. The theory is that, since covetousness is sinful and not the use of money, drunkenness is sinful and not the use of alcoholic beverages.

Such consumption, however, is not parallel to the use of money, for persons must have reasonable financial security in order to provide for their needs. The same is not true with alcoholic beverages. In fact, persons are often unable to provide for their needs because of their use of such beverages. Money is an essential medium of exchange, while alcoholic beverages are not. The theory therefore is without merit.

Alcohol and Gluttony

The view is expressed that the "moderate" intake of alcoholic beverages is parallel to the consumption of food. The theory is that, as gluttony is sinful and surely not the consumption of food, drunkenness is sinful and not the "moderate" use of alcoholic beverages. It is reasoned that since both are mentioned together in such passages as Proverbs 23:20–21, Matthew 11:18–19, and Luke 7:33–34, they must be parallel.

The two are not parallel, however, because ethyl alcohol is damaging to the functions of the mind, and thus hinders persons from discerning between good and evil, even when imbibed in small amounts.[1] The same is not true of food, which is essential to human growth and development. Although it is true that gluttony is sinful, it does not lead men to abuse their wives, neglect their children, or commit adultery, while "social" drinking often leads to these and numerous other evils.

According to the theory it would follow that since things are mentioned in the same passage or context they are parallel. Please note the following questions, based on the account of Matthew. (1) Are "your righteousness" and "the righteousness of the scribes and Pharisee" parallel?[2] (2) Are "thy neighbor" and "thine enemy" parallel?[3] (3) Are "treasures upon the earth" and "treasures in heaven" parallel?[4] Obviously, in each instance the two are not parallel. It does not follow, therefore, that since things are mentioned in the same passage or context they must be parallel.

Promotion of Alcoholic Sales

Those who promote the sale of alcoholic beverages and those who sell them, often claim that they are only promoting and selling a product which they are not forcing persons to purchase. They further claim that they should not be restricted because persons imbibe "excessively."[5]

---

1. Lev. 10:8–10; Is. 28:7.
2. Mt. 5:20.
3. Mt. 5:43.
4. Mt. 6:19–20.
5. Actually the idea of imbibing such beverages to an excessive degree is a misnomer, for the intake of any amount is excessive!

The illogical and foolish nature of their position may be demonstrated by a simple analogy. Those who operate establishments of prostitution and others who promote the sales of narcotics can employ the same reasoning as that of the liquor industry. Those involved in these shameful vocations do not force persons to buy their products either! Respectable persons, however, most assuredly do not sanction their sales! The purchase of such beverages is not *strictly* a matter of free choice. Because ethyl alcohol is habit forming, it becomes increasingly more difficult, if not virtually impossible, for many who imbibe it to resist without intense effort! Christians, therefore, should combine their efforts and work actively against the liquor industry.

Alcohol and Food Value

It is claimed that ethyl alcohol is of nutritional value to the human body and thus "moderate" consumption is permissible.

Food and Energy

Since proper nourishment is essential to physical health, it is important to know how ethyl alcohol functions in the human body. Whether it is considered a food depends on the way the term is defined. Relative to this point W. Russell Shull stated,

> Food is a substance performing one or more of the following functions: (1) It builds body tissue. (2) It repairs waste tissue. (3) It furnishes energy and heat. (4) It can be stored for future use. Number 3 is the only one of these qualifications that ethyl alcohol meets, and there is much doubt that it operates, even in this, for net gain. While it produces heat in the body, alcohol causes dilation of arteries and veins, leading to loss of heat through the skin. The usual net result of the use of alcohol is a lowered temperature of the body.[1]

Some medical scientists hold the view that ethyl alcohol supplies quick energy and permits the conservation of other sources of energy. However, the truth is its toxic and retarding effects make its use for this

---

1. W. Russell Shull, ed., *The Alcohol Problem Visualized* (Chicago: National Forum Inc., 1950), p. 47.

purpose highly questionable. Such may be seen from the following revealing quotations relative to the food value of ethyl alcohol.

> The heat and energy produced by burning alcohol in the body may be used to keep up the body temperature and to do work. In this way alcohol may be said to take the place of food . . . Since no more than two teaspoonfuls of alcohol can be burned up in the body in an hour, it can be used as a food in this way only to a very limited extent . . . It cannot be used to build up the body cells, nor can it be stored in some other form, as can sugars or fats.[1]

Estelle Bozeman is quoted as saying, "Alcohol is not a food and should never be relied on for this purpose even though its combustion (metabolism) in the body produces units of energy."[2]

Bozeman further states,

> Alcohol is a drug, not a food. Though it is burned in the body to yield energy, it differs from ordinary foods in several ways. It is a drug which depresses the nervous system and in large doses anesthetizes.[3]

It has been observed that "in using alcohol instead of food, the drinker is taking in a great many calories, but none of the essential bone and tissue-building protein."[4] Such beverages do not contain vitamins, minerals, fats, proteins, or usable carbohydrates.[5] The one exception is beer, although the amounts present are insignificant. On the contrary, calories are abundant in all such beverages with most of the caloric value coming from the alcohol itself. These, however, provide nothing toward good nutrition, but displace potentially wholesome foods from the diet. In fact, it is said that "the use of alcohol . . . as a substitute for food . . . is physiologically unsound."[6]

---

1. Emil Bogen and Lehmann Hisey, *What About Alcohol?* (Los Angeles: Angeles Press, n.d.), p. 35.

2. W. Russell Shull, ed., *The Alcohol Problem Visualized,* p. 49, quoting Estelle Bozeman, *Scientific Answers* (New York: Signal Press, 1947), p. 1.

3. Ibid.

4. *Family Health Guide and Medical Encyclopedia,* 1970 ed., s.v. "Why You Need a Balanced Diet," p. 35.

5. Leon A. Greenburg, "Alcohol in the Body," in *Drinking and Intoxication,* ed. Raymond Gerald McCarthy (Glencoe, Illinois: Free Press, 1959), p. 8.

6. *Alcohol: Its Action on the Human Organism* (London: His Majesty's Stationery Office, n.d.), n.p.

Those who imbibe such beverages often do substitute ethyl alcohol for food, and thus fail to get the proper nourishment which is so essential to physical health. This fact, and the extent to which ethyl alcohol does take the place of food, are key factors in the relations of ethyl alcohol to disease. Haven Emerson stated,

Alcohol lowers the resistance of the body to disease in two ways. First, it actually lowers the resistance of the body to disease germs. Some people argue that alcohol kills disease germs. There is some evidence that light drinkers have greater resistance to a few specified germs, but by far the larger portion of evidence reveals a lowered resistance of moderate drinkers. Authorities agree that the resistance of heavy drinkers is reduced. Secondly, alcohol lowers the resistance of the body to disease by causing the drinker to neglect his health when he is under the influence.[1]

Beer

Some persons hold the view that beer is liquid bread. It is true that the grain from which beer is made, like the fruit from which wine and hard cider are made, is valuable food. Fermentation, however, decomposes all but a very small proportion of the food material and leaves in its place the poison, ethyl alcohol. In discussing this point Emma L. Benedict Transeau states,

The only food substance in beer at all resembling that in bread is a small amount of solids called *extract*, which usually constitutes only from five to six percent of the beer. Not all even of this *extract*, only eight-tenths, is composed of protein, gum, dextrine, and maltose sugar, which alone have food value. This would bring the total food material in beer, according to standard analyses of ordinary samples, to about five percent. Over 90 percent is water. Bread, on the other hand, contains only about 38.5 percent water, 60 percent of good food substances, and no alcohol.[2]

The small amount of nutritive material in beer is more than offset by the alcohol content. Enough beer to furnish any significant amount of

---

1. Haven Emerson, ed., *Alcohol and Man* (New York: Macmillan Co., n.d.), p. 197.
2. Emma L. Benedict Transeau, p. 11.

nutriment would contain enough alcohol to cause considerable damage to the body.

It can thus be seen beyond doubt that ethyl alcohol is not of nutritional value to the human body. If it could be proved otherwise, however, it would not give credence to the view that so-called moderate consumption is sanctioned by the word of God.

PART TWO

AFFIRMATIVE ARGUMENTATION
OF THE PROBLEM

3

Major Affirmative Arguments

Degree Argument

There are degrees or stages of drunkenness, which fact will be proved in the course of this argument. This is an extremely important matter because many persons who advocate "social" drinking do so with the idea that the Bible condemns drunkenness, but not "social" drinking. The implication is, therefore, that there is a clear distinction to be made between intoxication and "moderation." As the writer has previously pointed out, there is no such thing as moderation when it comes to the imbibing of alcoholic beverages!

In describing the effects of ethyl alcohol often such terms as "dead drunk," "dog drunk," "sot drunk," and "stone drunk" are employed. Persons who are intoxicated are frequently referred to as "gassed," "high," "influenced," "lit," "looped," "loaded," "smashed," "soaked," "soused," "stoned," "stewed," "tight," "tipsy," or "woozy." It seems that society does not favor the Bible term "drunk." It should be noted, however, that each of the foregoing terms is descriptive of intoxication or drunkenness.

Deductive Reasoning

The argument for this section may be stated in a deductive manner, using a *modus ponens* form. The conclusion must be true if the argument is valid and the propositions are true.[1] The syllogism is as follows:

---

1. Irving Marmer Copi, *Introduction to Logic,* 4th ed. (New York: Macmillan Co., 1972), p. 23.

(1) If drunkenness implies the amount of ethyl alcohol which is consumed in "social" drinking, then "social" drinking is contrary to the law of God.

(2) Drunkenness implies the amount of ethyl alcohol which is consumed in "social" drinking.

(3) Therefore, "social" drinking is contrary to the law of God.

The argument is stated in valid form since the minor premise affirms the antecedent.[1] There will, no doubt, be little disagreement on the first proposition, which is true, based on many plain statements in the Bible.[2] Since the second proposition is the major point of disagreement, most of the material in this section will focus on it.[3]

Terms Defined

It should be remembered that "social" drinking is referred to in this book in the sense of imbibing non-medicinally light or small amounts of mind-altering or intoxicating drinks as beverages. Intoxication has been described as having begun when there is enough alcohol in the blood to produce a "perceptible change in a given psychological function."[4]

Stages of Drunkenness

It should be observed that intoxication does not have reference to any *exact* stage, which when reached, labels the imbiber as intoxicated or drunk. A noted toxicologist declares, "The higher nerve functions of the forebrain, such as reasoning, judgment, and social restraint are impaired by *very low concentrations* of alcohol in the blood,"[5] and the same is affirmed by

---

1. James Edwin Creighton, *An Introductory Logic,* 5th ed. (New York: Macmillan Co., 1926), p. 160.

2. New Testament prohibitions of drunkenness include Rom. 13:13; 1 Cor. 6:9–10; Gal. 5:19–21; and Eph. 5:18.

3. For additional arguments on this point, consult Appendix C, Additional Arguments, pp. 210–11.

4. Arnold Bruce Come, *Drinking, a Christian Position* (Philadelphia: Westminster Press, 1964), p. 7.

5. *Encyclopaedia Britannica,* 1959 ed., s.v. "Drunkenness," by Clarence Weinert Muehlberger, p. 683. Emphasis mine, WDJ. See also Rolla N. Harger, "The Response of the Body to Different Concentrations of Alcohol: Chemical Tests for Intoxication," in *Alcohol Education for Classroom and Community,* ed. Raymond Gerald McCarthy (New York: McGraw-Hill Book Co., 1964), p. 94.

another accomplished medical authority, Rolla N. Harger. A term which includes both slight and marked effects of ethyl alcohol, intoxication involves the abnormal state of exciting, confusing, or stupefying the mind to the point where physical or mental control is diminished. The issue therefore concerns the point at which this takes place.

Judgment and self-control represent the highest functions of the brain, and some impairment begins with concentrations of alcohol *below* those which will cause muscular incoordination.[1] Even the first few sips of an alcoholic beverage may cause changes in mood and behavior.[2] Dr. J. Murdoch Ritchie, Professor and Chairman, Department of Pharmacology, Yale University School of Medicine, indicates that as a result of a large blood supply, alcohol concentration in the brain quickly approaches that of the blood.[3] The maximum concentration is reached in one-half to two hours.[4] In regard to the rapidity of alcohol absorption Dr. Rolla N. Harger states, "Within two or three minutes after a few sips of whiskey or beer are swallowed, alcohol can be detected in the blood."[5] The small size of its molecule permits alcohol to diffuse rapidly through the various vessels and membranes inside the body. The symptoms of intoxication are caused by the depressant action of alcohol on nerve cells, acting in a manner similar to that of general anesthetics.

In a discussion concerning tests of the consumption of only *small* amounts of alcohol and its effect in regard to intellectual functioning, it has been determined that

> the cumulative evidence of tests on memory, association, judgment, reasoning, etc., definitely establishes the impairment of intelligence in alcoholic intoxication.[6]

---

1. Ibid., p. 93.

2. *First Special Report to the U.S. Congress on Alcohol and Health,* by Elliott L. Richardson, Chairman (Washington, D.C.: Government Printing Office, 1971), p. 37.

3. J. Murdoch Ritchie, "The Aliphatic Alcohols," in *The Pharmacological Basis of Therapeutics,* eds. Louis S. Goodman and Alfred Gilman (London: Collier-Macmillan, Limited, 1970), p. 141.

4. Maurice Victor and Raymond D. Adams, p. 668.

5. Rolla N. Harger, "The Sojourn of Alcohol in the Body," in *Alcohol Education for Classroom and Community,* ed. Raymond Gerald McCarthy (New York: McGraw-Hill Book Co., 1964), p. 79.

6. E. M. Jellinek and R. A. McFarland, "Analysis of Psychological Experiments on the Effects of Alcohol," *Quarterly Journal of Studies on Alcohol* 1 (1940):361.

In regard to the initial effects of alcohol consumption, Dr. Donald L. Gerard states,

> There is a general sequence of events which commonly occurs when a sober person begins to drink alcoholic beverages. These events are expressions of the *degree* to which a person has lost control over his speech, emotional expression, and motor behavior. The rate at which this effect takes place is related to the quantity of alcohol ingested, to the rapidity of absorption, and to the body weight of the drinker. With the *first few* "social" drinks, the individual's judgment and inhibitions are affected.[1]

In addition Dr. Gerard states, "*Many studies* have indicated that ingestion of relatively *small quantities* of alcohol not only affects the rate at which tasks are done but also diminishes efficiency and accuracy."[2]

It has been stated by Dr. Edith Lisansky, a lecturer in psychology, in Yale Center of Alcohol Studies, that imbibing an alcoholic beverage in small or large amounts does affect one's behavior and feelings.[3]

Persons can be intoxicated without staggering, slurring their speech, or disclosing in any way to the ordinary sense the fact that they are intoxicated,[4] and there is absolutely no doubt that it is the alcohol present in the brain itself that is responsible for the intoxicating effect.[5] Irving Fisher stated, "So-called moderate drinking merely means moderate intoxication. A mild drinker denies that he is drunk, if he does not stagger, but a man who has drunk one glass of beer is one-glass-of-beer drunk."[6]

---

1. Donald L. Gerard, "Intoxication and Addiction," in *Drinking and Intoxication*, ed. Raymond Gerald McCarthy (Glencoe, Illinois: Free Press, 1959), p. 27. Emphasis mine, WDJ.

2. Ibid., pp. 29–30.

3. Edith S. Lisansky, "Psychological Effects," in *Drinking and Intoxication,* p. 18.

4. Harvey W. Wiley, "Legislative Hearing," *Scientific Temperance Journal* 3 (May 1920):2. See also *How to Talk to Your Teenager About Drinking and Driving* (Washington, D.C.: Government Printing Office, 1981), p. 10.

5. Leon A. Greenburg, "The Concentration of Alcohol in the Blood and Its Significance," *Alcohol Science, and Society: Twenty-Nine Lectures with Discussions as Given at the Yale Summer School of Alcoholic Studies* (Westport, Connecticut: n.p., 1945), p. 46.

6. Irving Fisher, *Prohibition at Its Worst* (New York: Macmillan Co., n.d.), p. 135.

The Brain

Impaired efficiency is the basic effect of *any amount* of alcohol on the brain and on its related structures in the central nervous system. According to Dr. Henry W. Broslin, a fundamental mental derangement or lost contact with reality is a type of psychosis. Organic psychosis, which is a physical disorder of the brain, is experienced by persons who are under the influence of alcoholic beverages.[1] Ethyl alcohol depresses the central nervous system in a *progressive* and *continuous* way, and the higher brain centers or cortex are depressed first.[2] Regarding the kinds of feelings which are experienced, Wayne E. Oates states,

> Through the narcotic action of alcohol on inhibitions, a person tends to feel that he can express himself more freely, act with more confidence and less uncertainty, with more ease and less self-restraint . . . The finer capacities of attention, judgment, comprehension, and reflection are dulled.[3]

Even low concentrations dull the highest levels of brain functions and lead to excited and even exuberant behavior because they retard the activities of the most highly specialized and sensitive part of the brain, the cortex.[4] Dr. J. Murdoch Ritchie indicates that

> the first mental processes to be affected are those that depend on training and previous experience and that usually make for sobriety and self-restraint. The finer grades of discrimination, memory, concentration, and insight are dulled and then lost.[5]

---

1. *Encyclopaedia Britannica*, 1959 ed., s.v. "Psychosis," by Henry W. Broslin, p. 722.

2. Kenneth L. Jones, Louis W. Shainberg, and Curtis O. Byer, *Drugs and Alcohol,* 2nd ed. (New York: Harper and Row, Publishers, 1969), pp. 126–27.

3. Wayne E. Oates, *Alcohol In and Out of the Church* (Nashville: Broadman Press, 1966), p. 9.

4. Nello Pace, "Planning for Alcohol Education," *Proceedings of a Conference Jointly Sponsored by the Departments of Public Health, Education, and Mental Hygiene, Division of Alcohol Rehabilitation* (Berkeley: Department of Public Health, 1960), p. 20. See also Margaret Bacon and Mary Brush Jones, *Teen-Age Drinking* (New York: Thomas Y. Crowell Co., 1968), p. 134.

5. J. Murdoch Ritchie, "The Aliphatic Alcohols," p. 136.

Dr. Ritchie proceeds to point out that

> mood swings are uncontrolled and emotional outbursts frequent. These changes are accompanied by sensory and motor disturbances. For example, spinal reflexes are at first enhanced because they have been freed from central inhibitions; *as intoxication becomes more advanced,* however, this first phase of enhanced reflex activity is succeeded by a general impairment of nervous function and a condition of general anesthesia prevails.[1]

Among other things it may be observed from Dr. Ritchie's statement that intoxication is definitely a matter of degree!

Dr. James E. P. Toman, Professor and Chairman, Department of Pharmacology, Chicago Medical School, and Jean P. Davis have indicated that alcohol produces a slowing of the brain wave rhythm, and that this effect becomes particularly prominent as *intoxication develops.*[2]

There is an extremely subtle barrier to the best intentions to imbibe "moderately," because the desire for alcohol increases with indulgence, and every increase of alcohol in the blood progressively suppresses the operation of those areas of the brain on which persons depend for clear insights and rational decisions. The longer the desire is gratified, the more potent must be the beverage that will satisfy its craving and, according to Dr. T. Rothrock Miller, orthopedic surgeon, "the more one drinks, the more it takes to constitute the same degree of intoxication."[3] It should also be noted that the habituated individual can drink more and show fewer effects than the "moderate" drinker or abstainer.[4]

The Effects

As previously indicated, the finer grades of judgment, concentration, and understanding are the first to be affected. Such effect, which may occur after as little as one drink, increase rapidly as the alcohol concentra-

1. Ibid. Emphasis mine, WDJ.
2. James E. P. Toman and Jean P. Davis, "The Effects of Drugs Upon the Electrical Activity of the Brain," *Pharmacological Review* 1 (1949):425–92. Emphasis mine, WDJ.
3. Donahue TV Program, 24 November 1980.
4. Maurice Victor and Raymond D. Adams, "Alcohol," p. 669.

tion in the blood is raised by additional drinks.[1] Furthermore, the toxic effects linger for some time.

George B. Wallace reported that when one quart of 10 percent wine was taken by an abstainer on an empty stomach, the concentration of alcohol in the blood did not reduce below 0.1 percent until seven hours later.[2]

Tests by delicate instruments have indicated that small doses of ethyl alcohol also affect the functions of sight, hearing, and touch sensation, in each instance by the depressant or narcotic action upon the central nervous system. Delay in important reflexes or trained responses to signals, ranged from 5 to 15 percent of the usual response time after the use of doses so small that those tested were scarcely aware or knowledgeable of the existence of any resulting physiological change attributable to alcohol.[3]

This is the reason, that after an extensive study, it has been determined that the efficiency of operating an automobile is affected progressively from the first measurable quantity of alcohol in the blood.[4] Drs. John J. Hanlon and Elizabeth McHose state,

> As far as automobile driving is concerned, there is a clearly consistent increase in the probability of accident with an increase in the amount of alcohol in the blood. As little as 0.03 percent of alcohol in the blood reduces driving skill.[5]

Judgment of time is impaired by alcohol. Judgment of one's own performance is also affected and this is a most significant danger in imbibing alcoholic beverages even in *small* amounts while driving. When

1. Frances Todd, *Teaching About Alcohol* (New York: McGraw-Hill Book Co., 1964), p. 68.

2. George B. Wallace, in *Alcohol and Man,* ed. Haven Emerson, p. 59.

3. Haven Emerson, *Alcohol: Its Effect on Man* (New York: Appleton-Century Co., nd.), p. 47.

4. G. C. Drew, W. P. Colquhoun, and Hazel A. Long, "The Effects of Small Doses of Alcohol on a Skill Resembling Driving," *Traffic Safety Review* 3 (1959):4–11.

5. John J. Hanlon and Elizabeth McHose, *Design for Health,* 2nd ed. (Philadelphia: Lea and Febiger, 1971), p. 180. At the time of writing, Dr. Hanlon was Assistant Surgeon General, Public Health Service U.S. Department of Health, Education, and Welfare; Dr. McHose was Professor Emeritus of Health, Physical Education, and Recreation, at Temple University.

the estimates of driving skills are enhanced by even *small* quantities of alcohol, the setting has been prepared for an accident.[1] Another study indicates that those who imbibe to a blood-alcohol level of only 0.05 to 0.06 percent are involved in more automobile accidents than others. An important and similar study placed the significant blood-alcohol level at 0.05 to 0.10 percent.[2] A study by the Department of Police Administration at the University of Indiana indicates that where the alcohol level in the blood of a driver reaches 0.15 percent the chances of that driver's having an accident increase twenty-five times.[3]

Moderation, a Misnomer

Those who have imbibed are as oblivious as their observers to their dulled mental faculties after taking an amount of alcohol, which to them seems insignificant. They are satisfied with themselves because the dulling has weakened their power of self-criticism. With it has gone troublesome anxieties and sense of responsibility. As caution and self-control become partially paralyzed, such persons are often induced to continue with seeming moderation until they are stupefied to an even greater degree.

The idea, therefore, which is often advanced that there is no harm in "moderate" consumption of alcoholic beverages is a misconception. The fact that there is no definite amount of alcohol which is moderate in the sense of being entirely harmless for every person is evidence of the danger in experimenting with it. Especially is this true in view of the fact that ethyl alcohol is a habit-forming drug.

The idea that maintaining "moderation" is a mere matter of self-control, similar to refraining from eating too much, is also erroneous. The fallacy is because of the fact that ethyl alcohol as a drug has an adverse effect upon those very centers of the brain which exercise self-

1. K. Bjerver and L. Goldberg, "Effects of Alcohol Ingestion on Driving Ability," *Quarterly Journal of Studies on Alcohol* 11 (1950):1.
2. Wolfgang Schmidt and Reginald G. Smart, "Drinking-Driving Mortality and Morbidity Statistics," *Alcohol and Traffic Safety* (Washington, D.C.: Government Printing Office, 1963), p. 33.
3. John S. Sinacore, *Health, a Quality of Life,* 2nd ed. (New York: Macmillan Publishing Co., Inc., 1974), p. 388.

control, while food and other matters of indulgence, which can be safely left to self-control, do not weaken the very seat and center of it.

It is perfectly normal, therefore, for imbibers not to care what they do because with the loss of self-criticism goes loss of the sense of responsibility. Self-control is weakened because it belongs to the group of higher powers which are first impaired by small amounts of ethyl alcohol. A depressed brain, persuasive associates, and the strength of an acquired craving, each combine with the beverage in an attack upon self-control. Both the Bible and medical science are in clear opposition to the theory that a distinction should be made between "social" drinking and drunkenness.

The Bible

There are several Greek terms which are translated "drunk," "drunken," and "drunkenness" in the New Testament. Along with several others, W. E. Vine makes an interesting distinction in regard to *methusko*. He defines it as "to make drunk, or to grow drunk (an inceptive verb, marking the process of the state expressed in *methuo),* to become intoxicated, Luke 12:45; Ephesians 5:18; 1 Thessalonians 5:7a."[1]

Robert Young, along with W. A. Haynes, defines it as "to begin to be softened."[2] S. T. Bloomfield views the term as meaning, "to moisten, or to be moistened with liquor, and in a figurative sense, to be saturated with drink."[3] E. W. Bullinger says *methusko* means, "to grow drunk (marking the beginning of *methuo.")*[4] The renowned Joseph Henry Thayer states that the term means, "to get drunk, become intoxicated."[5]

---

1. "Drunk," in *An Expository Dictionary,* 1:341. See also Francis Brown, Samuel Rolles Driver and Charles Briggs, *A Hebrew and English Lexicon of the Old Testament,* 8th ed. (Oxford: Clarendon Press, 1976), p. 1016; William Frederick Arndt and Felix Wilbur Gingrich, *A Greek-English Lexicon of the New Testament* 4th ed. (Chicago: University of Chicago Press, 1957), p. 500; and Edward Robinson, *Greek and English Lexicon of the New Testament* (New York: Harper and Brothers, Publishers, 1877), p. 448.

2. Robert Young, *Analytical Concordance to the Bible* (New York: Funk and Wagnalls Co., n.d.), p. 275; Wilson Albinus Haynes, *Beautiful Word Pictures of the Epistle to the Ephesians* (Caney, Kansas: Busy Man's Bible Co., 1911), p. 173.

3. Samuel Thomas Bloomfield, vol. 2, p. 214.

4. Ethelbert William Bullinger, *A Critical Lexicon and Concordance to the English and Greek New Testament* (London: Samuel Bagster and Sons, Limited, 1969), p. 238.

5. Joseph Henry Thayer, p. 396.

These definitions clearly establish beyond a doubt that drunkenness is something that can grow, progress from one state to another, be considered as a state of becoming softened, and, therefore, that it is the beginning of even an advanced degree. The implication is that persons begin to be drunk when they begin to drink. No doubt the reason that some fail to see this fact is because of what they literally *see*. They have built into their systems the idea that persons must be staggering or in a stupor to be drunk. If they *see* them in such condition, they consider them as drunk, and otherwise they do not. This is not, however, the basis upon which the Bible determines drunkenness. Medical science also testifies in regard to alcoholic influence.

Medical Science

Medical science has determined that intoxicating beverages are consumed primarily for their peculiar effects, especially so by those habituated to their use. The amounts necessary to produce a given effect vary with different persons, and there is no absolute uniformity in effects.[1] No two persons will experience the same concentration, even from identical beverages. Individual bodies, moods, temperaments, and personalities differ.

Alcohol influence depends upon (1) the time over which a given amount is consumed, (2) the amount of food in the stomach, (3) the amount of food substance in the beverage,[2] (4) the weight of the drinker, (5) the drinker's temperament, (6) the learned ability to control one's reactions, and (7) the degree of social control that is present.[3]

Body size is a factor because the larger the blood stream into which alcohol passes, the more diluted it will be. In regard to the weight factor it has been stated,

> A 125 pound party-goer who tries to match drinks with a 200 pound companion will soon be in difficulty. The smaller person must consume a good deal less alcohol if he expects to stay as sober as his friend. The reason for this is obvious. The 200 pound

---

1. Albion Roy King, p. 97.
2. Distilled spirits, such as whiskey, do not contain food substance.
3. Arnold Bruce Come, p. 5.

person has a greater volume of fluid in his tissues, and the same number of drinks will not produce as high a concentration of alcohol in him as it will in a smaller person.[1]

John S. Sinacore indicates that the same amount of alcohol will have differing effects on a person as compared to another and may even differ in the same individual from week to week.[2] This being the case, if drunkenness is not but a matter of degree, it follows that persons can conceivably imbibe a certain quantity on one occasion and be drunk and the same amount on another occasion and not be drunk. In view of this, those who claim there are not degrees or stages of drunkenness have no way of knowing the limit of sobriety at a given instance.

Absorption

Beer contains solids which retard absorption, whereas, the effervescent wines are absorbed much more rapidly. The rate of absorption is determined, among other things, by the alcoholic content of the beverage, the emptying rate of the stomach, the kind of beverage, and the combination of materials it contains, as well as the rate of blood-flow through the gastrointestinal tract.[3] These variables make it *impossible* to formulate a rule that will safeguard *even one person!*

When persons consume an alcoholic beverage, some 20 percent of the alcohol in it is usually absorbed immediately into the blood stream through the stomach walls. The other 80 percent of the alcohol enters the bloodstream almost as fast, after being quickly processed through the gastrointestinal tract. Once alcohol enters the blood stream, contrary to a wide impression, nothing can be done about its effects except to wait until it is metabolized by the body.[4]

---

1. Margaret Bacon and Mary Brush Jones, p. 133.

2. John S. Sinacore, p. 324. See also *Alcohol: Some Questions and Answers* (Washington, D.C.: Government Printing Office, 1981), p. 6; Edith S. Lisansky, "Psychological Effects," in *Drinking and Intoxication*, p. 24; Edith S. Lisansky, "The Psychological Effects of Alcohol," in *Alcohol Education for Classroom and Community*, ed. Raymond Gerald McCarthy (New York: McGraw-Hill Book Co., 1964), p. 108.

3. Salvatore Pablo Lucia, ed., *Alcohol and Civilization* (New York: McGraw-Hill Book Co., 1963), p. 22.

4. *Alcohol: Some Questions and Answers*, p. 8.

The rapidity with which ethyl alcohol induces intoxication is related to the speed of its absorption from the stomach and small intestine, and to the drinking history of the individual.[1] Alcohol does not require digestion and thus can move rapidly into the blood. In fact, medical authorities state that within four minutes after persons have taken an alcoholic beverage, alcohol is found in the blood. Life-saving blood travels throughout the body in slightly less than one minute, and immediately after ethyl alcohol reaches the brain, persons are intoxicated or poisoned.[2]

The concentration of alcohol in the blood is determined by the rate of absorption, elimination, and oxidation. The rate of absorption is dependent upon the factors of speed of drinking, type of beverage, and body condition. The rate of elimination and oxidation is relatively fixed and unaffected by the pattern of drinking.[3]

Intolerance

Approximately 80 to 90 percent of alcohol in the body must be disposed of through oxidation, the rate of which is relatively constant and rather slow. Various experiments have revealed that persons must imbibe large amounts over a long period of time to produce changes in feelings and behavior which they had previously attained with smaller amounts.[4] In light of this, if abstinence is not binding, whereas such persons formerly sinned in becoming drunk with lesser amounts, they may now imbibe more ethyl alcohol before they sin. This in no way, however, means that a tolerance for alcohol can be created regardless of the length of time persons practice drinking. Experienced drinkers may learn how to slow the concentration of ethyl alcohol in the blood by slowing drinking when the stomach is filled with food, but they cannot change its effects when it reaches the blood.[5]

Relative to alcohol dilution Berton Roueche quotes Howard W. Haggard and E. M. Jellinek as follows:

---

1. *First Special Report,* p. 37.
2. Marguerite Skidmore and Carolyne LaGrange Brooks, *Boys and Girls Learning About Alcohol* (Nashville: Abingdon-Cokesbury Press, n.d.), p. 69.
3. Douglas Jackson, *Stumbling Block* (Nashville: Parthenon Press, 1960), p. 12.
4. *First Special Report,* p. 38.
5. Douglas Jackson, p. 14.

When a strong alcoholic beverage is taken into the stomach, the secretion of that organ dilutes it. When the alcohol passes into the blood, it is diluted by that fluid, and when it spreads from the blood to the fluid in and about the cells of the tissues, it is still further diluted. The extent to which alcohol is eventually diluted after absorption depends upon the amount of body water and this in turn is influenced by body weight. Inasmuch as the effects of alcohol vary in general with its concentration in the blood, it follows that, for the same amount of alcohol in their bodies, large individuals are less affected than small ones.[1]

Pertaining to this, Edith S. Lisansky likewise states, "Alcohol dosage is not equal if two subjects, one weighing 125 pounds and the other 225 pounds, are given the same amount of alcohol."[2] Since this is the case, if consumption above the degree which is reached in "social" drinking is required to constitute drunkenness and, therefore, sin, large persons can consume more than small persons without sinning!

Drunkenness

When persons imbibe any amount of alcoholic drinks, according to the definition of the biblical term *methusko* and the determinations of medical science, they are softened, intoxicated, and drunk to that degree. There is absolutely no other basis upon which drunkenness can be properly determined.

In regard to degrees of drunkenness it has been said that if such logic were applied to eating, persons would be full after one bite. Such a statement however but accomplishes the reverse of what its advocates intend, for to apply the principle to eating would but indicate that persons have *begun* the *process* of fullness after one bite. As they would be to that degree drunk after one drink, so they would be to that degree filled after one bite!

Those who hold the view that "social" drinking is permissible, despite both biblical and scientific evidence to the contrary, cannot successfully

---

1. Berton Roueche, *Alcohol, Its History, Folklore, and Its Effect on the Human Body* (New York: Grove Press, Inc., 1960), p. 66.
2. Edith S. Lisansky, "Psychological Effects," in *Drinking and Intoxication,* p. 19.

deny that persons do not know their personal limit of resistance until they indulge. A leading medical journal indicates,

> Blood alcohol of 1/10 of one percent can be accepted as *prima facie* evidence of alcohol intoxication recognizing that many individuals are under the influence in the 5/100 of one percent range . . . There is no minimum (blood-alcohol concentration) which can be set at which there will be absolutely no effect.[1]

This statement simply means that imbibers are drunk to the extent of the amount they consume. There is no minimum amount of alcohol in the body fluids which can be accepted as indicating absolutely no impairment by alcohol. Different things happen at the various levels of alcohol concentration in the blood, which reflects the concentration of alcohol in the brain more directly than does any other obtainable fluid.[2] Documentary evidence bearing testimony to this fact is abundant.

If persons cannot feel the effects of alcoholic beverages, there is no point in imbibing them; if they can, they are mentally impaired to that degree. Persons cannot willfully impair their minds in such fashion without violating the law of God.

Sections of the Brain

The brain is composed of three basic sections which are referred to as the cerebrum, cerebellum, and medulla. The cerebrum is the seat of emotions, intelligence, and will. It is the part of the brain which affects personality and ability to act and think correctly. The cerebellum controls consciousness, while the medulla is the center which controls respiration, circulation, and other important processes.

The effects of alcohol may be compared to dropping water on a sponge. It soaks in from the top, passing through the various sections to the innermost part. Its first effect is to numb the restraining power, the section which informs persons to not do those things which they have learned from years of spiritual, moral, and legal standards that they should not do. With the first section drugged, persons become more

---

1. Minutes of the 1960 annual meeting of the American Medical Association, and "Are You Fit to Drive?" *Journal of the American Medical Association.*

2. Leon A. Greenberg, p. 47.

confident and less capable. Alcohol then soaks into the second section, which controls reaction, vision, and hearing. With the cerebellum affected, persons become sedated. Eventually, if the alcohol soaks into the third section, which controls the heart and breathing, it may prove fatal. All thinking persons therefore can see the dangers which are inherent in imbibing intoxicating beverages.

Based on the following information, those who defend "social" drinking are obligated to reveal at what point imbibers violate the biblical injunction against drunkenness.

(1) The frontal lobe of the cerebrum, which is one's reason and self-control, is affected by 0.01%-0.10% alcohol causing removal of inhibitions, loss of self-control, weakening of will power, impaired judgment, etc. (2) The parietal lobe of the cerebrum, which is one's sensory control, is affected by 0.10%-0.30% alcohol causing dulled or distorted sensibilities, unsteadiness of movement, inability to write, etc. (3) The occipital lobe of the cerebrum, which controls one's visual sensations, is affected by 0.20%-0.30% alcohol causing loss of color perception, distortion, double vision, etc. (4) The cerebellum, which is one's coordination center, is affected by 0.15%-0.35% alcohol causing serious disturbances of equilibrium and coordination. (5) The thalamus and medulla, which control one's respiration and circulation, are affected by 0.25%-0.50% alcohol causing depression of respiration, failure of circulation, stupor, shock, and death.[1]

The reason more persons do not die from immediate alcohol intake, is because they usually pass out before a deadly amount is consumed.

Alcohol Concentration

Indications are that 0.005 percent is about the smallest concentration of alcohol in the blood which can be measured in terms of its effect on some areas of the brain. This constitutes only one drop of alcohol in 20,000 drops of blood. The first measurable effects on adults who are

----

1. *Beverage Alcohol, What Does It Do to You?* (Nashville: United Tennessee League, n.d.), a pamphlet. Similar blood-alcohol percentages are cited by Albion Roy King, in *Basic Information*, pp. 95–106.

occasional drinkers is 0.01 percent.[1] Most physical symptoms of drunkenness are seen after the level goes beyond 0.05 percent.

One source indicated that two cocktails or two cans of beer taken in less than an hour usually produce 0.05 percent concentration of alcohol in the blood.[2] This amount anesthetizes the upper brain, the source of inhibitions and critical evaluations. Being free to act without these restraints is what creates the impression that ethyl alcohol is a stimulant. The freedom to speak or to carry on conversation and to do what persons feel like, is the sense of release which most imbibers value in lesser degrees of intoxication.

It has been demonstrated that the very first introduction of alcohol into the brain causes sedated sleep to descend over that portion which controls the intelligence, reason, judgment, and moral and religious convictions of persons.[3] The delicate capacities of intellectual decision, choice, discretion, and willpower are those faculties which are first retarded and then completely anesthetized by alcohol because they are the least capable of withstanding its toxic effects. On this point W. E. Dixon indicates that attention, judgment, and the higher intellectual processes are retarded *immediately* by even small amounts of ethyl alcohol.[4]

Brain Damage

Symptoms which are characteristic of drunkenness may result from many causes including diabetes, epilepsy, kidney disease, and brain injury. Persons who suffer brain damage in automobile accidents frequently experience physical symptoms of alcoholic intoxication, such as a dulling of the mind, loss of equilibrium, and unsteady speech; yet, such symptoms do not constitute sin. Persons sin when they willfully, for no justifiable reason, sedate their intellects, wills, and consciences, thus causing losses of the powers of inhibition. Medical science has proved that this is the *first* step in drunkenness, not the last. For this

1. Haven Emerson, *Alcohol: Its Effect on Man,* p. 92. Emil Bogen and Lehmann Hisey give similar information in *What About Alcohol?* pp. 79–82.

2. Arnold Bruce Come, p. 6.

3. Haven Emerson, *Alcohol: Its Effect on Man,* p. 37.

4. Courtenay C. Weeks, *Alcohol and Human Life,* 2nd ed. (London: H. K. Lewis and Co., 1938), p. 84, quoting W. E. Dixon, Pharmacology, 6th ed., 1935.

reason, it is affirmed in this argument that persons are drunk to the degree of their consumption.

Those who insist that drunkenness is sinful, and at the same time that it is not a matter of degree, should answer the following pertinent questions: (1) Can a person who is drunk (drunk according to your definition of the term) become more drunk? If you answer no, how do you explain that which happens to a person who is obviously drunk, and upon additional consumption, loses complete motor control and, perhaps, even falls into a stupor? If you answer yes, and thus admit that a person can become more drunk, how do you conclude that drunkenness is not but a matter of degree? (2) How much ethyl alcohol does it take to cause drunkenness? If you state that you *do not* know and yet agree that drunkenness is sinful, are you not making yourself liable to sin if you imbibe? If you state that you *do* know how much it takes to become drunk, since you do not hold the view that drunkenness is but a matter of degree, how did you determine the amount without becoming drunk and thus committing sin?

Medical research has indicated that "social" drinkers along with heavy drinkers incur some loss of brain cells every time they drink, and that these cells are irreplaceable. The only difference between the losses of "social" drinkers and heavy drinkers are those of degree.[1]

According to Dr. A. C. Ivy, when persons begin to drink occasionally, they take one-in-nine chances of becoming addicted drinkers and chronic alcoholics.[2] In view of the admonition, "keep thy heart with all diligence; for out of it are the issues of life,"[3] individuals should abstain. Persons cannot imbibe alcoholic beverages, even in small amounts, and abide by this charge to give careful and continual attention to their thinking, reasoning, and understanding faculties. On the other hand, persons should not attempt to justify the consumption of that which has deceived

---

1. Albert Q. Maisel, "Alcohol and Your Brain," *Reader's Digest* 96 (June 1970):68, refers to experiments of Professor Melvin H. Knisely and Drs. Herbert A. Moscow and Raymond C. Pennington, of the Medical University of South Carolina.
2. A. C. Ivy, "Alcohol as a Depressant," *Twentieth Century Christian* 18 (January 1956):20–21.
3. Prov. 4:23.

so many persons, when the Bible teaches so much about the dangers of being deceived.[1]

A Medical Consideration

It may be claimed that if there are degrees to drunkenness, those who take medicine containing alcohol are intoxicated to a degree. Although in a technical sense this is true, it should be noted that the purpose is *medicinal* and therefore *approved* in the Bible. It should also be noted that those who claim this as an argument, in so doing, logically admit there are degrees of drunkenness.

The Implication

In this section attention has been given to the various degrees of intoxication, and it has been shown that "social" drinking involves enough consumption of alcohol to affect the policy-making areas of the brain. In view of these facts, it can be seen that drunkenness, as the second proposition states, implies the amount of ethyl alcohol which is consumed in "social" drinking. Since the argument is valid and the propositions are true, it follows that "social" drinking is contrary to the law of God. Those who engage in such activities are guilty of sin against God.

The claim that the Bible sanctions the "moderate" use of ethyl alcohol as a *beverage* is *merely* a claim![2] It is not supported by a single positive statement. There is not *one* instance in either the Old Testament or the New Testament where the condemnation of drunkenness is joined with *any* approval of so-called moderation!

Physical Effects Argument

The Bible teaches that it is contrary to the law of God to abuse or harm the human body.[3] Although it is usually admitted that heavy consumption of intoxicating beverages is detrimental to physical health, in this section it will be proved that enough ethyl alcohol is imbibed in "social" drinking to produce harmful effects.

---

1. cf. Lk. 21:8; Rom. 7:11; 1 Cor. 6:9; 15:33; Gal. 6:7; Eph. 5:6.
2. There is no such thing as moderation in the use of those things which, under the conditions named, are wrong.
3. cf. Rom. 12:1; 1 Cor. 3:16; 6:15–20; 10:31.

A Modus Ponens *Statement*

The argument may be stated in *modus ponens* form as follows:

(1) If the consumption of ethyl alcohol to the degree which it is consumed in "social" drinking is harmful to the human body, then "social" drinking is contrary to the law of God.

(2) The consumption of ethyl alcohol to the degree which it is consumed in "social drinking is harmful to the human body.

(3) Therefore, "social" drinking is contrary to the law of God.[1]

Toxic Effects

Some of the immediate results of the intake of intoxicating beverages are widely known, while many basic issues are hidden beneath prejudice, misunderstanding, and ignorance. Before proceeding further, it should be observed that the reason alcoholic beverages are harmful to the human body, even in small amounts, is because ethyl alcohol is poisonous, as has been indicated previously. In fact, the term commonly applied to the abnormal conditions produced by alcohol, "intoxication," is derived from the Latin term *toxicum,* meaning "poison." In reference to this fact, Dr. Emil Bogen stated, "Alcohol is the most dangerous poison widely included in the human diet."[2]

Although the term "poison," is even frequently used as a synonym for alcohol in medical literature, various persons have held that it is a poison only when taken in large quantities. The implication is that the nature of a substance changes with quantity. On this point Dr. August Ley states,

> Without doubt, and here it is the laboratory that speaks, alcohol is poison. With this view all modern works are in accord. It is equally certain that for all poisons—for example, morphine, cocaine, strychnine—one may find a dose extremely minute in which the poison would not cause serious trouble in the body. It is the same with alcohol. An infinitesimal dose of alcohol does not

---

1. A similar argument is advanced by Phil Thompson in "Social Drinking: Right or Wrong?," a paper presented to Professor Thomas Bratton Warren, Harding Graduate School of Religion, December 1977, p. 9.

2. Haven Emerson, ed., *Alcohol and Man,* p. 150, quoting Dr. Emil Bogen.

act upon the body as a poison. But from the practical point of view, in ordinary life, *alcohol is always a poison.*[1]

The public news media has often declared that impure beverages constitute the principle cause of health problems. Although such beverages have no doubt caused some problems, tests made in various laboratories of samples of illegal alcoholic beverages have shown that ethyl alcohol is the chief poisoning agent. In fact, examinations have disclosed there are few things more toxic than ethyl alcohol.

Furfural is slightly more poisonous in an equal quantity than is ethyl alcohol, and, according to Dr. Frank Overton, amyl alcohol or fusel oil is "far more poisonous" than is ethyl alcohol.[2] Concerning such agents and their effects, Donald Guyer Zink indicates that although isoamyl alcohol constitutes 85 percent of the amyl alcohols present in fusel oil, such oil also contains n-amyl, active amyl, isopropyl, n-propyl, n-butyl, and isobutyl alcohols, with traces of various esters. Used in manufacturing solvents, lacquer, and plastics, they cause thirst and headache in small doses, and are convulsive poisons in larger doses.[3]

It is quite generally thought that the process of aging tends to rid distilled alcoholic beverages of various secondary poisons, but such is not the case, for some of these are increased rather than diminished by aging. Dr. Herman C. Lythgoe states,

> It is a well-known fact that when distilled spirits are permitted to age in charred oak barrels, there is an increase in secondary bodies which are slightly more toxic than is alcohol. The work of Crampton and Tolman showed that during an aging period of eight years, the fusel oil increased 40 to 70 percent; the aldehydes increased 200 to 300 percent; the furfural increased 150 to 250 percent; the acids increased 700 to 1,800 percent; and the esters increased 250 to 450 percent. The increase in fusel oil is due solely to evaporation; the extract is obtained from the barrel and the increase in other ingredients is due to chemical compounds produced from the alcohols by the aging process. The greatest increase in secondary

---

1. Emma L. Benedict Transeau, p. 3, quoting Dr. August Ley. Emphasis mine, WDJ.

2. Frank Overton, *Applied Physiology Including the Effects of Alcohol and Narcotics* (New York: American Book Co., n.d.), p. 45.

3. *Encyclopaedia Britannica,* 1959 ed., s.v. "Fusel Oil," by Donald Guyer Zink, p. 952.

bodies occurs during the first year. In an aged whiskey there is about 99.4 percent of alcohol and water; the other 0.6 percent consists of 0.26 percent of solids extracted from the barrel and 0.34 percent of fusel oil, aldehydes, acids, esters, and furfural.[1]

It can be seen, therefore, that the process of aging does not rid distilled liquors of the secondary poisons.

Evidence Examined

The syllogism which was introduced at the beginning of this section is stated in valid form because the minor premise affirms the antecedent. The first proposition is true, based on the fact that the passages cited teach that it is sinful to abuse or harm the human body.

Evidence for the second proposition will now be introduced to prove that the consumption of ethyl alcohol to the degree which it is consumed in "social" drinking is harmful to the human body and, therefore, involves those in sin who so imbibe.

Alcohol and the Nervous System

Various substances, when taken into the body, affect the nervous system in different ways. Some stimulate or increase action; some depress or retard it; others have no effect. The nervous system is composed of thousands of cells which constantly carry messages from all parts of the body to the brain.

The previously mentioned Dr. Ritchie indicates that alcohol injures cells by precipitating and dehydrating protoplasm, and that the central nervous system is more markedly affected by alcohol than is any other system of the body.[2] It is known that alcohol, like other general anesthetics, is a primary and continuous depressant of the central nervous system. According to Dr. Haven Emerson, a professor in the College of Physicians and Surgeons, of Columbia University, "Alcohol is a narcotic drug."[3]

---

1. Herman C. Lythgoe, *New England Journal of Medicine,* n.p., n.d.
2. J. Murdoch Ritchie, "The Aliphatic Alcohols," p. 135.
3. Haven Emerson, *Alcohol: a Food, a Drug, a Poison* (Newark, New Jersey: Foundation for Narcotic Research and Information, Inc., n.d.), p. 1.

Narcotics have a retarding effect on the nervous system, while stimulants excite or increase activity within the nervous system. Scientists have proved that ethyl alcohol depresses or retards the activity of the highest brain centers. In fact, scientists have found it is easier to establish the fact that ethyl alcohol depresses than to determine how it depresses. Through the years many theories have been advanced and tested, but no theory fully explains it.[1] In regard to this point Dr. Ritchie states, "The apparent stimulation results from the unrestrained activity of various parts of the brain that have been freed from inhibition as a result of the depression of inhibitory control mechanisms."[2]

The cortex or higher brain center, however, is likely not the part of the brain that is the most sensitive to the action of alcohol. Indications are that it exerts its first depressant action upon a part of the brain known as the reticular activating system.[3] According to J. D. French, this seems to be the system that is responsible for much of the integration of activity in the various portions of the nervous system.[4] Drs. Peter J. Cohen, Professor and Chairman, Department of Anesthesiology, University of Colorado School of Medicine, and Robert D. Dripps, Professor and Chairman, Department of Anesthesia, University of Pennsylvania School of Medicine, indicate that the "reticular core of the brain stem contains neurons and pathways involved in the maintenance of consciousness, the so-called reticular activating system."[5]

Medical science has further indicated that the reticular core also contains an inhibitory system that discharges upward, thereby reducing the level of excitability of the cortex. It has also been observed that both activation and inhibition of the cortex by the ascending reticular systems are active processes which can be blocked by anesthetics. Since alcohol

1. Those interested in these theories will find a detailed discussion of them in Courtenay C. Weeks, *Alcohol and Human Life,* 2nd ed. (London: H. K. Lewis and Co., 1938).

2. J. Murdoch Ritchie, "The Aliphatic Alcohols," p. 135.

3. H. Kalant, "Some Recent Physiological and Biochemical Investigations on Alcohol and Alcoholism," *Quarterly Journal of Studies on Alcohol* 23 (1962):52–93.

4. J. D. French, "The Reticular Formation," in *Handbook of Physiology,* vol. 2, ed. H. W. Magoun (Washington, D.C.: American Physiological Society, 1960), n.p.

5. Peter J. Cohen and Robert D. Dripps, "Signs and Stages of Anesthesia," in *The Pharmacological Basis of Therapeutics,* eds. Louis S. Goodman and Alfred Gilman (London: Collier-Macmillan, Limited, 1970), p. 54.

is a general anesthetic, it is interesting to note that it is the ascending activating influence of the brainstem core that may be primarily impaired by most general anesthetics.[1]

The nervous system guides and controls other systems of the body, and alcohol has a special attraction for the nerve cells. Its affect on these, as on other cells, is to slow their activity and to depress instead of stimulate. Seeming stimulation is prevalent because alcohol weakens first the highly developed nerve centers, which release the lower centers from control. Tests involving small quantities of ethyl alcohol have shown these centers to be affected.[2] It is also significant to note that alcohol cannot be stored in the body or used in the replacement of destroyed tissue.[3]

Alcohol and the Stomach

Ethyl alcohol is capable of injuring the stomach. Even "social" drinkers often get inflammation of the lining of the stomach, known as gastritis, especially when they imbibe beverages of a high alcoholic content on an empty stomach. The fact that the stomach is empty allows the alcohol to act directly on the stomach lining.

There is another cause of gastritis which may be secondary among imbibers, namely, deficiency of vitamins and minerals. Such persons often fail to take sufficient food. W. Russell Shull stated, "Liquor does not contain the essential vitamins and minerals found in the foods of a normal diet. This lack of vitamins not only causes gastritis but also loss of appetite, which in turn leads the drinker to take liquor without food."[4]

Other Members of the Body

The effect of alcoholic beverages upon the brain, the nervous system, and the stomach, constitutes only a part of their action upon the whole body. The heart and blood vessels are responsible for carrying alcohol to

1. H. S. Davis, W. F. Collins, C. T. Randt, and W. H. Dillon, "Effects of Anesthetic Agents on Evoked Central Nervous System Responses: Gaseous Agents," *Anesthesiology* 18 (1957):634–642.

2. Emma Benedict Transeau, pp. 25–26.

3. Maurice Victor and Raymond D. Adams, "Alcohol," p. 668.

4. W. Russell Shull, p. 49.

all parts of the body. Though a very tough and powerful organ, the heart is affected by alcohol. Medical research has determined that three ounces of alcohol will increase the fatty substance in the blood of those who drink. This substance has been linked with artery disease, heart attacks, and strokes. In such fashion alcohol retards the utilization of oxygen. A panel of doctors, including Dr. William P. Castelli of the National Heart, Lung and Blood Institute, has taken issue with reports that two drinks a day may protect against heart attack. The panel stated that the risk is too great to justify ever recommending liquor.[1]

Alcohol also serves to enlarge the blood vessels near the body surface, in addition to being harmful to the liver. A recent government report substantiated the fact that such medical problems as gastro-intestinal, cardiac, muscle, hematologic, and metabolic disorders often develop as a result of "social" drinking.[2]

Drs. E. Mansell Pattison and Edward Kaufman, who are professors in the University of California, Irvine, serving in the Department of Psychiatry and Human Behavior, state, "Alcoholism is the third most prevalent public health problem in our society."[3] "Social" drinking leads to alcoholism.

It has been determined that persons who imbibe even small quantities of alcoholic beverages are more difficult to anesthetize for surgery than are those who are abstainers.[4] This is because alcohol, as a component part of ether, which was formerly employed in surgery, serves to deaden the senses of those who imbibe, to a certain degree.

The effects of alcohol on digestion, heart action, kidneys, and liver, may remain unnoticed until these organs are required to meet unusual

---

1. "Doctors Debunk Liquor as an Rx," *Nashville, The Tennessean,* 16 November 1979, n.p.

2. *First Special Report,* pp. 38, 45–54.

3. E. Mansell Pattison and Edward Kaufman, "Alcohol and Drug Dependence," in *Psychiatry in General Medical Practice,* eds. Gene Usdin and Jerry M. Lewis (New York: McGraw-Hill Book Co., 1979), pp. 306–307.

4. Personal interview with Dr. Roy Douglas, surgeon gynecologist in residence in Jackson-Madison General Hospital, in Jackson, Tennessee, 31 January 1978. See *Third Special Report to the U.S. Congress on Alcohol and Health,* by Ernest P. Noble, ed. (Washington, D.C.: Government Printing Office, 1978), p. 197; B. Kissin, "Interactions of Ethyl Alcohol and Other Drugs," in *The Biology of Alcoholism,* vol. 3, *Clinical Pathology,* eds. B. Kissin and H. Begleiter (New York: Plenum Press, 1974), pp. 109–61.

strain during illness or shock. The effects on such organs, however, for the "social" drinker, are minor in comparison with the effects on the brain and the other parts of the nervous system. Such effects differ with individuals, and with time and circumstances. Ethyl alcohol, however, even in small amounts, with continued use, slowly though imperceptibly harms all cells and tissues which it touches, although not all of the tissues of the body are affected to the same extent. Robert E. Fleming has stated,

> The higher centers of the central nervous system are particularly sensitive to concentrations of alcohol much lower than the thresholds for other tissues such as muscle, glands, etc. It is for this reason that symptoms involving disturbances of thought processes, of mood, of sensation, and of coordination are among the first to appear after the ingestion of alcohol.[1]

Alcohol and Other Drugs

In the past thirty-five years there has been an extremely large increase in the use of drugs, including illicit and self-prescribed over-the-counter drugs, as well as those which are commonly prescribed by physicians. During this time, a large increase in the use of alcohol has occurred. There is, therefore, now a greatly increased probability that alcohol and another drug will be acting simultaneously in many persons. Such alcohol-drug combinations can result in very severe health problems, and even death. Although such alcohol-drug interactions are most likely to occur after heavy and continuous drinking, with some drugs even *a single drink* can cause adverse reactions.[2]

G. A. Zirkle and several associates have determined that the consequences of imbibing *even small amounts* of alcohol following the ingestion of various other drugs may be severe or even fatal. In fact, psychopharmacological agents are now so widely employed that it is important for physicians to warn patients who have been given such medication of

---

1. Robert E. Fleming, "On Certain Medical Aspects of Alcoholism," *Bulletin of the Academy of Medicine of New Jersey* 1 (15 June 1956):14–15.

2. D. Bailey, "Some Undesirable Drug-Alcohol Interaction," *Journal on Alcohol* 9 (1974):62–68.

the increased effect of ethyl alcohol and of the consequent increased dangers of imbibing.[1]

Many common and legitimate drugs are potentially hazardous when combined with alcohol. These include antibiotics, antihistamines, antidepressants, sedatives, stimulants, tranquilizers, antidiabetic agents, analgesics, drugs used in the treatment of cardiac disease, and many others.[2]

The harmful consequences of combined alcohol-drug use are not always strictly medical, but many include behavioral effects. A study[3] showed that driving impairment was significantly greater when alcohol was taken with small doses of various sedatives, minor tranquilizers, or marijuana, even when blood-alcohol concentration was low. Similar findings were obtained in another driver study[4] involving alcohol in combination with marijuana, and antihistamines, or minor tranquilizers.

Combining alcohol with drugs is a special problem. Drugs which are taken specifically for their effects on the nervous system have considerable potential for interaction with alcohol. An interaction between alcohol and a drug is defined as any alteration in the pharmacologic properties of either because of the presence of the other. Interactions may be one of three types, namely: (1) Antagonistic, resulting in a blocking or reduction of the effects of either or both drugs: (2) additive, so the net effect of the two drugs is the sum of the effects of each; (3) supra-

1. G. A. Zirkle, P. D. King, O. B. McAtee, and R. Van Dyke, "Effects of Chlorpromazine and Alcohol on Coordination and Judgment," *Journal of American Medical Association* 171 (1959):1496–99; G. A. Zirkle, O. B. McAtee, P. D. King, and R. Van Dyke, "Meprobamate and Small Amounts of Alcohol," *Journal of American Medical Association* 173 (1961):1823–25.

2. In regard to this, consult F. A. Seixas, "Alcohol and Its Drug Interactions," *Annual on Internal Medicine* 83 (1975):86–92, and B. Kissin, "Interactions of Ethyl Alcohol and Other Drugs," in *The Biology of Alcoholism,* vol. 3, *Clinical Pathology,* eds. B. Kissin and H. Begleiter (New York: Plenum Press, 1974), pp. 109–61.

3. R. Burford, I. W. French, and A. E. Leblanc, "The Combined Effects of Alcohol and Common Psychoactive Drugs. I. Studies on Human Pursuit Tracking Capability," in *Alcohol, Drugs, and Traffic Safety,* eds. S. Israelstam and S. Lambert (Toronto: Addiction Research Foundation of Ontario, 1975), pp. 423–431.

4. A. Smiley et al., "The Combined Effects of Alcohol and Common Psychoactive Drugs. II. Field Studies with an Instrumented Automobile," in *Alcohol, Drugs, and Traffic Safely,* eds. S. Israelstam and S. Lambert (Toronto: Addiction Research Foundation of Ontario, 1975), pp. 433–438.

additive, so the net effect of the two drugs in combination is greater than it would be if the effects were merely additive.

The third type of interaction is probably the most important from a public health standpoint, since the hazards of these combinations are greater than expected. Antagonistic interactions, however, may also be important when the therapeutic effects of one drug are being reduced by the other agent.

Antagonistic, additive, and supra-additive interactions can be direct or indirect. Direct interactions involve the basic pharmacologic effects of alcohol and the other drug at the same site of action. Thus, alcohol, a central nervous system depressant, is counteracted by drugs that stimulate the central nervous system, and augmented by drugs that are themselves central nervous system depressants.[1] Indirect interactions occur when one agent affects the absorption, distribution, excretion, or metabolism of the other to produce antagonistic, additive, or supra-additive effects.[2]

The well-known danger to life from combined use of alcohol and barbiturates appears to result from a supra-additive interaction.[3] In an investigation of eighty-five barbiturate-related deaths in Glasgow, Scotland,[4] alcohol and barbiturates were found together in 42 percent of the cases. The lethal dose was nearly 50 percent lower in the presence of alcohol than when used alone, which means that a fatal overdose of barbiturates is more likely when alcohol is used simultaneously than when it is not.

Minor tranquilizers such as Valium and Librium are most likely to be combined with alcohol by the general population. Persons are generally unaware that tranquilizers are central nervous system depressants that can increase the effects of alcohol on performance skills and alert-

1. B. Kissin, "Interactions of Ethyl Alcohol and Other Drugs," in *The Biology of Alcoholism,* vol. 3, *Clinical Pathology,* eds. B. Kissin and H. Begleiter (New York: Plenum Press, 1974), pp. 109–61.

2. P. G. Dayton and J. M. Perel, "Physiological and Physicochemical Bases of Drug Interaction in Man," *Annual of New York Academy of Science* 179 (1972):67–87.

3. C. R. B. Joyce et al., "Potentiation of Phenobarbitone of Effects of Ethyl Alcohol on Human Behavior," *Journal of Mental Science* 105 (1959):51–60.

4. J. Bogan and H. Smith, "Analytical Investigation of Barbiturate Poisoning— Description of Methods and a Survey of Results," *Journal of Forensic Science* 7 (1967):37–45.

ness. One investigator[1] has placed minor tranquilizers in the same psychopharmacologic class as barbiturates.

Alcohol has been shown to act supra-additively with meprobamate to depress performance tasks.[2] Major tranquilizers such as chlorpromazine and thioridazine are powerful drugs which are used in connection with serious emotional disturbances. These and other such tranquilizers, when used in combination with alcohol, produce severe, possible fatal, depression of the respiratory center. It has been determined that alcohol, when combined with any of the major tranquilizers, impairs performance skills.[3]

The consumption of alcoholic beverages in some instances brings about addiction to other forms of narcotic drugs. In regard to this fact Dr. Jerome H. Jaffe states,

> In Western society individuals who later become addicts invariably have experiences with alcohol prior to using opiates. A considerable number of such persons also experimented first with marijuana, amphetamines, barbiturates, and tranquilizers.[4]

Nationally, alcohol in combination with other drugs is the second most frequent cause of drug-related medical crises. The minor tranquilizers are the drugs most frequently combined with alcohol and can increase the pernicious effects of alcohol on performance skills and alertness. In combination with alcohol, some of these tranquilizers can depress heart functioning and respiration fatally. A wide variety of drugs, not limited to psychoactive agents, can interact with even *small amounts* of alcohol.[5] It should also be noted that in regard to a combination of

---

1. M. H. Seevers, "Psychopharmacological Elements of Drug Dependence," *Journal of American Medical Association* 206 (1968):1263–66.

2. L. Goldberg, "Effects of Ethanol in the Central Nervous System," in *Alcohol and Alcoholism,* ed. R. E. Popham (Toronto: University Press, 1970), pp. 42–56. See also G. A. Zirkle et al., "Meprobamate and Small Amounts of Alcohol: Effects on Human Ability, Coordination, and Judgment," *Journal of American Medical Association* 173 (1960):1823–25.

3. G. A. Zirkle et al., "Effects of Chlorpromazine and Alcohol on Coordination and Judgment," *Journal of American Medical Association* 171 (1959):1496–99.

4. Jerome H. Jaffe, in *The Pharmacological Basis of Therapeutics,* eds. Louis S. Goodman and Alfred Gilman (London: Collier-Macmillan, Limited, 1970), p. 291.

5. *Third Special Report,* p. 207.

such stimulants as caffeine and alcohol, studies[1] have shown that caffeine is at best only a weak antagonist of the depressant effects of alcohol.

Children

Small quantities of alcohol affect children to even a greater degree than adults. Drs. Pattison and Kaufman indicate that in France it was one time the custom to give young children in school diluted wine with their meals. Consequently, many young French children developed cirrhosis.[2] According to two pediatricians, Dr. William Altemeier, Director of Pediatrics Services, in Nashville General Hospital, and Dr. John Wilson, a Vanderbilt University Medical School professor, children who drink as little as one can of beer or one mixed drink could suffer irreversible brain damage or retardation. These men, eminently qualified in their field, further indicated that ethyl alcohol is a special danger because it tends to cause hypoglycemia, which is a drop in blood sugar, resulting in possible permanent damage unless medical attention is received immediately.[3]

Barbara Luke, a clinical specialist in maternal nutrition, stated, "Alcohol consumption during pregnancy is known to result in approximately 6000 defective births each year."[4] Relative to the effects of ethyl alcohol on expectant mothers, Dr. Clyde Capps, medical director of the Care Unit Program at St. Mary's Medical Center, in Knoxville, Tennessee, stated, "The more alcohol a pregnant woman drinks, the greater are the risks of giving birth to an abnormal baby."[5]

---

1. H. W. Newman and E. J. Newman, "Failure of Dexedrine and Caffeine as Practical Antagonists of the Depressant Effect of Ethyl Alcohol in Man," *Quarterly Journal of Studies on Alcohol* 17 (1956):406–10. See also F. W. Hughes and R. B. Forney, "Dextro-Amphetamine, Ethanol and Dextro-Amphetamine-Ethanol Combinations of Performance of Human Subjects Stressed with Delayed Auditory Feedback (DAF)," *Psychopharmacologia* 6 (1964):234–38; R. B. Forney and F. W. Hughes, "Effect of Caffeine and Alcohol on Performance Under Stress of Audio-Feedback," *Quarterly Journal of Studies on Alcohol* 26 (1965):206–12.

2. E. Mansell Pattison and Edward Kaufman, p. 308.

3. "Alcohol Danger for Youths Told," *Memphis, The Commercial Appeal,* 25 April 1977, p. 3.

4. "Medical Experts Back Alcohol Warning," *Memphis, The Commercial Appeal,* 1 February 1978, p. 20. See also Marian Sandmaier, *Alcohol and Your Unborn Baby* (Washington, D.C.: Government Printing Office, 1981).

5. "Alcohol Affects Unborn Babies," *Cookeville, Tennessee, The Herald-Citizen,* 26 September 1979, p. 7.

In addition, it was indicated that more than 5000 babies born in the United States this year will have one or more symptoms of Fetal Alcohol Syndrome, a pattern of mental and physical defects. Some 1500 babies will experience the full syndrome, which has been linked with alcohol on the part of mothers. Dr. Capps further stated, "One of five Fetal Alcohol Syndrome children die in the womb or within the first twenty-eight days after birth. Of the children that do survive, almost all are seriously mentally retarded as well as physically deformed."[1]

In addition to Fetal Alcohol Syndrome, drinking on the part of expectant mothers has been linked to other problems in their children. Between five and seven million school-age children suffer from Minimal Brain Dysfunction, a pattern of behavior and learning problems.

Also researchers at the University of Washington have found that "social" drinking during the first five months of pregnancy can affect the natural behavior of newborn babies. In another study, children of "social" drinkers were reported to have weighed less at birth than is considered normal.[2]

In explaining and emphasizing the function of ethyl alcohol Dr. Capps stated, "Alcohol is a powerful, addictive drug. When a woman takes a drink, the alcohol crosses the placenta to the fetus. The alcohol travels through the baby's bloodstream in the same concentration as in its mother's."[3]

In other words, the baby, yet unborn, is as drunk as the mother! Because the unborn baby's delicate system does not tolerate alcohol well, growth is arrested and brain damage can occur. Some cases have been so extreme that babies have been born with alcohol on their breath and have had to suffer through alcohol withdrawal!

It has been observed that women who drink between only one and three ounces of ethyl alcohol risk having children with some Fetal Alcohol Syndrome symptoms or Minimal Brain Dysfunction. It is indeed revolting to think of the harm that has been done to innocent babies because of the intake of such beverages!

---

1. Ibid.

2. Ibid.

3. Ibid. See also "Mother's Alcohol Use Linked to Brain Damage in Infants," *Nashville, The Tennessean,* 1 March 1981, p. 17A; "Official Warning: Pregnant Women Shouldn't Drink," *Cookeville, Tennessee, The Herald-Citizen,* 19 July 1981, p. 9.

Indirect Harm

Not only is "social" drinking directly harmful to the human body, but indirectly as well. Likely most persons are aware of the fact that many statistics could be cited to indicate that even light consumption contributes to automobile accidents and highway deaths.[1]

Alcohol in Medicine

Persons may reply to the view that ethyl alcohol is harmful to the human body by stating that it is employed in medicines. Although this is true, it is not used nearly as much as formerly because more is known of its toxic effects. Andrew Poznanski states:

> Numerous medical writers, including Galen, used wines in medicine and gave recipes for their production. Arnold of Villanova (1235–1311), physician, surgeon, botanist, alchemist, and philosopher, is perhaps the first to have written a book about wines. In his *Treatise on Wine* he discusses how the various wines should be prepared, and discusses their medicinal attributes.[2]

Although alcohol was long prescribed as a tonic, a sedative, and a soporific, its traditional role in medicine has now been taken over largely by the barbiturates, minor tranquilizers, and other sedatives and hypnotics.[3] It should also be observed that in antiquity the range of pharmaceutical products was much more limited than in modern times. On the other hand, various other drugs are employed in medicines, which should be taken only after having been prescribed by competent physicians.

Early distillers claimed that alcoholic beverages possessed great medicinal powers, even to the extent of being a virtual cure for all maladies. Consequently, various forms of alcoholic beverages were quite generally employed as household remedies. Physicians, in fact, employed whiskey for practically every known ailment, until medical scientists

---

1. Joel Fort, *Alcohol: Our Biggest Drug Problem* (New York: McGraw-Hill Book Co., 1973), p. 107.

2. Andrew Poznanski, "Our Drinking Heritage," in *McGill Medical Journal*, (1956):35–41.

3. Edward M. Brecher, *Licit and Illicit Drugs* (Boston: Little, Brown and Co., 1972), p. 245.

began to correct the theories upon which such medicinal use was chiefly founded.

In modern society, with vastly improved and advanced medical technology, alcohol is not commonly used in medicine. As has already been observed, modern processes of fortifying and distilling alcohol have greatly increased its toxic effect.

When scientists discovered that ethyl alcohol is a depressant which, consequently, lowers body temperature and lessens the power of normal resistance to disease. Other remedies, which were devoid of the depressant effects, were employed to accomplish the desired results.

For many years whiskey was a desired household prescription for snakebite. For more than seventy-five years, however, warnings against the use of ethyl alcohol in snakebite cases have been prevalent in medical literature. As long ago as 1908, Dr. Prentiss Willson denounced its use. The American Medical Association issued the following comment on Dr. Willson's report:

> Alcohol poisoning is often enough more serious than the snake poisoning. Nothing could be more irrational and dangerous than the popular notion concerning the antagonism of whiskey and snake-bite, and Willson reports that several fatalities in his series were directly due to alcohol rather than to the bite.[1]

In recent years Dr. Ivan L. Bennett, Jr., Director, New York University Medical Center, stated, "Alcohol has no place in the treatment of snake-bite."[2] In June 1917, the American Medical Association passed the following resolution:

> Whereas we believe that the use of alcohol is detrimental to the human economy, and its use in therapeutics as a stimulant has no scientific value; therefore, be it resolved that the American Medical Association is opposed to the use of alcohol as a beverage; and be it further resolved that the use of alcohol as a therapeutic agent shall be further discouraged.[3]

---

1. *Journal of the American Medical Association,* n.p., 11 July 1908.

2. Ivan L. Bennett, Jr., "Disorders Caused by Venoms, Bites, and Stings," in *Harrison's Principles of Internal Medicine,* eds. Maxwell M. Wintrobe, et al. (New York: McGraw-Hill Book Co., 1970), p. 692.

3. J. Hericourt, *The Social Diseases* (London: Routledge, 1920), p. 22. See also *Family Health Guide and Medical Encyclopedia,* 1970 ed., s.v. "Alcohol," p. 21.

The Proposition Proved

From the foregoing material the proposition is proved that the consumption of ethyl alcohol to the degree which it is consumed in "social" drinking is harmful to the human body. Since the syllogism is stated in valid form, and both propositions are true, it follows that "social" drinking is contrary to the law of God.

Influence Argument

Romans 14:21

If it were not contrary to the divine law of God to privately imbibe light or small quantities of alcoholic beverages,[1] the Bible clearly indicates dangers which are prevalent with "social" drinking. Paul said, "It is good not to eat flesh, nor to drink wine, nor to do anything whereby thy brother stumbleth."[2] The text indicates that to eat with offense is to eat under circumstances which cause persons to stumble. There is very little danger today that eating meat will cause persons to stumble, but by "social" drinking individuals may lead others to also violate the law of God. Christians should contemplate the possible influence of their actions before engaging in any activity which will likely cause others to stumble.

Christian Influence

The church is a kingdom of influence.[3] The New Testament metaphor pertaining to salt[4] indicates that followers of Christ are to be influential in preserving the world from corrupt and destructive devices. Christians are to shine as lights,[5] in overcoming darkness. Actions which involve righteous deeds, sound teaching, and godly thoughts, will dispel spiritual darkness.

---

1. Dedicated Christians believe that it is contrary to the law of God to imbibe such beverages, even in a private setting.

2. Rom. 14:21.

3. Mt. 13:33.

4. Mt. 5:13.

5. Mt. 5:14–16.

Persons should consider how their actions relate to the desires of Christ. Any view as to how Christ would regard the consumption of alcoholic beverages today, must be based upon His total attitude toward the purpose of life and toward human personality. The Son of God desires that persons live the very best life possible.[1]

Persons who sanction the imbibing of intoxicating beverages should realize that there are many persons who are not Christians who do not subscribe to *even* "social" drinking. If such persons are converted by a member of the church who is a "social" drinker, or by one who does not drink but defends the rights of others to so do, either the new convert must be convinced that his former position in regard to drinking is wrong and, therefore, it is indeed permissible, or the one doing the converting must conceal the fact that he condones "social" drinking. It is a fact that "social" drinking not only *can* but *does* destroy influence for the cause of Christ!

Christian Expediency

If the Bible substantiates the use of intoxicating beverages within the limits of sobriety, as it is held to do by those who claim there was no such thing as unintoxicating wine in the first century, then the doctrine of Christian expediency, in its application to the issue, is absolutely worthless!

To break the force of this natural and logical conclusion, it has been said that times have changed to the extent that the circumstances of the present day and land are so different from those of the times and land of the Bible, that such should not be made a duty now.

In reply to such reasoning, it may be said that if times have changed, who has changed them? It is a certain and irrefutable fact that the Bible has most assuredly not changed! Paul admonished elders and deacons in the early church of the dangers of intoxicating wine. If those men could involve themselves in teaching others while drinking such wine without hindrance, provided they did not get drunk or become intoxicated, as some persons advocate they could do, they could do this before converts, some of whom had no doubt but immediately left the revellings and drunkenness of heathendom, and in the full light of the doctrine of Christian expediency!

---

1. Mt. 5:48.

If this were true, and those who contend that wine is not wine unless intoxicating, and that intoxicating wine is allowed and approved, as to its so-called moderate use, must think it to be true—where are the circumstances in which abstinence because of influence may be the duty of others? The writer would like the proof from those who think they have divine sanction and approval throughout the Bible for the use of alcoholic beverages within the limits of so-called moderation, if this does not take the very heart out of the doctrine of Christian expediency or influence! If not, why not?

The apostle Paul enumerates among the sins of his time, drunkenness and revellings, and he urges the saints at Rome not to walk in "revelling and drunkenness."[1] He counsels the Corinthians to avoid the company of the drunkard, though he be called a brother.[2] Among gross offenders he names drunkards, adding: "Such were some of you."[3] He urges the Ephesians to "be not drunken with wine,"[4] and the Thessalonians to be sober and not drunken.[5]

These passages prove beyond all question that drunkenness was a common sin in the time of Christ and the apostles. Such warnings, counsels, and exhortations have no meaning otherwise! The force of these facts cannot be impaired by any response about distilled and adulterated beverages. Persons may travel to the very lands of the Bible where the wine is the same and its effects the same and human nature the same as nearly two thousand years ago and observe that "revelling" and "drunkenness" are the same as they were then. Yet no Christian missionary worthy of the name in Bible lands today, could hold his place in the confidence of supporters who are faithful to Christ, who would publicly and repeatedly endorse the so-called moderate use of alcoholic beverages so long as persons avoid drunkenness.

The writer does not believe that what the Bible refers to as a mocker, a deceiver, a breeder of woe, sorrow, and contention, and which at the last "biteth like a serpent and stingeth like an adder," Jesus made in large quantity on a public festive occasion and gave to persons who had

---

1. Rom. 13:13.
2. 1 Cor. 5:11.
3. 1 Cor. 6:10–11.
4. Eph. 5:18.
5. 1 Thess. 5:4–8.

already freely indulged. The writer does not believe that Paul declared it morally obligatory not to drink wine for the sake of a stumbling brother, and then in the midst of prevailing drunkenness, and multitudes of stumblers, wrote publicly to churches, elders, deacons, and aged women, endorsing their "moderate" use of wine! Those who do think these things to be true, and therefore indict the Son of God and His word, should remember that the indictment comes from their misuse of the Bible, although sincere they may be, and not from the writer's exegesis of the eternal verities of God!

One principle which many persons fail to recognize is the fact that, according to the Bible meaning of expediency, those things which can be proved as expedient are authorized and are therefore matters of faith. Since matters of faith are binding, if a principle can be determined to be expedient, it is as equally binding.

Christian Restraint

Persons in Bible times likely knew little, if anything, about the action of ethyl alcohol inside the human body, and how it acts on the brain and central nervous system, as is known today. They were, however, keen observers of how persons acted when they were under the influence of alcoholic beverages.[1] Restraint therefore is enjoined clearly and emphatically throughout the Bible, and self-control is listed as the only real safeguard against fleshly indulgences.[2] The motives for self-control are numerous, but the greatest source of self-control is a determination to do the will of God. Despite everything which may be written or said in regard to abstinence or indulgence, restraint from imbibing alcoholic beverages depends on persons themselves.

It is right to provide for the comfort, growth, health, and preservation of the human body, but no provisions should be made for gratifying the lusts of the flesh.[3] It is difficult enough to control lusts and passions of the flesh when unexpectedly and suddenly persons are tempted through them. On the contrary, when persons contemplate, plan, and provide for

---

1. 1 Sam. 1:12–15; 25:1–37; 1 Kings 20:1–20; Ps. 104:15; Prov. 20:1; 23:21, 29–35; 31:6–7; Is. 5:11–12.

2. cf. 1 Cor. 9:25–27; Gal. 5:16–17, 24; Col. 3:5–17; 2 Pet. 1:1–11.

3. Rom. 13:13–14.

their personal gratification, they should not expect to escape the condemnation of God.

Not only does the Bible warn against the evil influences which are connected with the use of such beverages, but it warns persons not to associate with those who imbibe them.[1] God, however, allows persons to choose for themselves whether they will be corrupted by evil influences. They must be moved to action by the admonitions of the Bible, led by the goodness of God, and constrained by the love of Christ in order to function properly. Nothing else is so powerful in helping persons shun temptations and exhibit reverence for God and His word, as a sense of personal responsibility in the sight of God. It is indeed tragic, however, when young children are brought up in a less than ideal home environment, an environment where reverence for God and His word is not daily demonstrated.

Christian Homes

Every infant has a God-given right to grow to maturity in a righteous environment, which is characterized by Christian influence. It is a fact that many Christians by precept or practice advocate the use of intoxicating beverages. Many of those who imbibe strongly contend for Christian liberty in the matter. It is also a fact that the public example of such Christians has been the occasion of many young person's first step to ruin. Many children have, no doubt, been brought to the degradation and doom of drunkenness through habits they have observed at their own parent's table! In fact, many young persons imbibe alcoholic beverages because their parents do, and even to the same frequency.[2] Likely not one such Christian parent would say that he ever knowingly placed a stumblingblock or an occasion to fall in his children's way. Nevertheless, this is precisely what has been done! Persons are responsible to God for their influence, conscious or unconscious, whether it extends to those whom they know or to those whom they have never met!

Young persons in particular face some difficult decisions in the present ultra-permissive society. Mysteries surrounding the prevailing

---

1. cf. Prov. 23:20–21; 1 Cor. 15:33.

2. Marston M. McCluggage et al., "Summary of Essential Findings in the Kansas Study," in *Drinking and Intoxication,* ed. Raymond Gerald McCarthy (Glencoe, Illinois: Free Press, 1959), pp. 211–18.

ideas in regard to light drinking are not helpful to youth, even those who do not imbibe, because it is likely that the majority of them will at some time face the question of how to conduct themselves in situations where others are imbibing.

Young persons often undergo tremendous peer pressure, and for many of them imbibing is, no doubt, largely a matter of exhibiting a certain style. Motivational factors often involve the desire to appear to be manly, sophisticated, or grown-up, when in reality the imbibing of alcoholic beverages is indicative of sheer immaturity! Parental training is the key to maturity. Until young persons reach a certain age, parents often are not cognizant of the fact that the realities of life are imminent, and the consequences of failure to train their precious children properly can be overwhelming!

In recent years there has been considerable emphasis given to the study of teenage drinking.[1] A relatively recent survey of 7345 students attending thirty-four New England colleges indicated that in most cases both heavy and light drinking college students were following a pattern set during their high school years when they drank. Those who abstained from alcohol, a group comprising only 5 percent of those surveyed, did so in high school as well. The study also showed a correlation between the drinking habits of students and their parents, with drinking students being less likely to have parents who did not drink, while college abstainers came from predominately non-drinking families.[2] There are as many as "1.1 million young people who can be considered problem drinkers,"[3] although most young persons who drink do so to a lesser degree.[4]

---

1. Various studies include Margaret Bacon and Mary Brush Jones, *Teenage Drinking* (New York: Thomas Y. Crowell Co., 1968), pp. 209–21; Jim Orford, Seta Walker, and Julian Peto, "Drinking Behavior and Attitudes and Their Correlates Among University Students," *Quarterly Journal of Studies on Alcohol* 35 (December 1974):1370–74; Robert Straus and Seldon D. Bacon, *Drinking in College* (New Haven, Conn.: Yale University Press, 1953; reprint ed., Westport, Conn.: Greenwood Press, 1971), p. 37.

2. "Patterns of College Drinking Linked to High School Habit," *Memphis, The Commercial Appeal,* 16 March 1978, p. 12.

3. "Youth and Alcohol," in *Alcohol Topics in Brief,* vol. 1 (n.p.: National Institute on Alcohol Abuse and Alcoholism, n.d.), n.p.

4. In a spiritual sense, of course, imbibing to any degree constitutes a problem.

Some persons think that it is simply and solely their own business if they drink. They are mistaken, however! What about the suffering which is brought to wives, husbands, and children by those who drink? What about innocent victims in automobile accidents which are caused by drivers under the influence of ethyl alcohol?

What function does alcohol serve for various persons? Perhaps several reasons are in order: (1) Some drink because others do and it seems easier to conform than to be labeled as different. (2) Others no doubt drink to celebrate happy occasions, for pure pleasure, and out of good spirits. (3) Some who are tense and apprehensive drink to feel more relaxed and secure. (4) Some drink because it makes them feel less lonely. (5) Some drink because it makes them feel more comfortable and capable in coping with work and in social life. (6) Some persons drink to free themselves of guilty feelings.

Different persons no doubt drink for these and other reasons, and all drink for different reasons at different times.[1]

Alcoholic beverages are often enticing because of the techniques and terminology connected with imbibing. Such consumption has its own language with terms like "bonded," "on the rocks," and "jigger," along with numerous others. Various rituals include shaking and stirring, which along with special terminology, creates an atmosphere in which many young persons, in particular, who are most likely anxious to appear to be greatly sophisticated and knowledgeable, cast aside every restraint. The ancient Roman philosopher and senator Seneca wrote in or around A.D. 50 that drunkenness brings vice into view. He said, "The haughty man increases his arrogance, the ruthless man his cruelty, and the slanderer his spitefulness. Every vice is given free play and comes to the front."[2]

In regard to the influence of alcohol upon society, Dr. Edith S. Lisansky indicates that imbibing for most persons who thus do is a social act. Whether one partakes with family, business associates, friends, the casual acquaintances at a cocktail party, or with those standing around a bar, drinking for most persons means so-called social drinking.

---

1. For a valuable study concerning this point, consult A. Myerson, "Alcoholism: The Role of Social Ambivalence," in *Drinking and Intoxication,* ed. Raymond Gerald McCarthy (Glencoe, Illinois: Free Press, 1959), pp. 306–12.

2. Seneca's Epistle LXXXIII: On Drunkenness. Classics of the Alcohol Literature, *Quarterly Journal of Studies on Alcohol* 3 (1942):302.

Likely for most of such persons alcohol serves as a social lubricant and facilitates much of American party life because it serves to diminish those inhibitions which keep some persons reserved and cautious when meeting people. Such persons can behave a little more as they did when they were children, before the processes of socialization taught them to control their feelings to a certain extent.[1]

Proper influence in the home cannot be stressed too much or over-emphasized. Many emotional, mental, and physical ills which are suffered by modern society may be traced to influence exerted in homes. Parents are entrusted with the lives of their children, and even with their souls to a certain extent. It is imperative, therefore, that children be taught and trained carefully. Parents cannot forfeit or neglect such responsibility without violating the law of God.[2]

Although relatively little has been written by members of churches of Christ through the years toward educating persons in regard to the dangers involved in alcohol, various treatises in scientific journals may be useful, and in addition there are several extremely well-documented books which can prove to be helpful in working with both young and adult heavy drinkers and alcoholics.[3] It should be noted that the writer does not endorse everything that is taught in these journals and books.

---

1. Edith S. Lisansky, "Psychological Effects," in *Drinking and Intoxication,* ed. Raymond Gerald McCarthy (Glencoe, Illinois: Free Press, 1959), p. 24.

2. cf. Prov. 22:6; Eph. 6:4.

3. The scientific journals include G. Nicholas Braucht et al., "Drug Education: A Review of Goals Approaches and Effectiveness, and a Paradigm for Evaluation," *Quarterly Journal of Studies on Alcohol* 34 (December 1973):1279–92; Gail Gleason Milgram, "A Descriptive Analysis of Alcohol Education Materials." *Journal of Studies on Alcohol* 36 (March 1975):416–21; Robert D. Russell, "Alcohol and Other Mood-Modifying Substances in Ecological Perspective: A Framework for Communicating and Educating," *Quarterly Journal of Studies on Alcohol* 35 (June 1974):606–19. The books include Robert A. Blees, *Counseling with Teen-Agers,* Successful Pastoral Counseling Series (Englewood Cliffs, New Jersey: Prentice-Hall, 1965); Howard J. Clinebell, Jr., *Understanding and Counseling the Alcoholic,* revised and enlarged ed. (Nashville: Abingdon Press, 1968); John E. Keller, *Ministering to Alcoholics* (Minneapolis, Minn.: Augsburg Publishing House, 1966); Derek Miller, *Adolescence: Psychology, Psychopathology, and Psychotherapy* (New York: Jason Aronson, 1974). In regard to definitions, various books will prove to be quite helpful in relation to the extremely technical terminology which is often employed in the study of alcohol. One such book is Mark Keller and Mairi McCormick, *A Dictionary of Words About Alcohol* (New Brunswick, New Jersey: Publications Division, Rutgers Center of Alcohol Studies, 1968), pp. 1–227.

The Bible, of course, is the best book concerning the evils of alcoholic beverages.

Christian Examples

The arguments presented in defense of "social" drinking are fallacious and are not worthy of the valid reasoning which its advocates apply in other phases of their lives. Most persons who defend "social" drinking would not likely affirm that (1) they can successfully teach others about Christ while under the influence, (2) their marriage has been more spiritual-minded since ethyl alcohol entered it, (3) they can wield a better influence on their children with a drink in their hand, (4) they have lost absolutely no fervor for spiritual activities since they began drinking, and (5) when Christ comes they would be perfectly willing to meet Him with ethyl alcohol on their breath.

In light of these facts, therefore, "social" drinkers influence persons in a way which is contrary to the law of God. Not only will such advocates, who fail to repent, suffer for their personal acts, but for their evil influences upon others. The consequences of engaging in such activities are so far reaching that persons should think carefully before they begin to follow such a corrupt course which will ultimately lead to eternal destruction.

An Additional Observation

Although "social" drinking is to be condemned because of its evil influence upon others, it is not correct to condemn it *solely* on the basis of its evil influence.[1]

Syllogistic Reasoning

Those who claim that one's influence upon others is the *only* basis for abstinence must accept the following:

(1) If influence upon others is the only basis upon which the imbibing of light quantities of ethyl alcohol as a beverage can be considered

---

1. Although the following material would ordinarily be included in Part One under "Negative Argumentation of the Problem," the writer feels that since the matter of influence is under consideration in this section, it is in order to consider it with the present material.

as sinful, then one who is isolated from others may imbibe light quantities of ethyl alcohol as a beverage without sinning.

(2) Influence upon others is the only basis upon which the imbibing of light quantities of ethyl alcohol as a beverage can be considered as sinful.[1]

(3) Therefore, one who is isolated from others may imbibe light quantities of ethyl alcohol as a beverage without sinning.

In regard to the first proposition, (1) if influence upon others is the only basis upon which the imbibing of light quantities of ethyl alcohol as a beverage can be considered as sinful, then one who is isolated or separated from all other persons, or at least from those who do not sanction such imbibing themselves, could so imbibe without sinning.

In regard to the second proposition (2), although the writer *does* hold the view that influence upon others is *a* basis upon which the imbibing of light quantities of ethyl alcohol as a beverage can be considered as sinful, he does *not* hold the view that it is the *only* basis upon which such imbibing can be considered as sinful!

In regard to the conclusion (3), which necessarily follows, the claim is untenable because its espousal constitutes the acceptance of the false doctrine of situation ethics. It should be observed at this point that the espousal of *any* view that constitutes the acceptance of false doctrine (*any* false doctrine) is wrong and, therefore, sinful!

Light Consumption

As has been previously noted,[2] even the consumption or intake of light or small quantities of ethyl alcohol as a beverage constitutes a degree of drunkenness or intoxication, which condition is plainly taught in the Bible to be sinful or contrary to the law of God.[3]

In addition, those who accept the above claim reject the fact that even the consumption of light quantities of ethyl alcohol as a beverage are harmful to the human body, which fact has also been previously

---

1. Please note that this, and the conclusion which follows, is not the writer's view!
2. See Chapter 3, pp. 98–115.
3. Hab. 2:15; Lk. 21:34; Rom. 13:13; 1 Cor. 6:9–10; Gal. 5:19–21; Eph. 5:18.

noted,[1] and, the fact that those things which are harmful to the human body are sinful.[2]

The fact that one situation or another might prevail does not negate Bible teaching in regard to drunkenness or harm to the human body.

Situation Ethics

The doctrine of situation ethics is false because it is designed to gain an advantage over all law, which is, of course, foreign to biblical teaching. That God demands respect and adherence to His law is abundantly evidenced in the Bible.[3] In fact, persons can scarcely examine the contents of Psalm 119 without becoming aware of the profound significance of God's law! Although it is true that much of the Old Testament has reference to God's law in regard to the Mosaic economy, the principle of respect and adherence still applies, even today.

Those who sanction the intake of light quantities of ethyl alcohol as a beverage in an isolated situation give credence to the false doctrine of situation ethics, which would have persons to keep law in a subservient position in order that personal desires may be gratified. Such is the case whether it is intended or not. Those who espouse the situational view do not commonly appreciate such terms as "absolute," "always," and "complete" in reference to law. Persons are placed at the center of concern rather than principles. The law of God makes a very clear and indelible distinction between right and wrong! The apostle Paul, in Romans 7, amply illustrates the importance of God's law.

There are two laws in action. One is the law of God, which is regulated by a system of rules, while the other law is that of the flesh. Persons are either under the law of God, or they are under the law of the flesh. Neither law can be rejected without embracing the other. The law of God, with its rules, describes the law of the flesh, with its detrimental consequences. There is no way that persons can keep the spirit of the

---

1. See Chapter 3, pp. 115–130.

2. cf. Rom. 12:1; 1 Cor. 3:16; 6:15–20; 10:31.

3. Gen. 26:1–5; Ex. 13:9; 16:4; Deut. 17:18–20; 27:1ff; 32:46; Neh. 10:29; Job 23:11–12; Ps. 1:1–3; 19:7; 40:8; 78:1; Prov. 3:1–6; Is. 1:10; 8:19–20; Jer. 31:31–34; Mt. 4:4; Rom. 2:12–16; 8:1–4; Jas. 1:25; 2:12; 1 Jn. 3:4.

law of God and at the same time ignore the stringent demands of the law.[1]

Respect for the law of God demands observance of the law! Those, therefore, who have the spirit of the law of God cannot but have the letter of the law. Those who have the letter of the law of God will have the spirit of the law, because the letter of the law demands that persons manifest a respectful spirit toward the law. Regardless of what the situation may be or of how difficult it may be to do right, sin is always wrong! There are absolutely *no* exceptions!

It should be additionally noted that, *if* influence upon others is the only basis upon which the imbibing of light quantities of ethyl alcohol as a beverage can be considered as sinful, and *if* persons who so advocate will not accept the position that the imbibing of light quantities of ethyl alcohol as a beverage is permissible in an isolated setting, *then* they are inconsistent in their view because they do not think there is an additional reason for not imbibing.

It likewise follows that *if* influence upon others is the only basis upon which the imbibing of light quantities of ethyl alcohol as a beverage can be considered as sinful, and *if* persons who so advocate hold the view that drunkenness is sinful and yet condone the imbibing of light quantities of ethyl alcohol as a beverage in an isolated setting, *then* in order to be consistent, they must accept the false position that drunkenness is *not* a matter of degree.

There is absolutely no situation under which the imbibing of even light quantities of ethyl alcohol as a beverage (in an isolated setting or otherwise) can be considered as in harmony with the law of God! Those, therefore, who reverence God and thus respect His law will strive to be obedient in every situation of life.

Relative to this same situational principle, the view has been advanced at various times that since persons in such places as Africa, France, and Germany imbibe in social settings as a custom or as a common practice, and have done so for many years, it is permissible for persons who travel to these or other similar areas to so imbibe.

In the first place, the fact that such a view can be thought of as plausible is virtually beyond the comprehension of this writer! In the

---

1. cf. Jn. 14:15–24.

second place, and this is the important point, it makes *utterly no difference* what custom persons in the above nations (or any other nations, for that matter) practice in regard to the present issue, or even may have been practicing for centuries! In fact, *if every person on earth* engaged in "social" drinking as a custom, and even if *all* persons have been thus engaged *from the beginning of time,* the practice is still sinful, for it violates the law of God! Given this view regarding customs, it would logically follow that persons who may travel to areas where polygamy or cannibalism is practiced could so engage.

Again, the writer repeats a statement that is applicable under *every* conceivable condition—*Those, therefore, who reverence God and thus, respect His law will strive to be obedient in every situation of life.*

4

MISCELLANEOUS AFFIRMATIVE ARGUMENTS

Implicit Authority Argument

There are numerous passages which implicitly condemn the use of ethyl alcohol as a beverage. In fact, the greater part of the Lord's instructions were of this nature. He dealt infrequently with the minor details of duty, and did not attempt to cover every possible need by particular precepts. There were many wicked practices of His own day which He did not explicitly forbid. The New Testament, for instance, contains no explicit condemnation of slavery or gambling. Yet, without doubt, the Lord's spirit, example, and oral teaching served to condemn these and other practices. He did not even attempt to provide *specifically* against evils which might arise for the first time in subsequent generations. Christ did not explicitly forbid the use of distilled liquors[1] as beverages, but He did enunciate laws of personal duty which cover them and every other form of sinful indulgence.

Such laws are universal in their character. No condition of the present and no contingency of the future can exhaust their significance or exceed their application. It is difficult to understand how any unprejudiced mind can come into contact with the teaching of the Christ without recognition of this truth. Principles of human conduct are determined by various laws which include (1) the law of self-denial, (2) the law of the avoidance of temptation, (3) the law of love, and (4) the law of perfection.

---

1. The process of distillation had not even been discovered at the time.

Law of Self-Denial

The law of self-denial is announced in the following terms: "If any man would come after me, let him deny himself, and take up his cross, and follow me."[1] The self to be denied is the carnal nature, whose desires come often into conflict with the spiritual nature. The desire for ethyl alcohol is the desire for that which the human system does not need, and which it cannot receive without detrimental effects. Indulgence in such beverages dims religious perceptions, deadens devotional feelings, and diminishes spiritual powers. The denial which is enjoined in the above passage is absolute.

The verb rendered "deny" is from *arneomai,* indicating "to deny, to refuse, absolutely to say no, decline.[2] The term carries with it the strongest sense of renunciation, and involves in this instance the absolute abandonment of all that is opposed to Christian service.

The law of self-denial is reinforced by the Lord's declaration:

> And if thy right eye causeth thee to stumble, pluck it out, and cast it from thee: for it is profitable for thee that one of thy members should perish, and not thy whole body be cast into hell. And if thy right hand causeth thee to stumble, cut it off, and cast it from thee: for it is profitable for thee that one of thy members should perish, and not thy whole body go into hell.[3]

The phrases "pluck it out" *(exele),* "cast it from thee" *(bale apo sou),* and "cut it off" *(ekkopson)* indicate an instantaneous and utter abandonment of evil. The phrase "causeth thee to stumble" *(skandalizei)* signifies "to put a snare or stumblingblock in the way."[4] It is employed metaphorically in the passage to indicate "the stick in the trap that springs and closes the trap when the animal touches it."[5]

It cannot be successfully refuted that alcoholic beverages come within the scope of this definition. None other is so seducing in its nature or detrimental in its consequences. No doubt, more wretchedness, shame,

---

1. Mt. 16:24; Mk. 8:34; Lk. 9:23.

2. Henry George Liddell and Robert Scott, *A Greek-English Lexicon,* p. 103.

3. Mt. 5:29–30.

4 "Offend," in *An Expository Dictionary,* 3:130.

5. Archibald Thomas Robertson, *Word Pictures in the New Testament,* vol. 1, p. 46.

and sin have been consequent on the use of alcoholic beverages than on all other forms or self-indulgence. Relative to the eye and the hand, to "pluck it out" and to "cut it off" is equivalent to crucifying the flesh[1] and putting to death your members.[2] Persons, therefore, should deny themselves of "what is even the most desiring and alluring, and seems the most necessary, when the sacrifice is demanded"[3] for the good of their souls.

The passage under consideration negates all defenses of activities confessed to be injurious in their effects, but defended on the basis that they are not wrong per se. The eye and the hand are not only in themselves innocent, they are in their correct use very important. To deprive persons of them is both to injure persons and lessen their means of usefulness. The same principle may be applied to ethyl alcohol in its proper place as a chemical agent, and possibly in some instances, as a medicinal remedy. Whatever therefore tempts persons into sinful courses, even though it is not only in itself innocent, but in its right employment important, should be abstained from. The law of self-denial strikes not only at habitual evil, but at it in its very incipiency. Henry Alford views or regards Matthew 5:29 as "an admonition, arising out of the truth announced in the last verse, to withstand the first springs and occasions of evil desire, even by the sacrifice of what is most useful and dear to us."[4]

Alford further states: "Our Lord grounds His precept of the most rigid and decisive self-denial on the considerations of the truest self-interest—*sumtherei soi,* it is profitable for thee."[5]

No stronger enforcement of duty in this respect could be employed. It is often expressed, however, that this constitutes asceticism. It should be observed that there is a radical difference between the principles on which the practices of asceticism and abstinence are founded. Asceticism pretends to promote the development and dignity of the body. Abstinence, however, seeks to secure complete physical health and vitality in order

---

1. Gal. 5:24.

2. Col. 3:5.

3. Samuel Thomas Bloomfield, *Greek New Testament with English Notes,* vol. 1, p. 25.

4. Henry Alford, *The Greek Testament,* vol. 1, p. 48.

5. Ibid., p. 49.

that one may grow in holiness and power. The ascetic rejects alcoholic beverages because they are a luxury and a comfort, while the abstainer refuses them because they are a poison to his body and a curse to his soul.

Law of the Avoidance of Temptation

The law of the avoidance of temptation is expressed as follows: "Watch and pray, that ye enter not into temptation."[1] In connection with teaching His disciples how to pray the Lord stated, "And bring us not into temptation, but deliver us from the evil one."[2]

Plumptre indicates that the Greek term *peirasmon,* rendered "temptation," includes, "the two thoughts which are represented in English by 'trials,' i.e., sufferings which test or try and 'temptations,' allurements on the side of pleasure which tend to lead us into evil."[3]

The term is here used in reference not only to the act of tempting or of being tempted but to any situation in which, because of our own weakness and Satan's cunning, we should succumb to sin.

In this sense it is applicable to intoxicating beverages. It is their peculiarity that they act as a dangerous enticement to those who imbibe for the first time, and the danger increases with every subsequent indulgence. An unnatural and insatiable craving is created. As this craving is gratified the more imperious become its demands, until in time it will eliminate every restraint and completely captivate those who indulge. Such is the natural history of alcoholic beverages. It is one of the physiological actions of alcohol that its very presence in the human body maintains the desire for it and overcomes the will. At the entrance to the path of alcoholic indulgence, therefore, is the law of the Lord. He forbids persons to cross the threshold of temptation. His word of warning is "Watch and pray, that ye enter not into temptation."[4]

---

1. Mt. 26:41; Mk. 14:38; Lk. 22:40, 46.
2. Mt. 6:13; Lk. 11:4.
3. E. H. Plumptre, *St. Matthew, St. Mark, and St. Luke,* A Bible Commentary for English Readers, ed. Charles John Ellicott (New York: Cassell and Co., n.d.), p. 36.
4. Mt. 26:41.

The only safety for any person, and the single duty for all persons, is abstinence! It is the only possible application of the law of the avoidance of temptation, so far as alcoholic beverages are concerned.

The two principles considered to this point concern our personal duties, those which we owe to ourselves. There is another covering our relative duties, those which we owe to others. It is the law of love.

Law of Love

The law of love may be stated as follows: "Thou shalt love thy neighbor as thy self."[1] The frequent enunciation of this law, both by the Lord and by His apostles, indicates its significance. Paul explicitly declared the importance of this law when he stated, "Love worketh no ill to his neighbor."[2]

The objects of this law are inclusive of the human race. It embraces all persons. It requires persons to be as regardful of their neighbor's interests as of what belongs to themselves. If persons are to deny their own sinful desires, they are to be equally careful not to excite or minister to such desires in others. If persons are to be careful that they do not enter into temptation, they are to be of the same concern not to lead others into it. No doubt this law is in no way more often or more flagrantly violated then by setting bad examples before others! Likewise, no example is more pernicious than that of persons who imbibe alcoholic beverages, even in what is commonly referred to as "moderation." On every hand persons have the weak and the tempted as their neighbors, and if it were possible[3] that they do not need to abstain on their own account, the obligation of abstinence for the sakes of others is still imperative. Paul plainly indicates that the law of love covers this principle by stating: "Now we that are strong ought to bear the infirmities of the weak, and not to please ourselves."[4]

W. E. Vine states that "infirmities" *(asthenemata)* are "those scruples which arise through weakness of faith. The strong must support the

---

1. Mt. 19:19; 22:39; Mk. 12:31; Lk. 10:27; Rom. 13:9; Gal. 5:14; Jas. 2:8.
2. Rom. 13:10.
3. It is not! WDJ
4. Rom. 15:1. See also Rom. 14:21.

infirmities of the weak *(adunatos)* by submitting to self-restraint."[1] Likely no stronger or more comprehensive announcement of this principle can be made than that of Paul in this text.

There have, however, been protests lodged against indiscriminate application of the passage to the duty of abstinence, as may be seen from the following objection. "The abstinence so repeatedly and forcibly inculcated is always for the sake of those who are ethically weak— weak in the possession of an overscrupulous conscience."[2]

It is perhaps true that such is the immediate application of the principle. On the other hand, however, it cannot be confined to such a narrow range. It is ample enough to include within its scope every case and circumstance where the main point is involved—the temptations and sins of others. The principle applies to those who are volitionally weak, whose consciences are not "overscrupulous," but properly sensitive on this matter, and yet whose general moral power is weakened by indulgence.

In reference to the term "weak" *(asthenei),* Meyer observes that it denotes one who is "morally, powerless to withstand temptation and to follow his moral conviction."[3] Those who are of such a persuasion who proceed to violate their moral convictions, sin in so doing. Others are under an obligation to abstain for the sakes of such persons. The principle is broad in scope to the extent that it covers all cases where the soul's highest interests are at stake.

It has been alleged that "in an appeal to that portion of Paul's precepts which inculcate benevolent abstinence, the precepts declarative of Christian liberty are ignored."[4]

In answer to this charge it may be said that in the use of alcoholic beverages Christian liberty is not involved. Christian liberty is brought to bear only within the sphere of things innocent or indifferent in themselves. Outside that limit it has no range. It has already been established beyond a doubt that alcoholic beverages do not belong to the category of things innocent or indifferent. To attempt the application of the principle

---

1. "Infirmity," in *An Expository Dictionary of New Testament Words,* 2:257.

2. Horace Bumstead, p. 97.

3. Heinrich August Wilhelm Meyer, *The Epistle to the Romans,* Meyer's Commentary on the New Testament (New York: Funk and Wagnalls, Publishers, 1884), p. 520.

4. Horace Bumstead, p. 115.

of Christian liberty to them is to make a gross mistake. This very mistake is corrected by Paul when he writes to the church at Corinth. Because he had maintained the right of individual liberty in regard to eating things offered to idols, Paul had been quoted as an authority for liberty regarding fornication.[1] Therefore, in 1 Corinthians he proceeds to show that this principle of Christian liberty "does not refer to matters which are absolutely wrong, and that even in its application to indifferent masters it must be limited, and guarded by other Christian principles."[2]

Thus even if it were to be agreed to admit the use of alcohol as a beverage to be an intrinsically innocent procedure, the difficulty would remain. Christian liberty is conditioned by the stipulation that it is not to be used "for an occasion to the flesh" and, by the general law, "through love be servants one to another."[3] Its sphere is bounded not simply by the limits of things lawful[4] for one's self, but by the more limited lines of things expedient for others.[5] Persons do not have scriptural right to go outside of this boundary. Persons may not *lawfully* do what is *inexpedient* to be done! An act, however innocent in itself, if it be injurious in its influence upon others, is thereby rendered not merely inexpedient, but, by very reason of its inexpediency, unlawful. Personal liberty ceases to be liberty when it becomes an occasion of temptation to others. To attempt its exercise under such circumstances is to turn it into license, and as has been preciously observed, Christian liberty does not give persons license to do as they please but only the freedom to do as God pleases! Upon those thus guilty, the Lord pronounces the condemnation, "Woe unto the world because of occasions of stumbling! for it must needs be that the occasions come; but woe to that man through whom the occasion cometh!"[6]

---

1. Heinrich August Wilhelm Meyer, *The Epistles to the Corinthians,* pp. 137–38.

2. T. Teignmouth Shore, *The First Epistle to the Corinthians,* A Bible Commentary for English Readers, ed. Charles John Ellicott (New York: Cassell Co., n.d.), p. 304

3. Gal. 5:13.

4. "Lawful" in 1 Corinthians 6:12 is from *exesti,* which literally signifies "it being permitted." "Lawful," in *An Expository Dictionary,* 2:316.

5. "Expedient," in 1 Corinthians 6:12, is from *sumphero,* which means "it is profitable." Ibid., 2:62.

6. Mt. 18:7; Lk. 17:1. For an additional discussion of the concept of Christian expediency, see pp. 131-33.

If there is any other principle applicable to the consumption of ethyl alcohol as a beverage, it may be summed up in the law of perfection.

Law of Perfection

Jesus announced His law of perfection in the following terms: "Ye therefore shall be perfect, as your heavenly Father is perfect."[1]

"Ye therefore shall be perfect," is grammatically in the future tense but the force is that of an imperative. The term "perfect" must not be taken in the sense of either possessing all the perfections of God or of attaining sinless perfection, for to claim the former is blasphemy and to claim the latter is to make God a liar.[2] In the context the Lord is emphasizing that children of God should not imitate the publicans and Gentiles, but the heavenly Father. The same principle, of course, applies to persons today, including those who would imbibe alcoholic beverages.

"Perfect," from *teleios,* is expressive of "being whole," which manifests itself in concrete behavior. In the text, "whole" applies to conduct in relation to men.[3] "Wholeness" is the Old Testament background to the term, with 1 Kings 11:4 providing a most notable example. In advanced years, Solomon's heart was not "perfect" with God as was the heart of his father David. David, however, who was not sinless, had a heart which was given in holiness or without reservation to God, although through weakness on occasion he committed sin. Sinlessness is not attainable on earth, but those who would honor God must determine to constantly follow after it.[4]

Those who defend the intake of alcoholic beverages, even in privacy, under the guise that it is not wrong because they are not influencing other persons to so do, are not following after this noble goal! The deportment of Christians must rise above worldly standards, or the true meaning of Christianity will not be revealed to the world.

---

1. Mt. 5:48.

2. 1 Jn. 1:8, 10.

3. Gerhard Delling, "Teleios," in *Theological Dictionary of the New Testament*, ed. Gerhard Friedrich (Grand Rapids: Wm. B. Eerdmans Publishing Co., 1972), 8:74.

4. cf. Phil. 3:12–14.

Cremer indicates that *teleios* is used in a moral sense of being "perfect, complete, blameless."[1] Applied to persons, of course, the term has reference to completeness of parts or a situation where no part is defective or lacking. The Old Testament character, Job, is said to be "perfect."[2] This does not mean that he is as holy as God, or sinless, for fault is found with him,[3] but rather that his piety was proportionate. His piety had a completeness of parts, and was thus consistent and regular.

In regard to Matthew 5:48, Lenski states that the term *as* indicates that persons are to make God their "model in all His perfections and follow Him in spirit and in truth; not, however, that complete equality is demanded. For God's attributes are infinite while our virtues are finite and, compared with God's, a mere shadow."[4]

Those who are opposed to "social" drinking *solely* on the basis of its influence upon others should consider what it means for God to be our *personal* model! Persons who have embraced biblical principles and who have built them into their character will sin on occasion or commit isolated acts of sin, but as time passes will continue to develop in godliness because they have become "partakers of the divine nature, having escaped from the corruption that is in the world by lust."[5] Without successful refutation, it follows that those who would sanction the imbibing of alcohol as a *beverage* to *any* degree or under *any* circumstance, in *private isolation* or *otherwise,* are most certainly *not* partakers of the divine nature of Almighty God!

Paradoxical Argument

Wine is referred to in the Bible in unmistakable language. As has been previously noted, in one class of passages it is considered as a blessing and in another as a curse; it is approved and condemned; it is allowed and interdicted; it is exhibited as possessing seemingly opposite influences, as productive of good and bad effects; it symbolizes consolation

---

1. Hermann Cremer, *Biblio-Theological Lexicon of New Testament Greek* (Edinburgh: T. and T. Clark, 1872), p. 568.

2. Job 1:1.

3. Job 9:20; 42:6.

4. Richard C. H. Lenski, *The Interpretation of St. Matthew's Gospel,* p. 252.

5. 2 Pet. 1:4.

and vengeance, and joy and woe. The natural inference is therefore that two different articles are designated by such diverse characterizations. Attempts are often made, however, to meet this argument by citing other things which, it is claimed, are mentioned in similar fashion.[1]

Claims

Rain is referred to as a blessing given to both the just and unjust, and as a curse sent to destroy persons during the flood of Noah's day. The tongue, which is spoken of as "a world of iniquity," is also indicated as an "unspeakable benefit." Knowledge is referred to as that which "puffeth up" as well as that which is "excellent." The Bible both approves and disapproves of marriage. God is spoken of as "love" and as "a consuming fire." Christ is mentioned as both a "Savior" and a "stone of stumbling," and leaven, which is likened to the kingdom of heaven, is also referred to as the symbol of Pharisaic doctrine.

Those who would challenge the argument which indicates that there are two types of wine referred to in the Bible, often ask if it is to be inferred in these cases that there are two kinds of rain, tongues, and knowledge, or whether the distinction is in the uses of the various objects. Relative to the rain, tongue, and leaven, it is evident that they are used figuratively, and that in no instance is the object itself intended to be described as intrinsically good or bad. For example, it is not denied that the best gifts may be abused, and that even as worthwhile as knowledge is, it may become a means of pride. On the other hand, however, an isolated instance of warning against the abuse of a good thing affords no logical parallel to the numerous biblical warnings against the use of intoxicating wine. The same principle is true with marriage, which is commended in the Bible, except in certain circumstances where it is considered as inexpedient. The references to God and Christ, in their twofold attitudes toward sin and the persistent sinner on the one hand, and toward the penitent person on the other, are in no way pertinent to this particular case.

The Bible teaches that there are two kinds of wine, which are totally distinct in their characteristics and compositions. The two types of

---

1. Horace Bumstead, p. 65; Dunlop Moore, p. 83.

passages, the commendatory and the condemnatory, cannot be indiscriminately applied to the two kinds of wine. Unfermented wine would not be prohibited since it is completely natural and healthful as a beverage and, therefore, would not be made the symbol of wrath and destruction. On the contrary, fermented wine could not properly be commended for employment as the symbol of blessing and life. It has been previously shown that ethyl alcohol in any form or quantity is foreign and harmful to the human body. In addition to various scientific pronouncements, it is also pronounced a poison in the Bible, as is signified by the Hebrew term, *chemah*.[1]

God does not condemn and approve the same object. Such action on His part would but reflect a state of utter inconsistency, and to claim that God is inconsistent is a reflection on His integrity. It is therefore logical to conclude that when wine is approved, unfermented wine is meant, and when wine is disapproved, fermented wine is meant. The position or view that all first-century wines were alcoholic in content because such is the case with modern wines is unwarranted by the evidence. The evidence, in fact, conclusively points to the contrary!

Book of Revelation

In the final book of the New Testament, Revelation, several references to *oinos* may be observed. In two instances, *oinos* is employed symbolically in the expression "wine of the wrath of her fornication,"[2] which signifies a love-potion, with which a harlot seduces to fornication (idolatry), and then brings upon them the wrath of God. In one instance, *oinos* is used symbolically in the expression "wine of her fornication,"[3] which means the same. Any thinking person can see the contempt which Christ puts upon the intoxicating liquid by using it in such a figure as this! The Lord's abhorrence of it in the phrases (1) "Fallen, fallen is Babylon the great, that hath made all the nations to drink of the wine of the wrath of her fornication,"[4] (2) "they that dwell in the earth were

---

1. Deut. 32:33; Jer. 25:15; Hos. 7:5; Hab. 2:15.

2. Rev. 14:8; 18:3.

3. Rev. 17:2.

4. Rev. 14:8.

made drunken with the wine of her fornication,"[1] and (3) "for by the wine of the wrath of her fornication all the nations are fallen,"[2] is exceeded only by His use of it as a symbol of His own wrath, in the threatening, "If any man worshippeth the beast and his image, and receiveth a mark on his forehead, or upon his hand, he also shall drink of the wine of the wrath of God, which is prepared unmixed in the cup of his anger."[3]

The phrase "without mixture" *(kekerasmenou akratou),* the King James Version rendering, or "unmixed," the American Standard Version rendering, is indicative of fiery, potent, undiluted wine, emphasizing by all the power of language, the terrors of God's cup of wrath!

In light of the foregoing studies the writer is compelled to affirm that the Bible prohibits the use of ethyl alcohol as a beverage. Considering the informal manner in which the subject is discussed in the word of God, in the use of several terms of different etymological significance; by commendation here, prohibition there; in narrative, in prophecy, in illustration, and in symbol; here enforcing a promise, and there a threatening, it is difficult to see how the judgment of God through inspired men could have been more forcibly or more decisively expressed!

General Arguments

Comparison of Alcoholic Beverages

There is a great distinction to be made between the intoxicating beverages of the first and twentieth centuries.

It is important to remember that the culture of the first century was basically that of a quite simple agrarian society in which wine was a noncommercial product. The wines of that period, which were primarily for ceremonial, dietary, and medicinal purposes were far less potent than the intoxicants of the present time. Although many of them were intoxicating, a much larger quantity was required to equal the level of modern distilled and heavily fortified intoxicants.

Several interesting comparisons may be drawn between the use of wine in the first century and the employment of alcoholic beverages in the twentieth century. (1) In the first-century period, wine had a place

---

1. Rev. 17:2.

2. Rev. 18:3.

3. Rev. 14:9–10.

as a food and drink because water and milk were often unsafe to drink. In the twentieth century, sanitation methods and refrigeration serve to make unnecessary any reliance on intoxicating beverages. (2) In the first century fermented wine had an alcoholic content of but 4 to 15 percent. In the twentieth century, intoxicating beverages have an alcoholic content as high as 54 percent. (3) In the first century intoxication was the chief ill-effect from consumption, and it did not occur to a great degree unless approximately one quart of wine was consumed without food. In the twentieth century, small amounts of alcohol are dangerous, for example, in reducing self-control and driving skills. (4) In the first century the production of wine was a normal and limited part of an agricultural economy, with each family producing their own supply. In the twentieth century, the manufacture of alcoholic beverages is an extremely organized business operation, which seeks as much profit as possible from sales schemes. (5) In the first century, imbibing, which was a family practice set within the normal restraints of family guidelines, was engaged in as a friendly and leisurely activity. In the twentieth century, although consumption may be in a family setting, to a large degree it occurs in taverns and at parties where family and other restraining guidelines do not operate. (6) In the first century pressurized advertising demands to purchase various drinks were not practiced. In the twentieth century, advertising seeks to create a demand for the use of alcoholic beverages. (7) In the first century imbibing in such a simple, slowly moving agricultural environment was harmful chiefly to the consumer and those immediately dependent upon him. In this century drunkenness, even to a small degree, in the midst of a highly industrialized and mechanized society, has been recognized as having serious consequences for all persons.[1]

Lyman Abbot, who was not an advocate of abstinence, described the wines of Palestine as follows:

> First, there was fermented wine. It contained, what is the only objectionable element in modern wines, a percentage of alcohol. *It was the least common,* and the percentage of alcohol was small. Second were the new wines. These, like our new cider, were *wholly without alcohol,* and were not intoxicating. They were easily

---

1. Douglas Jackson, p. 70.

preserved in this condition for several months. Third were wines in which, by boiling or by drugs, the process of fermentation was prevented and alcohol excluded. These answering somewhat in composition and character to our raspberry shrub, were mixed with water and constituted *the most common drink of the land.*[1]

From the foregoing statements it can be clearly seen that there are considerable differences in the various wines and customs of antiquity and those of the present time. The term "wine" is employed today to denote beverages which always contain a considerable portion of alcohol, not only that produced by fermentation, but alcohol which is added to increase its potency. Persons have absolutely no right to take the present use of the term in interpreting the Bible. They should constantly strive to adapt their thinking to the exact circumstances of those times, ascertain what idea the term conveyed to those who used it then, and apply that sense to the term today. The significance of this principle may be seen in the following statement by John Stuart Mill, a nineteenth century logician.

> A generic term is always liable to become limited to a single species if people have occasion to think and speak of that species oftener than of anything else contained in the genus. The tide of custom first drifts the word on the shore of a particular meaning, then retires and leaves it there.[2]

Although the intoxicating effect of wine in antiquity could be increased by the addition of various drugs and spices,[3] modern methods of distillation, which were unknown in the ancient world, can increase the alcohol content far beyond that which could be achieved by mere fermentation.[4] For example, when fermented wine is made stronger in the process of distillation, it is heated, after which the alcohol content will turn to vapor in larger proportions than the water content, it is in

---

1. Lyman Abbot, *A Life of Christ,* 2nd ed. (New York: Harper and Brothers, 1882), p. 109. Emphasis mine, WDJ.

2. William Patton, pp. 63–64, quoting John Stuart Mill, *System of Logic.*

3. J. F. Ross, "Wine," in *Interpreter's Dictionary of the Bible,* ed. George Arthur Buttrick (New York: Abingdon Press, 1962), 4:850.

4. R. J. Forbes, *Studies in Ancient Technology,* vol. 3 (Leiden: E. J. Brill, 1955), pp. 60–70.

such fashion that water-wine vapor, which is condensed again to a liquid, produces an even stronger wine.

The art of distillation was known to the East long before it was introduced into the West. It was introduced to Italy and from there to France and Spain. Despite the Arabic origin of the term, and the fact that the Arabian physician Rhazes is credited with the discovery of distillation in the tenth century,[1] the separation of alcohol from wine was not likely known to Arabian alchemists then. Marcellin Berthelot and Edmund O. Von Lippmann state,

> The earliest known use of distillation as a means of producing alcohol is recorded in a twelfth century Latin manuscript, *Mappae Clivicula,* and it is safe to assume that alcohol was first produced by distillation in the wine districts of Italy about A.D. 1200.[2]

Albertus Magnus of Cologne[3] has left a clear description of the process for distilling and converting wine to brandy, and it has been said that "distilled whiskeys were first introduced to Europe about A.D. 1500"[4] It is known that "the distillation of alcoholic beverages from fermented liquors, became general throughout the whole of Europe during the sixteenth and seventeenth centuries . . ."[5] At that time it was a very expensive process, and it was not until the Industrial Revolution of the nineteenth and early twentieth centuries that it became an industry. Through the process of distillation beverages were introduced which contained as much as 50 percent ethyl alcohol, which has increased somewhat in modern times.

The term "proof" is descriptive of the strength of various distilled alcoholic beverages. It is derived from an old English test for the strength of whiskey. Gunpowder, which would explode after having been saturated with whiskey, gave proof that the whiskey contained the proper concentration of alcohol. Proof figures given in the United States today are

---

1. Raymond Gerald McCarthy, *Drinking and Intoxication,* p. 43.

2. Wayne E. Oates, *Alcohol In and Out of the Church* (Nashville: Broadman Press, 1966), p. 3.

3. A.D. 1193–1280.

4. John S. Sinacore, *Health, a Quality of Life,* p. 320.

5. *Encyclopaedia Britannica,* 1959 ed., s.v. "Whiskey," by Francis G. H. Tate, p. 569.

double the percentage of alcoholic content. Therefore, 100 proof indicates that the beverage contains 50 percent alcohol. In England 100 proof spirit contains 57.1 percent by volume of alcohol.

In reference to alcoholic beverages of antiquity, a special government report indicates that until about the sixteenth century intoxicating beverages were derived from fermentation and consisted of wines and beers containing at most about 14 percent alcohol.[1] Of such beverages Samuel W. Small states,

> The intoxicants of antiquity were mild, being principally composed of the pure unfermented juice of the grape, with none of the deleterious matters subsequently added. There is abundant reason to believe, also, that the unfermented juice of the grape was largely employed as a beverage.[2]

It can therefore be seen that intoxicants of antiquity were devoid of many of the harmful additives of the present day.

The Tabernacle

The principle is stated in the Old Testament[3] that priests who served under the Levitical priesthood were commanded to abstain from imbibing alcoholic beverages while serving in the tabernacle, as a perpetual requirement. Flavius Josephus mentions this same requirement.[4] The reason assigned for their abstinence was "that ye may make a distinction between the holy and the common, and between the unclean and the clean; and that ye may teach the children of Israel all the statues which Jehovah hath spoken to them by Moses." Such beverages would have dulled their judgment so that, likely, the priests would have done things not commanded.[5]

---

1. *First Special Report,* p. 6.
2. Samuel W. Small, *The White Angel of the World* (Philadelphia: Peerless Publishing Co., n.d.), p. 143.
3. Lev. 10:8–11.
4. *Flavius Josephus Antiquities* 3. 12; *Against Apion* 1. 22.
5. cf. Ezek. 22:26.

The tabernacle of the Old Testament is a type of the church of the New Testament.[1] If God would not allow Levitical priests to imbibe alcoholic beverages while serving, modern advocates of "social" drinking should not think God will allow members of the Christian priesthood[2] to serve under such conditions. There is one difference, however, the priests of ancient Israel were not on continual duty in the tabernacle, but members of the Christian priesthood are on continual duty in the church! Peter instructed Christians to "abstain from fleshly lusts which war against the soul."[3] Since it cannot be successfully refuted that ethyl alcohol involves a fleshly lust, and that it wars against the soul, Christians should abstain from imbibing.

Proverbs 23:31–32 and Habakkuk 2:15

In the Old Testament the very look of approval upon strong drink is prohibited.[4] The Bible therefore cannot be employed to license "social" drinking. Often the objection is raised that passages from the Old Testament applied only in Old Testament times. In the light of Romans 15:4, however, it can be said that the *principles* in the Old Testament constitute things which were written for the learning of persons today, and are thus applicable.

The prophet Habakkuk pronounces woe upon a person who does three things: (1) He "giveth his neighbor drink," (2) he "puttest thy bottle to him," and (3) he "makest him drunken also."[5] That "social" drinking involves each of these, in the writer's view, cannot be successfully refuted.

Injunctions to Sobriety

Injunctions to sobriety occur frequently in the epistles of Peter and Paul. Each writer employs two different terms to express this quality, both of which are rendered "sober." They are not synonymous, but in strict usage denote (1) mental sobriety and (2) physical sobriety or absti-

---

1. Heb. 8:5; 9:13–24; 10:1.
2. 1 Pet. 2:9.
3. 1 Pet. 2:11.
4. Prov. 23:31–32.
5. Hab. 2:15 (KJV).

nence. The terms however are very closely correlated in their meanings, which are often merged or interchanged. This is explained by the fact that each term regards the same virtue, but from two different standpoints.

Physical abstinence is the condition of the clearest mental sobriety, and mental sobriety is the characteristic of the strictest physical abstinence. The term therefore signifying mental sobriety is employed metaphorically for physical abstinence, and vice versa. For illustrative purposes and in order to give more clarity, each term shall be considered separately.

Mental Sobriety

Mental sobriety is noted by *sophron,* rendered "sober-minded;"[1] *sophrosune,* rendered "soberness" and "sobriety;"[2] *sophroneo,* rendered "in his right mind,"[3] "to think soberly,"[4] "of sober mind,"[5] "of sound mind,"[6] and "sober-minded;"[7] *sophronizo,* rendered "train;"[8] and *sophronos,* rendered "soberly."[9]

An examination of each of these terms will reveal that they convey the idea of being "in one's right mind," or "of sound mind, sane in one's judgment," or, in addition, "curbing one's desires and impulses, self-controlled, temperate."[10]

In a discussion of the important distinction between shamefacedness and sobriety, Richard Chenevix Trench states of sobriety *(sophrosune)* that it is that "habitual inner self-government, with its constant rein on all the passions and desires, which would hinder the temptation to this from arising."[11]

---

1. 1 Tim. 3:2; Tit. 1:8; 2:2, 5.
2. Acts 26:25; 1 Tim. 2:9, 15.
3. Mk. 5:15; Lk. 8:35.
4. Rom. 12:3.
5. 2 Cor. 5:18.
6. 1 Pet. 4:7.
7. Tit. 2:6.
8. Tit. 2:4.
9. Tit. 2:12.
10. Joseph Henry Thayer, *Greek-English Lexicon of the New Testament,* pp. 612–13.
11. Richard Chenevix Trench, *Synonyms of the New Testament* (Grand Rapids: Associated Publishers and Authors, Inc., n.d.), p. 68. In regard to the term "this," in the quote, Trench has reference to giving in to passions and desires, WDJ.

While always retaining the strong idea of mental soundness, this term never departs from the thought or idea of bodily abstinence or self-restraint in which the mental quality has its physical basis. In various passages[1] there can be no doubt that sober-mindedness is enjoined with explicit reference to the physical abstinence on which its existence and exercise are conditioned. This is evidenced, if in no other way, by the close connection in which it stands with such phrases and terms as "not given to wine"[2] *(me paroinon)* and "temperate" *(enkrate* and *nephaleon).*

Physical Sobriety

Physical sobriety is denoted by *nephaleon,* rendered "temperate."[3] The verbal form, *nepho,* occurs several times, and is rendered "be sober."[4] W. E. Vine indicates that *nepho* signifies "to be free from the influence of intoxicants."[5] James Strong defines the term, "to abstain from wine (keep sober), i.e. (fig.) be discreet—be sober, watch."[6] Liddell and Scott define *nephalios,* an early form of *nephaleon,* as "sober: and of drink, without wine, wineless."[7] Edward Robinson refers to the term as meaning, "sober, temperate, especially in respect to wine."[8]

When Paul states, "let us watch and be sober" *(gregoromen kai nephomen),*[9] and Peter says, "Be sober, be watchful" *(nepsate, gregoresate),*[10] there can be no doubt that abstinence is involved. In each instance *gregoreo* denotes the mental state and *nepho* its physical condition. Both terms represent abstinence as the price of vigilance.

---

1. 1 Tim. 3:2; Tit. 1:8; 2:2; 1 Pet. 4:7.

2. KJV.

3. 1 Tim. 3:2, 11; Tit. 2:2.

4. 1 Thess. 5:6, 8; 2 Tim. 4:5; 1 Pet. 1:13; 4:7; 5:8.

5. "Sober," in *An Expository Dictionary,* 4:44. See also G. Abbott-Smith, *A Manual Greek Lexicon of the New Testament,* pp. 302–303; John Parkhurst, *A Greek and English Lexicon of the New Testament* (London: William Baynes and Son, 1826), p. 376; Ethelbert W. Bullinger, *A Critical Lexicon and Concordance to the English and Greek New Testament,* p. 713.

6. James Strong, *Dictionary of the Greek Testament* (n.p., nd.), p. 50.

7. Henry George Liddell and Robert Scott, *A Greek-English Lexicon,* p. 977.

8. Edward Robinson, *A Greek and English Lexicon of the New Testament,* p. 480.

9. 1 Thess. 5:6.

10. 1 Pet. 5:8.

In regard to 1 Peter 5:8 the scholarly Adam Clarke states,

> There is a beauty in this verse, and a striking apposition between the first and last word, which I think have not been noticed: Be sober *(nepsate)* from *(ne),* not, and *(piein),* to drink; do not drink, do not swallow down: and the word *(katapin),* from *(kata),* down, and *(piein),* to drink. If you swallow strong drink down, the devil will swallow you down.[1]

Social Acceptance and Anxiety

As has already been discussed to some degree, social acceptance is a major motive underlying the consumption practices of many persons in the United States. Persons imbibe to achieve social status or to retain status. Also different social classes have different consumption patterns, and many persons adopt patterns associated with the class to which they wish to belong.[2] On this point Raymond McCarthy stated, "Most drinking in the United States no doubt is brought on by the stimulus of the social setting, rather than a desire for the pleasurable effects or the consequences."[3] On the other hand, David Horton points to the need to reduce anxiety as an important motivation to imbibe alcohol.[4]

Although no reason adequately explains the use of alcoholic beverages, the demand for excitement, the modern need for relaxation, the desire for sociability, and the desire for escape, all are involved in the reasons persons drink.[5]

So far as is known, man is the only creature with a marked capacity for anxiety. Many persons seek relief from mental strain and physical fatigue, which is caused by worry, through the use of alcoholic beverages. Dr. Ernest H. Starling stated that "under the influence of alcohol past

---

1. Adam Clarke, *Romans to Revelation,* A Commentary and Critical Notes, vol. 6, p. 869.

2. Vance Packard, *The Status Seekers* (New York: David McKay Co., 1959), pp. 143–46.

3. Raymond Gerald McCarthy, ed., *Drinking and Intoxication,* p. 232ff.

4. David Horton, "Alcohol, Science, and Society," *Quarterly Journal of Studies on Alcohol* 15 (1954):158.

5. Albion Roy King, p. 35.

troubles cease to repeat themselves and to reverberate in the drinker's mind."[1]

Those who trust in God are enabled to exercise and experience self-control which otherwise would be most difficult. This is the case because such persons are willing to rely upon the wisdom of God and therefore comply with His will.[2] Inward peace is the result of peace with God.[3] Anxiety is a symptom of which little faith is the cause.[4] In an attempt to mix wickedness with righteousness, persons have experienced insecurity, discontent, and restlessness. Such will continue as long as persons are filled with greed, hate, and malice. The principles of Christianity form the only basis for future hope. Multiple difficulties could be resolved, and the peace of mind which persons so earnestly desire could be a reality, if they would apply the law of God to the daily exercises of life. Persons should exercise whatever degree of restraint may be necessary in order that their manner of life may be worthy of the gospel of Christ.[5] Those who face problems squarely will eventually be victorious. Those who do not, will be given to apprehension, which cultivates worry. Worry, in turn, leads to tension and anxiety, which renders persons less capable to cope with the problems and trials of life. Ethyl alcohol does not provide the answer, but only multiplies the problem.

Emotional strain over a prolonged period of time, caused by anxiety, brings depression. Anxiety can be avoided by a proper relation with God.[6] The root of this most serious problem is sin, which produces the greatest disappointments, blights the finest hopes, and dims the happiest outlooks. Sin begins innocently, but soon enslaves. Persons who imbibe alcoholic beverages for the first time to experience the feeling, or for any reason, do not mean to become addicted, but over a period of time the habit often becomes so strong that they become its slave.[7]

---

1. Ernest Henry Starling, *The Action of Alcohol on Man* (London: Longmans, Green and Co., n.d.), p. 76.

2. cf. 2 Tim. 1:12.

3. Prov. 3:5–6; Is. 26:3.

4. cf. Mt. 6:33–34; Phil. 4:19.

5. Phil. 1:27.

6. Phil. 4:6.

7. cf. Rom. 6:16–18; 2 Pet. 2:19.

Concluding Observations

Magnitude of the Problem

Dedicated Christians are genuinely concerned with the alcohol problem, for it now is an issue of tremendous magnitude. Dr. Jerome H. Jaffe, Associate Professor of Psychiatry, University of Chicago, Pritzker School of Medicine, stated, "In Western society, alcohol has the unique distinction of being the only potent pharmacological agent with which self-induced intoxication is socially acceptable."

Dr. Jaffe further stated,

> The large role that the production and consumption of alcoholic beverages plays in the economic and social life of Western society should not permit us to minimize the fact that alcoholism is a more significant problem than all other forms of drug abuse combined.[1]

Ethyl alcohol constitutes the fourth major health problem in the United States. Approximately 7 percent of all persons who begin to imbibe become alcoholics. A 1977 report from the President's Commission on Mental Health indicates that an estimated ten million persons have a significant and recent alcohol related problem and that another ten million have experienced some type of alcohol related problem in the past.[2]

No one can doubt the serious medical, social, and economic consequences of alcoholism. The cost to the United States has been estimated

---

1. Jerome H. Jaffe,"Drug Addiction and Drug Abuse" in *The Pharmacological Basis of Therapeutics,* eds. Louis S. Goodman and Alfred Gilman (London: Collier-Macmillan, Limited, 1970), p. 291.

2. Sandra C. Malanga, *The Illness Called Alcoholism* (Monroe, Wisconsin: American Medical Association, 1973), p. 2

to be twenty-five billion dollars a year because of absenteeism, health and welfare services, and property damage and medical expenses.[1]

According to Bill Belvin, Jr. of the South Carolina Commission on Alcohol and Drug Abuse, some nursing homes, particularly understaffed ones that desire to keep patients sedated, often turn their backs on families wishing to keep their aged relatives supplied with ethyl alcohol.[2] Thus the self-destructive element of such beverages is overlooked by those who prefer to think that imbibing is one of the few pleasures left to aged persons and they should be allowed to obtain pleasure in what few alternatives remain.

In light of the complexities of modern society, with its subsequent anxieties, the breakdown of negative sanctions against "social" drinking, and the increasing availability and cultural attractiveness of ethyl alcohol as a means of problem-solving, dedicated Christians have more reasons than ever before to oppose "social" drinking.

Crime

No nation in the midst of crime, irreverence, and moral dissipation can remain strong and long endure such attacks upon its basic structure. The imbibing of alcoholic beverages is one of the greatest contributing factors to the moral contamination of modern society. Anything which contributes to such contamination should be eliminated, not promoted. In some sections of the United States organized crime is a major business. It costs the American public more than all education and welfare programs combined, and is increasing with such rapidity that in many areas there is open division and anarchy.

Beverage alcohol has a part in crime. In virtually every city in the nation it is a dangerous practice to be on the sidewalks after dark. Dr. Richard H. Blum states that the role between alcohol and murder is in keeping with the most probable effects of alcohol as a depressant of inhibition control centers in the brain, leading to release of impulses.[3] Several years ago Dr. M. E. Wolfgang reported that among 588 murders in Philadelphia,

---

1. Ibid., p. 3.
2. "Alcoholism: Another Problem for Aging Americans," *Nashville, The Tennessean,* 9 November 1980, p. 6A.
3. Richard H. Blum, Appendix B, *Task Force Report: Drunkenness,* p. 41.

alcohol was *absent* from both killer and victim in only 36 percent of the cases. In 9 percent of the cases, alcohol was found only in the corpse of the victim; in 11 percent it was found only in the blood-stream of the killer, and in 44 percent of the cases, both killer and victim had been drinking.[1]

Law enforcement agencies do not have adequate funds or the personnel to arrest even a fraction of the criminal element. Many persons in positions of responsibility are busy pretending that the devastating events of today are not happening. Multitudes are desperately attempting to escape the realities of the pressures of modern society through the consumption of alcoholic beverages.

A National Problem

Alcohol-related problems, which cost the United States nearly forty-three billion dollars in 1975,[2] are increasing on an annual basis, and it has been said that alcohol addiction is second only to nicotine addiction in incidence and prevalence in the United States today.[3] Furthermore, in at least nine states, alcoholic disorders lead all other diagnoses in mental hospital admissions.[4]

In the fifteen years following World War II, 1945 through 1960, consumption of beverage alcohol in the United States was fairly stable at slightly more than two gallons of absolute alcohol per person in the drinking-age population.[5] In the years since then the total consumption has risen over 25 percent,[6] and since 1971, per capita alcohol consumption

1. M. E. Wolfgang, cited by Richard H. Blum, Appendix B, *Task Force Report: Drunkenness,* President's Commission on Law Enforcement and Administration of Justice (Washington, D.C.: U.S. Government Printing Office, 1967), pp. 40–41.

2. R. E. Berry, Jr. et al., *The Economic Costs of Alcohol Abuse / 1975,* Draft Report Prepared for National Institute on Alcohol Abuse and Alcoholism, 1977. See also J. Valley Rachal et al., *A National Study of Adolescent Drinking Behavior, Attitudes and Correlates* (Research Triangle Park, North Carolina: Research Triangle Institute, Center for the Study of Social Behavior, 1975), p. 140.

3. Edward M. Brecher, *Licit and Illicit Drugs,* p. 260.

4. Thomas F. A. Plaut, Appendix I, *Task Force Report: Drunkenness,* pp. 120–31.

5. Marvin A. Block, *Alcohol and Alcoholism* (Belmont, California: Wadsworth, 1970), p. 9.

6. V. Efron; M. Keller; and C. Gurioli, *Statistics on Consumption of Alcohol and on Alcoholism,* 1974 ed. (New Brunswick, New Jersey: Rutgers Center of Alcohol Studies, 1974), p. 1.

in the United States, as measured by sales data, has been the highest recorded since 1850.[1] By 1978, total consumption had risen to more than 2.7 gallons per year per person fourteen years of age and older.[2] Several years ago a United States governmental report indicated that wine contributed only about 12 percent of the total absolute alcohol consumed in the United States,[3] and in a prior report the consumption of beer was stated to have risen by less than 11 percent since 1947 while the intake of distilled spirits had risen by the amount of 50 percent.[4] As has been observed previously, distilled spirits are far more potent than are such beverages as wine and beer.

In the last twenty-five or thirty years, the number of women in the United States who drink alcoholic beverages has increased greatly. A 1958 Gallup survey reported that 55 percent of American women drank alcoholic beverages, while a study in 1976 indicated that the amount had risen to 71 percent.[5]

In a speech delivered at the Fourth Southeastern Conference on Alcohol and Drug Abuse, Dr. Lewis K. Reed, who has been internationally associated with alcohol treatment programs for many years, stated that alcoholism "certainly is on a distinct increase." Reed further stated that about half of the alcoholics in the United States are women.[6]

Alcoholism is composed of a number of stages or patterns. E. M. Jellinek, a Yale University biometrician, has described five major categories of alcoholism in which there are varying combinations and degrees of (1) psychological dependence, (2) nutritional complications, (3) physical dependence, (4) loss of control, and (5) episodic use.[7]

With regard to the choice of beverage, it is clear that Americans are drinking more beer than either wine or distilled spirits. Per capita con-

1. *Third Special Report,* pp. 9–10.

2. *Fourth Special Report to the U.S. Congress on Alcohol and Health,* by John R. De Luca, ed. (Washington, D.C.: Government Printing Office, 1981), p. 1.

3. *Second Special Report,* p. 4.

4. *First Special Report,* p. 12.

5. James H. Winchester, "The Special Problems of Women Alcoholics," *Reader's Digest* 112 (March 1978):207–12.

6. "Ten to Twelve Million Americans Said Alcoholics; Numbers Rising," *Nashville, The Tennessean,* 6 December 1979, n.p.

7. E. M. Jellinek, *The Disease Concept of Alcoholism* (New Haven, Conn.: Hillhouse Press, 1960), n.p.

sumption, when averaged over the United States population aged fourteen and older, by 1980 averaged nearly thirty gallons of beer each year. This is equivalent to 320 12-ounce cans of beer. Americans consume nearly as much ethanol from beer[1] as from wine[2] and distilled spirits combined.[3]

International Comparisons

A comparison of the consumption trends in the United States from those in other industrialized countries in recent years indicates that in some respects the United States is reflecting overall trends but not in others.[4] In fact, twelve of the sixteen European and British Commonwealth countries shown in Table Three outranked the United States in the period from the late 1950s to around 1970 in the percentage increase of wine use. The total consumption of alcoholic beverages rose enough in the same period in some of the other countries so that the United States was outranked by eight of the sixteen in average annual percentage increase in overall consumption.

On the other hand, by 1974 the United States outranked all but two of the twenty-five other countries, from which reports were available, in per capita consumption of distilled spirits.[5] In terms of total per capita consumption of alcohol, among twenty-six nations surveyed between 1976 and 1978 the United States ranked fifteenth, but ranked third in the consumption of distilled spirits.[6] Although proportional increases in spirits consumption have been higher in several other countries in recent years, the United States is somewhat exceptional in its persistent high levels of spirits consumption, compared to the general twentieth century trend toward beer drinking in industrialized countries with a history of heavy spirit consumption.[7]

---

1. 49 percent.
2. 12 percent.
3. 39 percent. *See Fourth Special Report,* p. 16.
4. See Appendix B, Table Three, pp. 204–05.
5. *Statistics on Consumption,* p. 5.
6. *Third Special Report,* p. 5. See also *Statistics on Consumption.*
7. P. Sulkunen, "Changes in the Consumption of Alcoholic Beverages in the 1960s," *Alkoholipolitiikka* 38 (1973):147–54; P. Sulkunen, "The Production and Consumption of Alcoholic Beverages," *Alkoholipolitiikka* 38 (1973):111–17.

The abstinence rate in the United States does not appear to have been steady in recent years, at least in the adult male population, while it has been declining in other countries, a number of which have a very strong tradition of abstinence.[1]

It is important to note that statistics about the consumption of alcoholic beverages are available on less than half the world's population. There are none, for example, from two such large countries as China and the Soviet Union.[2] One investigator has pointed out that Europe, Japan, the United States, Chile, and Argentina, which have a quarter of the world's population, together account for four-fifths of the reported alcohol consumption. Although the consumption elsewhere can only be surmised, it seems likely that the foregoing comparisons involve most of the relatively heaviest drinking countries, and that the per capita consumption in the United States is above the median in the industrialized part of the world.

Social and Cultural Considerations

Social and cultural factors are strongly correlated with consumption patterns. Among such factors are sex, age, ethnic background, religious affiliation, education, occupation, and area of residence.

There was a time when consumers usually belonged to the lower socioeconomic class, lived in a large metropolitan area, and the drugs most often used were ethyl alcohol and heroin. Present day drug dependents, however, can be found in all socioeconomic classes in all major American cities, and with increasing frequency in many smaller cities and towns. Dr. Morris E. Chafetz indicated that the number of Americans who are under active treatment for alcoholism by public or private agencies are likely in the upper hundreds of thousands and that there may be as many as ten million persons whose imbibing has created problems for themselves, their families, their employers, or law enforcement agencies.[3] In regard to the foregoing view or observation,

---

1. R. Room and R. Roizen, *Drinking and Drug Practice Surveyor* (Berkeley, California: n.p., 1973), pp. 25–33.

2. P. Sulkunen, "The Production and Consumption of Alcoholic Beverages," pp. 111–17.

3. *Second Special Report,* p. 1.

it may be noted that any amount of imbibing creates a problem, a spiritual problem!

Sex

Approximately 68 percent of adults, age twenty-one and over, in the United States, imbibe alcoholic beverages, including 77 percent of the men and 66 percent of the women.[1] The proportion of adult women who imbibe has steadily and significantly increased since World War II.[2] Approximately 47 percent of adult women in the United States now drink once a month or more.

In a survey of 3376 internists, R. W. Jones and A. R. Helrich found that only 3 percent of them saw no alcoholics, whereas 16 percent saw over twenty alcoholics during a one month period. Significantly, half of the alcoholics were women.[3]

Age

The highest proportion of abstainers is found in those whose age is sixty-five or older. The highest proportion of imbibers are found among those aged from twenty-one to twenty-four years, but greater consumption among men is more frequent in eighteen to twenty year groups than in the twenty-one to twenty-four year groups.

Numerous studies of younger populations, mostly in high school, reveal that a substantial proportion of teenagers imbibe.[4] Estimates based on an aggregation of such surveys shows that in recent years from 71 to 92 percent of high school students have at least tasted intoxi-

---

1. D. Cahalan, I. H. Cisan, and H. M. Crossley, *American Drinking Practices: A National Study of Drinking Behavior and Attitudes* (New Brunswick, New Jersey: Rutgers Center of Alcohol Studies, 1969), p. 6.

2. *First Special Report,* p. 10.

3. R. W. Jones and A. R. Helrich, "Treatment of Alcoholism by Physicians in Private Practice: A National Survey," *Quarterly Journal of Studies on Alcohol* 33 (1972):117–31.

4. M. Bacon and M. B. Jones, *Teenage Drinking* (New York: Crowell Co., 1968), p. 1. See also G. L. Maddox and B. C. McCall, *Drinking Among Teenagers: A Sociological Interpretation of Alcohol Use By High School Students* (New Brunswick, New Jersey: Rutgers Center of Alcohol Studies, 1964), p. 4.

cating beverages.[1] In light of the common practice of imbibing in the American life-style, it is not surprising that the vast majority of teenagers have been introduced to alcoholic beverages of some description. In fact, a 1970 survey of young men a year following graduation from high school revealed that as many as 67 percent imbibed such beverages once a month or more.[2] The survey likewise indicated an increase in the frequency of "regular" consumption, those who imbibe once a week or more, from 33 percent during their high school years to a total of 44 percent the following year. The 1974 United States survey of high school students indicated that among seventh graders, as many as 63 percent of the boys and 54 percent of the girls had at least one drink. The proportion increased with each grade to 93 percent of the boys and 87 percent of the girls in the twelfth grade. The United States Department of Health, Education, and Welfare reports that with approximately ten million problem drinkers in our nation, 1.5 million are from preteen to twenty-one years of age. A 1977 national census revealed that a total of 27 percent of all high school students drank at least once a week.[3]

It is significant to note that the amount of regular drinking was higher among high school students who joined the military[4] than among those who took civilian jobs[5] or entered college.[6] The military sample not only began with higher rates of imbibers than most other groups but also indicated the highest rate of change from abstinence to consumption.

Beer is the most preferred drink, especially among boys. The imbibing of beer at least once a week increased from 10 percent among seventh grade boys to 42 percent among twelfth graders. Half of the boys reported consuming two drinks or less per drinking occasion, compared to one or less per occasion among girls. Generally, the quantity consumed at any

1. M. Bacon and M. B. Jones, *Teenage Drinking,* p. 1.

2. L. Johnson, *Drugs and American Youth* (Ann Arbor: University of Michigan, Institute for Social Research, 1973), p. 30.

3. Susan Nadler Gantry, "Gettin' Drunk on Saturday Night," *Nashville* 6 (November 1978):46.

4. 55 percent.

5. 48 percent.

6. 38 percent.

one time by both boys and girls increased with school grade, regardless of beverage type.

Ethnic Background

Heavy consumption rates tend to be low among groups whose drinking habits are well integrated with the rest of their culture. It is, therefore, not surprising that ethnic background and generational status or blended patterns of culture are important factors in determining consumption patterns in the United States.

Reports indicate that Irish-Americans have a greater percentage of heavy consumption than other Americans of the same social class, that little of their consumption is associated with important functions, and that intoxication is often deliberately sought.[1] On the contrary, Italian-Americans have strong sanctions against intoxication and apply little social pressure to imbibe.[2]

The amount, frequency, and style of imbibing differ according to sex, age, ethnic origin, religion, education, occupation, socioeconomic status, and residence. All strata of society, however, are affected. The more affluent, the better educated, and the urbanites are more likely to be addicted, while the younger and the poorer are more likely to experience severe problems, other than spiritual, in connection with their imbibing. Consistently, except if they become heavy imbibers, women imbibe less, and less often than men.[3]

In light of the monumental proportions of the awful problem, which affects human conduct to such a great degree, it should be dealt with, not minimized!

1. T. F. A. Plaut, *Alcohol Problems: A Report to the Nation by the Cooperative Commission on the Study of Alcoholism* (New York: Oxford University Press, 1967), p. 1.

2. G. Lolli, E. Serianni, G. M. Golder, and P. Luzzatto-Fegiz, *Alcohol in Italian Culture: Food and Wine in Relation to Sobriety Among Italians and Italian-Americans* (New Brunswick, New Jersey: Rutgers Center of Alcohol Studies, 1958), p. 3.

3. *Second Special Report*, p. 1.

Religious Affiliation

It is interesting to observe that religious motivations have been determined to be more successful than legal regulations in supporting abstinence.[1]

A national survey which placed religious groups in four classifications, namely, Roman Catholic, Jewish, Liberal Protestant, and Conservative Protestant, revealed that there were relatively high proportions of heavy imbibers among Roman Catholics.[2]

Although Jews had the lowest number of abstainers among the groups, they had a very large proportion of light imbibers and the lowest proportion of heavy imbibers. Liberal Protestants indicated a pattern rather similar to that of Roman Catholics in proportions of imbibers, except that there were fewer heavy imbibers among the Liberal Protestants. Conservative Protestants had the largest proportion of abstainers and the lowest proportion of heavy imbibers when the four groups were compared.

It is interesting to note that those who attended religious services more often were likely to report infrequent consumption. There was also a distinct inverse relationship between attendance of religious services and the amount of ethyl alcohol consumed per occasion—the more frequent such attendance, the less consumption per occasion, regardless of the type of alcoholic beverage.

The relation between religious participation and consumption patterns of youth has received considerable attention in several studies.[3] The frequency of attendance has been viewed as a behavioral measure of involvement in the adult social control system.[4] In a cross-study of consumer status in youth, one group of researchers reported that "religiousness" and frequency of attendance of such services were

1. *First Special Report,* p. 15.
2. D. Cahalan, I. H. Cisin, and H. M. Crossley, *American Drinking Practices: A National Study,* p. 7.
3. G. L. Maddox and B. C. McCall, *Drinking Among Teenagers: A Sociological Interpretation,* p. 4.
4. R. Jessor, T. D. Graves, R. C. Hanson, and S. L. Jessor, *Society, Personality, and Deviant Behavior: A Study of a Tri-Ethnic Community* (New York: Holt, Rinehart, and Winston, 1968), p. 5.

strongly related to abstinence.[1] In a study of high school students in Mississippi, those identified as "problem drinkers" scored lower than others on an index of religious participation.[2] In addition, in a review of two nationwide surveys of American youth, similar evidence was reported.[3]

Prohibition

Legislation and governmental legalization of anything which is sinful does not make it right. It has been stated that the arguments advanced in favor of prohibition before 1920 were overwhelming.[4] It is this writer's view that they are still overwhelming!

The Eighteenth Amendment, which brought prohibition, passed both houses of the United States Congress by the required two-thirds majority in December of 1917. Some thirteen months later it was ratified by the required three-fourths of the legislatures of the, then, forty-eight states. After thirteen years of prohibition, the Twenty-first Amendment, the Prohibition Repeal, was passed in Congress by the required two-thirds majority in February of 1933. Ratification by three-fourths of the state legislatures took less than ten months to secure. It was said that the United States learned more of the dangers of ethyl alcohol during prohibition than it had learned during previous decades. Nevertheless, prohibition was repealed. It was stated that *"the one decisive argument"* favoring the repeal, which the writer views as pragmatic, was the view that prohibition did not work![5]

Such reasoning is difficult to comprehend, and its fallacy is abundantly evident when the so-called "one decisive argument" is compared with murder, rape, armed robbery, and the like! Since these, along with numerous other equally sinful matters have been legislated against, yet unsuccessfully, and since the pragmatic view concerning alcoholic

1. R. Jessor and S. L. Jessor, *Problem Drinking in Youth: Personality, Social and Behavioral Antecedents and Correlates* (Boulder, Colorado: Institute of Behavioral Science, 1973), p. 14.

2. G. Globetti, "A Survey of Teenage Drinking in Two Mississippi Communities," *Preliminary Report* 3 (1964):3.

3. G. L. Maddox and B. C. McCall, *Drinking Among Teenagers: A Sociological Interpretation,* p. 5.

4. Edward M. Brecher, *Licit and Illicit Drugs,* p. 265.

5. Ibid. Emphasis mine, WDJ.

beverages has been resorted to, the same follows regarding murder, rape, armed robbery, and the like. Quite obviously legislation has been far from successful pertaining to these! In order to be consistent, therefore, legislation in their regard should likewise be repealed!

It has been stated that in some respects, and in some areas of the United States, perhaps, the situation was somewhat better during the period of prohibition, but that in other respects it was unquestionably worse. The same is equally true, however, concerning the aforementioned crimes or vices!

Further observation of the fallacious reasoning in regard to the Prohibition Repeal may be noticed in the following:

> The United States thus *learned* its lesson—with respect to alcohol More *remarkable,* the *mere memory of Prohibition,* forty years after Repeal, is still so *repellent* that no proposal to revive it would be taken *seriously.*[1]

In regard to this view, it may be stated that if America considers the legislation of alcoholic beverages as a "remarkable" lesson that has been "learned," and feels that the "mere memory of Prohibition" is "repellent," it has not merely pitched its tent toward Sodom, but rather is in Sodom! Persons need to learn the remarkable lesson that, "Righteousness exalteth a nation; but sin is a reproach to any people."[2]

It was also said that during the prohibition period, methyl alcohol, because ethyl alcohol was too costly, led to blindness and death, and also that "ginger jake," an ingredient in bootleg beverages, often produced paralysis and death.[3] Persons have but to investigate the alcoholic related deaths of the present generation to see the utter foolishness and fallacy of using such to remove prohibition!

In regard to prohibition, Edward M. Brecher states,

> The Twenty-first Amendment left power in the states to retain statewide alcohol prohibition—and made it a federal offense to ship alcoholic beverages into a dry state. Statewide alcohol prohibition, however, failed like national prohibition. State after state

---

1. Ibid., p. 266. Emphasis mine, WDJ.

2. Prov. 14:34.

3. F. R. Menue, "Acute Methyl Alcohol Poisoning," *Archives of Pathology* 26 (1938):79–92.

repealed its statewide alcohol prohibition laws; Mississippi's, in 1966, was the last to go.[1]

In reference to the Twenty-first Amendment and its application to federal and state laws, the principles found in the following passages no doubt apply. "Shall the throne of wickedness have fellowship with thee, which frameth mischief by statute?"[2] "Woe to him that buildeth a town with blood, and establisheth a city by iniquity."[3] Laws or statutes of men do not negate the law of Almighty God, and unquestionably, alcoholic beverages are doing much to make America an iniquitous nation!

Deceptiveness of Ethyl Alcohol

Ethyl alcohol is deceptive. First, a thirst must be created, then mental opposition must be broken down. It is a step-by-step process. A prime factor in bringing about indulgence is supposed friends, and as a rule the first drink is taken to merely please them. The challenge is to be a good sport or to do as others are doing. With good intentions persons take the first drink, and the second, until mental opposition is eventually destroyed, a craving is created, and a depraved desire is developed.

Both sacred and profane history attest to the fact that intoxicating beverages are harmful. One of the chief reasons for the disintegration of the Roman Empire, which ruled the world in the time of Christ, was the moral corruptness of its leaders. Before the Romans were the Greeks under Alexander the Great, who conquered the world but could not conquer his craving for alcoholic beverages. Ultimately he died a drunkard's death. Before the Greeks were the Persians, among whom was Ahasuerus, who at a drunken festival, attempted to make Vashti, his queen, do an immoral dance. There was David who, after committing adultery with Bathsheba, made Uriah, her husband, drunk in an effort to place the blame on Uriah for his own sin. Thus it can be seen when surveyed historically, that drunkenness is an old sin. Through the centuries, alcoholic beverages, along with other drugs, have proved to be devastating to home life.

---

1. Edward M. Brecher, *Licit and Illicit Drugs,* p. 266.
2. Ps. 94:20.
3. Hab. 2:12.

Crisis of the Home

One of the truly great needs of the present day is Christian homes. Nothing can take the place of the training and influence which comes from such homes. The tendencies of modern society, however, are to not build homes, but to destroy homes which now exist.

God's law is that the younger women "marry, bear children, guide the house, give none occasion to the adversary to speak reproachfully."[1] Aged women are to "train the young women to love their husbands, to love their children, to be sober-minded, chaste, workers at home, kind, being in subjection to their own husbands, that the word of God be not blasphemed."[2]

Husbands are to "love their wives, even as Christ also loved the church,"[3] and fathers are to "provoke not your children to wrath: but nurture them in the chastening and admonition of the Lord."[4] Children are to "obey your parents in the Lord: for this is right."[5] That there is a crisis in the American family today cannot be successfully denied.

Contributing Factors

The crisis can be attributed to a lack of respect for the word of God and a subsequent failure to adhere thereto. The family is the unit of society, and family life is an index to the strength and stability of the nation. The extent to which persons make good members of all other worthy institutions depends largely on how they were brought up in the home. The use of alcoholic beverages and other drugs often contribute to this crisis.

The present age is one in which there is a drug or pill for everything. In many instances parents have encouraged their children to explore their own pleasures without proper guidance. Consequently, there has been a deterioration of moral values, in which fathers have relinquished their God-ordained role of disciplinarian.

---

1. 1 Tim. 5:14 (KJV).
2. Tit. 2:4–5.
3. Eph. 5:25.
4. Eph. 6:4.
5. Eph. 6:1.

Ethyl alcohol and other drugs are underlying causes in more than half of all marriage failures. If they do not destroy homes by separation or divorce, they often destroy them by murder. News reports of husbands killing their wives, wives killing their husbands, or children killing their fathers or mothers because of ethyl alcohol or other drugs are numerous. The illicit and non-medicinal use of such drugs weaken persons mentally, morally, socially, and spiritually, and often bring them and their families to ruin.

The use of such agents is rapidly and dramatically increasing among young people. From junior high school through college age, many seem to be making strong commitments to their use and to the unreal world that they help to create. The question is not whether youth are using them as a way of escape, or even which ones they are using! These things are known! The significant question is: Why? Why do youth find it neces-sary to escape from the world around them? What happens that causes them to turn from society? Why do they choose to ignore the dangers of ethyl alcohol and other harmful agents? Perhaps the answer can be found in the home!

Parental Responsibility

Parents have a solemn responsibility to know some things about the devastation of such agents. At the same time, they should teach their children to care for their bodies, to recognize the purposes of life, and to pursue the means whereby these purposes may be achieved. Parents must therefore take the initiative in changing attitudes about the imbibing of intoxicants and the factors in home environment or otherwise, which motivate young people to seek them as a means of escape!

History of Drugs

The term *drug* does not have to be terrifying to persons. Webster defines the term as, "A substance used as a medication or in the preparation of medication."[1]

---

1. "Drug," in *Webster's New Collegiate Dictionary,* p. 350.

Over a period of many centuries, man has discovered plants which can be used for his well-being. Chinese medical history, which goes back about three thousand years, reveals that Emperor Shen Nung compiled the first Chinese listing of herbs useful in medicine. The beginning of chemistry and scientific pharmacy rose from the medical experience of ancient Jewish and Moslem physicians. In the fourth century B.C., the father of modern medicine, the Greek physician, Hippocrates, separated medicine from so-called magic.

Unfortunately, the good uses of many early medical discoveries have been deviated from by misuses. Therefore, the use of alcohol and other drugs have become dangerous through abuse. In the present day, when persons look for the most popular drugs in use, in addition to ethyl alcohol, they encounter marijuana, barbiturates, amphetamines, LSD, DMT, mescaline, codeine, methamphetamine, cocaine, morphine, and heroin, each of which along with ethyl alcohol have caused multiple problems in the home. Before leaving this area of thought, the writer desires to make one final observation in regard to the significance of parental duty.

Christian Instruction

Although there has been much written about the consumption of alcoholic beverages, they constitute but a symptom of the real problem. The real problem can be found in the failure to instruct, instill, and inculcate from infancy the genuine principles of Christianity through daily Christian deportment and oral teaching! The possibilities, therefore, which are opened to Christian parents are truly unlimited, and the accruing responsibilities are grave!

Persons must remember that every child is born with a God-given right to a Christian home. Children are indeed fortunate who, like Timothy, have parents and grandparents of "unfeigned faith."[1] In order to reach all spheres of life with its influence, such faith must pervade the home where manhood, womanhood, and citizenship are in the making.

---

1. 2 Tim. 1:5.

Cause of Suffering

Innocent persons frequently experience much intense suffering at the hands of those who imbibe intoxicating beverages. While under the influence of such beverages, persons are insane. Such detrimental agents or drinks are no respecter of persons. Wealthy socialites and common workers may equally suffer from the ravages of body, brain, and personality because of imbibing alcoholic beverages. At one time such persons had aspirations, ambitions, and aims, but ethyl alcohol led them to become helpless derelicts, headed in the direction of eternal destruction!

Those who sanction "social" drinking should consider its sounds and scenes. An infant cries out in the night because of the pains of hunger and disease; a grinding crash occurs on the highway and groans come from the lips of the dying; a mass of flesh staggers home late at night, cursing and reeling from one side to the other; a helpless and sad mother-to-be, without comfort from her husband, waits out the long hours of despair before what should be a wonderful event, but she has only tears and bitterness; and somewhere in a secluded place, a gun fires a bullet into the brain of a person hopeless and despondent, and the lifeless body falls to the earth—a suicide.

All of these scenes and more are frequently caused by persons who began their journey of physical, mental, and spiritual decay by engaging in "social" drinking! If persons could but see the end from the beginning, they would likely not take the first drink. Sin, however, is camouflaged by the multiple faces of frivolous, foolish, and fallacious reasoning! Perhaps no one thing contributes more to mental anguish and physical suffering by innocent persons than do alcoholic beverages.

Examples of Suffering

A Marriage

Several years ago Juvenile Court Judge Sam Davis Tatum of Nashville, Tennessee, spoke of a case in which four or five children were observed scrambling around in garbage cans in a back alley, looking for something to eat. An officer was sent to the area to pick up the children, whose ages ranged from eleven down to four. The children were filthy and their clothing was ragged. The father, who was a drunkard, had been gone from home for three weeks. The mother, who was a drunkard also, had been gone for two days and had sold the stove the day she left to secure money to purchase liquor. The children mentioned a baby at home, so an officer went with the oldest child to investigate. In a corner of a room, on a nasty and rotten mattress with torn bed clothing, looking more like a pile of coal than it did a bed, they found the little baby, a child about ten months of age. Malnutrition and rickets had already begun their work. A trained nurse was called, and it was discovered that, because it had lain in its own filth for so long, the fiber of the diaper had enmeshed itself into the tender flesh of the baby. It was taken to a hospital, where it lay in warm oil for many hours before the diaper could be removed. The father, it was learned, had at one time built up a good business as an electrician. The mother was from one of the finest families in the area from which they had moved. Their shameful journey down the primrose path had begun with "social" drinking. If on their wedding day someone had cautioned them about the dangers of ethyl alcohol, likely they would have thought they would not allow it to harm them or their children.

The children were placed in an orphan home. The parents were informed that the children would be cared for until they could get themselves in condition to reestablish their home. The father fought a terrific battle, attempting to break himself from the use of ethyl alcohol, and after several years he succeeded, and the children were returned to him. Their mother was so far gone that she was completely overcome by the beastly beverage. On numerous occasions she was observed going from one den of iniquity in the city to another, looking and acting more like an animal than a human. At times she would be sober enough to inquire about receiving her children back. She would be informed that her progress had not been sufficient enough to receive them. Upon learning that she could not receive them back, at times she desired to see them. Dates would be set and arrangements made to bring the children to a proper meeting place. The little children were brought in, and every time they heard someone in the hall they would go to the door eagerly anticipating the arrival of their mother. The mother never did come to see her children, and as far as is known, never saw them again.[1]

---

1. Sam Davis Tatum, *Words of Wisdom for Parents and Teenagers,* (Nashville: n.p., 1965), pp. 22–23.

Some persons may think this is an extreme case, and perhaps it is. Such cases, however, serve to illustrate the awful sorrow and shame which can come from "social" drinking.

An Employee

Clifford Payne gives a true graphic illustration as to the extent alcoholic beverages have become ingrained in modern society.

A large, reputable feed company had fired one of its salesmen, an intelligent, energetic, educated man, who was also a respected family man and dedicated worker in the Lord's church. Admittedly, the dismissal of such a person was strange, for why would a reputable company release a talented salesman of such high caliber? The company gave an unconvincing statement for their actions, but the real reason came to light later.

When the salesman had learned of his impending release, he suggested to a Christian friend that he apply for the job, which the friend did. Upon learning, however, that he was also a Christian, the company supervisor with whom the friend had an interview candidly informed him that the company would not consider him for the job. The supervisor proceeded to explain that he had been very unhappy with the previous salesman's anti-drinking convictions. He explained by saying that clients had informed him that the salesman would cordially entertain them by taking them out for sumptuous meals, but if they ordered an alcoholic beverage, he would politely explain that he would pay for the meal, but not for the beverage. Neither, of course, would he join them in imbibing, whether it was heavy or light. The supervisor went on to mention another specific incident which had displeased him.

At one of the company's conventions, all the salesmen had been solicited for a contribution in order that a gift could be purchased for one of the officials. Upon learning that the gift was to be a case of whiskey, the Christian salesman had declined to give, although he had courteously explained that if it were something else, he would gladly contribute.

The supervisor had made it indelibly clear that this kind of attitude toward alcoholic beverages absolutely prohibited the salesman from being favored by him, and that he would not consider anyone for the position who held such views.[1]

---

1. Clifford Payne, "Drinking: Can It Be Arrested?," *Firm Foundation* 78 (28 March 1961):196.

Such an incident is revolting to those who stand for decency and righteousness! It seems inconceivable that an excellent salesman's dismissal was facilitated and another man's possibility of employment destroyed because they refused to support in any way something as detrimental, dangerous, and degrading to humanity as alcoholic beverages. The tragic truth of the matter is that the consumption of such beverages has become so prevalent that those who do not conform are viewed as peculiar persons who may be penalized, especially if they actively oppose the imbibing of alcoholic beverages. Such deplorable actions but serve to confirm the teaching of Jesus: "Men loved the darkness rather than the light; for their works were evil. For every one that doeth evil hateth the light, and cometh not to the light, lest his works should be reproved."[1]

A Son

The following tragic event was reported by United Press International as it happened in Bradenton, Florida, on September 12, 1964.

A man who was sitting in a bar or tavern said to himself, "One more drink won't hurt." Thus he bought more alcohol to carry with him. He had always been a safe driver, so as he had done many times, he got into his car and started home. He had experienced a difficult day and was anxious to get home and see his young son who was in the fifth grade. He was proud of his son whom he felt was growing so fast, and he always enjoyed spending some time with him.

As he sped along, it seemed that he went faster and faster. He felt that perhaps the last drink had dulled his senses some, but that he was in control, and so he thought that it did not matter. Suddenly, from a side street a boy on a bicycle appeared in front of the car. The man swerved to miss, but struck the boy. For fear, perhaps, the man left the scene. Later, police officers came to his home and arrested him. The officers had found him in the attic with the bottle that he had purchased, crying, as he attempted to drown the terrible event out of his mind. They placed him in jail, but he was released to attend the funeral of the little boy his car had struck. This was the worst thing that had ever happened in his life.

---

1. Jn. 3:19–20.

The news media related the tragedy and added one more sad fact. The little boy who had been killed was the heartbroken man's only son![1]

Which of These Would You Desire To Be?

- Following a high school football game, many students were having a celebration. The gathering was exuberant for their team had been victorious over an arch rival. A number of the youth who were present were Christians and when other students offered them beer to celebrate the victory, some of them did not refuse the offer.

- A bill was presented to a state legislature which, if approved, would allow wine to be sold at a reduced price by the removal of certain taxes upon it. Another bill to be decided upon would allow billboard advertising of alcoholic beverages. Some members of the legislature were Christians. When they, along with the other members of the legislature, were asked to support these bills, several of them did not refuse. In fact, some of the brethren led the fight to get both bills passed.

- A Christian, who was quite successfully involved in business, sat across a table from a very important client. All was going well in the conversation. The client offered him an intoxicating beverage and he knew that if he accepted it, the client would be more responsive to him, and the sale for which he had so diligently worked, would likely be made. He did not refuse the offer.

- A Christian had assisted his neighbor with some yard work, in a hot afternoon sun. They had known each other for a long time and had often fished and played golf together. When they had completed the work in the yard they went into the neighbor's home to relax and cool off, with him offering the Christian a cold beer. He did not refuse the offer.

---

1. This event, reported by Kenneth Davis, was quoted August 2, 1981, in the bulletin of the Cape Fear Church of Christ, which meets in Fayetteville, North Carolina. Slight revisions have been made in the article by the writer, WDJ.

Some time back a report came from a Christian who was engaged in mission work in South Africa. He stated,

> One of our former graduates from Umtali Bible School, Douglas Dabangana, was killed by terrorists where he was preaching in Rhodesia. A group of terrorists tried to force him to drink beer, but he refused, saying he was a Christian and couldn't, so they shot him right then, killing him.

The time will come one day when the Christian youth, the Christian legislators, the Christian who was successful in business, the Christian neighbor, and Douglas Dabangana will "stand before the judgment-seat of God,"[1] at which time each will "receive the things done in the body, according to what he hath done, whether it be good or bad."[2] Which of these would you desire to be?[3]

A Personal Acquaintance

Ted Morris, a fine young Christian boy, and the only child of Frank and Elizabeth Morris, graduated in May 1982 from Trigg County High School in Cadiz, Kentucky. Having been a recent recipient of a scholarship to David Lipscomb College in Nashville, Tennessee, he, at the age of eighteen, had high hopes for a successful career following his college years. After having completed his first semester in college as a business administration major, he returned home to enjoy the Christmas holiday break with his parents and friends. During this period, he was happily employed, working part time with a music store in a shopping mall in Hopkinsville, Kentucky.

Ted and his parents were very close to one another. They did things together; the lives of Frank and Elizabeth were built around him, and Ted really loved and cared about them. The holiday season was a big thing with them. They had always enjoyed it together, and were anticipating an even greater one since Ted was at home for a brief time.

---

1. Rom. 14:10.

2. 2 Cor. 5:10.

3. This true story, written by Dan Jenkins, was quoted in *The Shell Street Sower* 1 (26 October 1980):2, a bulletin of the Shell Street Church of Christ, meeting in Healdton, Oklahoma. Slight revisions have been made in the article by the writer, WDJ.

It was seasonably cold in Hopkinsville on Thursday night, December 23, 1982, and Ted had agreed to work late in order that a coworker could have the evening off. That same day about five o'clock in the afternoon, a young man named Tommy, twenty-four years of age, had gotten off from work and gone to his apartment. Tommy had been a good student in high school several years before, having been an active member of the Key Club and also lettering in football. Although he too had envisioned high hopes for the future, he had begun drinking when he was about seventeen years of age, and a junior in high school. Tommy knew that, even then, it was not difficult for him to buy anything that he wanted—beer, whiskey, or anything—for alcohol dealers had desired his business. He also recalled that when he had begun, he had viewed drinking as the "grown up" thing to do, and had also been highly influenced by peer pressure. He had grown up in a home where alcohol was used, and after moving away at the age of nineteen, Tommy had been employed in a liquor store for a brief period of time.

On the night of December 23, Tommy had decided to attend a party about three miles from his apartment. Several young people were present. He had begun drinking shortly after getting home that afternoon, and by the time he arrived at the party at 8:30, he had drunk half of a fifth of whiskey and was very drunk. During the time he was at the party he had several more drinks, and eventually passed out when he started to leave. When he revived, some of those present offered to take him home, but he refused their offer, leaving by himself some time after ten o'clock, quite angry and extremely drunk.

In the meantime, the store where Ted worked closed for the day, and he, along with a friend, had gone to a local family entertainment center to play several video games. In a few minutes, in separate cars, they stopped at a local restaurant for a snack before going home. Because of the fact that he was at the restaurant, Ted started home by a different route from the one which he usually traveled.

Tommy by that time, about a mile from his apartment, had reached the same street, traveling on the wrong side at a high speed. Suddenly he observed headlights coming toward him. At 10:30, Ted Morris and Tommy met for the first time in their young lives—head on! The force was terrific! The crash was horrendous! The sound reverberated between the houses—then, silence.

Tommy's injuries were only minor, and although he was not totally conscious he could faintly realize that he was being removed from his wrecked car, although he was soon unconscious. With Ted, however, it was different. After some time, and in very critical condition, he was removed from his demolished car with the "Jaws of Life" rescue equipment. When Tommy revived at approximately two o'clock in the morning of December 24, he was given blood-alcohol tests by a police officer. The reading was measured at 0.28 percent, far beyond the degree for *legal* intoxication in Kentucky. His stepfather soon informed him that Ted had been rushed from the local hospital to Baptist Hospital in Nashville, Tennessee.

Frank and Elizabeth Morris dashed from their home and, when informed of the extremely critical condition of Ted, apprehensively followed the ambulance into Nashville. It seemed they would never get there, but finally they arrived and Ted was taken into the Intensive Care Unit. As they waited anxiously, it seemed that the report of the neurologist who had been summoned for the emergency would take forever. Finally, at 2:20, about an hour after their arrival on the morning of December 24, 1982, the neurologist came out to speak to them. Those who have never faced similar conditions and heard, "I am very sorry; we did all we could, but the injuries were fatal," cannot comprehend the sheer impact and awful finality of such a statement! Frank and Elizabeth Morris were devastated when informed that their only child had not made it! Things had occurred so rapidly that they did not even realize that a drunken driver had been responsible.

At this point in this sad story, the writer unapologetically injects a personal comment: Decent persons would have pity for any person who could have stood in the shoes of Frank and Elizabeth Morris at 2:20 on that fateful December morning, and yet attempt to defend the imbibing of the devilish drink to *any* degree! Had Tommy not taken the first drink several years before, this senseless death would not have occurred! Those who verbally sanction such give credibility to such horrendous happenings the same as those who themselves imbibe. Such tragedies are commonplace in our society. In fact, on the same day that Ted's funeral was conducted, two sisters, also students in David Lipscomb College, were slaughtered by a drunk driver!

When Tommy was informed that night that Ted had died, he cried the remainder of the night, having wished that it had been him, for he knew that it was his fault. He also at first could not believe that it had happened to him, recalling an incident in which a friend's twenty-two-year-old son had been killed by a drunk driver, and he distinctly remembered having said, "It will never happen to me!" But it did!

There were many times between the age of seventeen and twenty-four that Tommy could have been involved in such a tragedy. Everything, however, came together that terrible night. It was not Ted's custom to travel that street in going home, but on that particular night he had been in the area with a friend. Also if he had not worked later than usual, he would not have been there. Had Tommy have passed out at the party for a shorter or longer period, or had someone been successful in their offer to take him home, the death would not have occurred. The tragic event of that fateful night, however, could happen to anyone under the same conditions. What a terrible price, though, for one to pay who was under bondage to a beastly beverage, a price of shame, remorse, and a blighted memory for the remainder of his earthly life! In a split second's time, the mortal aims and ambitions of a fine young Christian boy were dashed, and his beloved parents were left with an indescribable emptiness in their lives.

Tommy's burden of guilt was later indelibly demonstrated. When asked if he had talked to Ted's parents, he had replied, "I don't know what to say to them, for if I just say, 'I'm sorry,' I don't think there is anything I could say to really make up for the loss." He further said that every time he saw someone, he felt they were perhaps thinking, "That is the guy that got drunk and killed somebody."

Later a special tape was found in the trunk of Ted's car, which was to have been a Christmas present for his father, Frank. Some time later, in his upstairs room at home, a cookbook which was to have been a Christmas gift for his mother, Elizabeth, was found. But Frank and Elizabeth Morris were not able to exchange gifts that holiday season with their son, their only child, or will they ever be able to again! For in the early hours of that cold December morning, Ted died the innocent victim of a horrible crime—death at the hands of a drunken killer!

Ted was highly respected in Cadiz, Kentucky, and in the surrounding area. Citizens were concerned. Some two weeks after his death, a group of his friends, including Rose J. Wyatt[1] of Cadiz, along with several concerned persons from the Hopkinsville area, initiated meetings which ultimately led to the forming of a MADD[2] chapter in that area. Membership was approved and the charter was granted from the national headquarters on August 11, 1983.

Tommy was originally charged with murder. On the advice of his attorney, he pleaded innocent. He eventually acquired another attorney, however, and changed his plea to guilty, saying, "I think I really admitted to myself, that I had done something wrong." In February 1983 the sentence was reduced to second-degree manslaughter.

With the Trigg County chapter of MADD actively at work, Judge Edwin White, in presiding over Christian County Circuit Court, in Hopkinsville, Kentucky, handed down one of the strictest probationary requirements ever given by the court. The probation contained fourteen separate stipulations. Tommy agreed to comply with the probation, which is for five years, rather than be sentenced to ten years in prison for the manslaughter charge. One of the requirements was that Tommy make scheduled talks to various school assemblies under the oversight of MADD, regarding his terrible experience. The story, however, is not over at this point.

When Mrs. Wyatt presented the first program at Trigg County High School for the new MADD chapter, Elizabeth Morris, Ted's mother, was present. A fourteen-year-old girl was also in attendance at the program. During the program, the young girl turned to a fellow-student seated next to her and remarked, "It will never happen to me." Little did she or anyone realize that in only four days she too would be hurled into eternity, and because of the same senseless reason as Ted was.

Barbi, a very popular sophomore in Trigg County High School, a member of the school band, and in the Beta Club, was returning home from a football game with another student and a former student in her school. On the night of November 4, 1983, at 9:45, the car, traveling at a very high speed, went out of control in a curve in the highway. A state trooper indicated that alcohol had been involved. She was ultimately rushed to Vanderbilt Hospital in Nashville, Tennessee, where severe

---

1. Rose J. Wyatt is a daughter of the writer.
2. MADD is the acronym for Mothers Against Drunk Driving.

head injuries proved to be fatal at 11:30 on Sunday morning, November 6, 1983, only four days following the comment to her classmate!

During his first school speech, Tommy stated, "I wish drunk drivers could feel the way I felt that night. You couldn't put it on a piece of paper. It doesn't have to happen!" Yet, Tommy and Barbi had both said, "It will never happen to me." Of one thing the writer is certain: Those who never take the first drink will neither die drunk, nor kill someone else while in a drunken stupor!

The beastly beverage has truly led to staggering statistics! Drunk drivers slaughter 26,000 persons per year, an average of seventy persons every day! Such drivers kill more persons in the United States annually than murderers do! In excess of 500,000 persons are injured every year in largely preventable alcohol-related automobile crashes! In the last ten years alone, an estimated 250,000 Americans have been killed and several million innocent persons have been seriously injured and disabled by drivers under the influence of ethyl alcohol! Between 50 and 55 percent of all fatal accidents involve a drinking driver or pedestrian. Statistics indicate that Americans between the ages of five and thirty-four are more likely to be killed in a traffic accident than any other single cause, and it is known that alcohol is involved in at least half of these fatal crashes. Such is the story of alcohol!

There is yet another chapter in Tommy's case. Good can sometimes come from shameful events, and it did with Tommy! On one occasion Frank and Elizabeth Morris, who are devout Christians, were taking Tommy to a MADD meeting. On the way, they began discussing the Bible. In January 1985, Tommy was baptized into Christ for the remission of his sins, by Frank Morris, whose son he had killed! On July 6, 1985, the writer's daughter stated that he faithfully attends all the services of the church and likewise takes an active part in serving the Lord's supper, reading the Bible, and leading in prayer. Thanks be to God![1]

---

1. Consult Peter Michelmore, "Could They Forgive Their Son's Killer?" *Reader's Digest* 128 (May 1986):136–40, for additional material concerning this event.

Proper Use of Things

It is often true that a moderate and proper use of things will be beneficial when their immoderate and improper use will be detrimental, dangerous, and sometimes deadly. Drugs, properly used, save lives; but improperly used, they destroy lives. Ethyl alcohol, scientifically or medicinally used for the correct purposes, may produce much good; used as a beverage, however, the results can be only harmful and evil.

Temperate persons have enough self-control to reject the wrong thing, and the wrong use of the right thing. Temporary gratification of fleshly appetites will never be worth the suffering, disgrace, and eternal condemnation which will follow. Thinking individuals will not jeopardize their entire future for the sake of one drink or for the approval of foolish, thoughtless, and deluded associates.

The best friends the alcoholic beverage industry has are compromising church members who are "social" drinkers. Such persons may continue to defend its use, but in reality it has no defense. It cannot be truthfully denied that "social" drinking is often used to promote sexual immorality. The difference between "social" drinking and alcoholism is but a matter of time and degree! Such drinkers influence others to think that they can indulge in safety, only to discover too late that there is no safe indulgence. Those who in any way promote "social" drinking are responsible for alcoholism, which could not be possible without an initial drink.

Answer to the Problem

In light of the tremendous problem inherent in the consumption of alcoholic beverages, men should preach the word of Christ,[1] equip themselves for its defense,[2] and adorn the doctrine of God.[3] Men should be afraid to be ashamed to teach what God would have them teach,[4] and on the other hand, they should be ashamed to be afraid to suffer the possible ill consequences of such teaching![5]

---

1. 2 Tim. 4:2.
2. 1 Pet. 3:15.
3. Tit. 2:10.
4. Rom. 1:16.
5. 1 Pet. 4:16.

It is indeed regrettable when persons are allowed to propagate theories and philosophies which are contrary to the eternal verities of God, with scarcely a voice or pen raised in opposition! Those who persist in defending such activities, socially or otherwise, and those who sanction such sins by cowardly silence, along with those who stand wholeheartedly for the truth will one day appear before the author of truth. Then the judgment of God will prevail!

A Final Plea

There are many innocent persons whose hearts are broken because of ethyl alcohol. There are many resources and abilities which are being wasted because of ethyl alcohol. There are many helpless victims whose lives have been demolished because of ethyl alcohol. The hills and vales of our great nation are being filled with the graves of those who are dead because of ethyl alcohol. The liquor traffic, which is a public cancer, is destroying the very vitals of society!

Blood, which is intended by God to be life-giving, therefore, may continue to stain the highways because of ethyl alcohol, but not by the approval of dedicated Christians! Ethyl alcohol may continue to bring shame and disgrace to the home, but not by the approval of dedicated Christians! Society may continue to crumble and decay because of ethyl alcohol, but not by the approval of dedicated Christians! Ethyl alcohol may continue to wound the innocent and promote health and moral problems by the score, but not by the approval of dedicated Christians! Disrespect for civil authorities and disintegration of decent and upright heritages may continue, but not by the approval of dedicated Christians! In fact, dens of iniquity may distribute ethyl alcohol on every street corner in every city in every nation, but not by the approval of dedicated Christians!

Dedicated Christians are diametrically opposed to the imbibing of alcohol as a mere beverage in any form and to any degree! Persons cannot be better persons than the Bible teaches them to be. The Bible does not teach persons to be given to alcoholic beverages but, regretfully, persons who are either woefully unaware or indifferent to biblical teaching do!

In concluding this book, please observe that the writer is clearly aware of the fact that there may be many so-called arguments favoring the imbibing of such beverages, of which he is unaware, and thus have not been explicated in the purview of this writing. May the reader be assured, however, that any such view or views can possibly be substantiated *only* after successful refutation of that which has been stated, for the Bible does not contradict itself!

The opportunities are many! The responsibility is great! The task is awesome! May God grant individuals the wisdom to recognize their opportunities, the courage to assume their responsibilities, and the zeal to press on with the task of promoting the truth in regard to the imbibing of alcoholic beverages. "Wine is a mocker, strong drink a brawler; and whosoever erreth thereby is not wise."[1]

The Bible plainly teaches this. The issue therefore is settled for all persons who respect and consequently accept the teaching of the Bible.[2]

---

1. Prov. 20:1.

2. Consult Appendix C, "Questions for Consideration," pp. 212-15 for a list of questions regarding the consumption of alcoholic beverages.

APPENDIX A

TABLE ONE

Terms Designating Wine or Related to Wine in the American Standard Version of the Bible

I. Hebrew Terms

  A. *Yayin*

    1. "Wine"
      Genesis 9:21, 24; 14:18; 19:32, 33, 34, 35; 27:25; 49:11, 12; Exodus 29:40; Leviticus 10:9; 23:13; Numbers 6:3, 3, 20; 15:5, 7, 10; 28:14; Deuteronomy 14:26; 28:39; 29:6; 32:14, 33, 38; Judges 13:4, 7, 14; 19:19; 1 Samuel 1:14, 15, 24; 10:3; 16:20; 25:18, 37; 2 Samuel 13:28; 16:1, 2; 1 Chronicles 9:29; 12:40; 2 Chronicles 2:10, 15; 11:11; Nehemiah 2:1; 5:15, 18; 13:15; Esther 1:7, 10; 5:6; 7:2, 7, 8; Job 1:13, 18; 32:19; Psalm 60:3; 75:8; 78:65; 104:15; Proverbs 4:17; 9:2, 5; 20:1; 21:17; 23:30, 31; 31:4, 6; Ecclesiastes 2:3; 9:7; 10:19; Song of Solomon 1:2, 4; 4:10; 5:1; 7:9; 8:2; Isaiah 5:11, 12, 22; 16:10; 22:13; 24:9, 11; 28:1, 7, 7; 29:9; 51:21; 55:1; 56:12; Jeremiah 13:12, 12; 23:9; 25:15; 35:2, 5, 6, 8, 14; 40:10, 12; 48:33; 51:7; Lamentations 2:15; Ezekiel 27:18; 44:21; Daniel 1:5, 8, 16; 10:3; Hosea 4:11; 7:5; 9:4; 14:7; Joel 1:5; 3:3; Amos 2:8, 12; 5:11; 6:6; 9:14; Micah 2:11; 6:15; Habakkuk 2:5; Zephaniah 1:13; Haggai 2:12; Zechariah 9:15; 10:7.

    2. "Wine-skins"
      Joshua 9:4, 13.

    3. "Wine-cellars"
      1 Chronicles 27:27.

4. "Banqueting"
   Song of Solomon 2:4.

B. *Tirosh*
   1. "New wine"
      Genesis 27:28, 37; Deuteronomy 7:13; 11:14; 12:17; 14:23; 18:4; 28:51; 33:28; Judges 9:13; 2 Kings 18:32; 2 Chronicles 31:5; 32:28; Nehemiah 5:11; 10:37, 39; 13:5, 12; Psalm 4:7; Proverbs 3:10; Isaiah 24:7; 36:17; 62:8; 65:8; Jeremiah 31:12; Hosea 2:8, 9, 22; 4:11; 7:14; 9:2; Joel 1:10; 2:19, 24; Haggai 1:11; Zechariah 9:17.

   2. "Vintage"
      Numbers 18:12; Micah 6:15.

C. *Shekar*
   1. "Strong drink"
      Leviticus 10:9; Numbers 6:3, 3; 28:7; Deuteronomy 14:26; 29:6; Judges 13:4, 7, 14; 1 Samuel 1:15; Proverbs 20:1; 31:4, 6; Isaiah 5:11, 22; 24:9; 28:7, 7, 7; 29:9; 56:12; Micah 2:11.

D. *Asis*
   1. "Sweet wine"
      Isaiah 49:26; Joel 1:5; 3:18; Amos 9:13.
   2. "Juice"
      Song of Solomon 8:2.

E. *Shemarim*
   1. "Wines on the lees" Isaiah 25:6, 6.
   2. "Lees"
      Jeremiah 48:11; Zephaniah 1:12.
   3. "Dregs"
      Psalm 75:8.

F. *Sobe*
   1. "Wine"
      Isaiah 1:22.

   2. "Drink"
      Hosea 4:18; Nahum 1:10.

G. *Chemer*
   1. "Wine"
      Psalm 75:8; Isaiah 27:2.

H. *Chamar*
   1. "Wine"
      Ezra 6:9; 7:22; Daniel 5:1, 2, 4, 23.

I. *Mesek*
   1. "Mixture" Psalm 75:8.

J. *Mimsak*
   1. "Mixed wine"
      Proverbs 23:30.
   2. "Mingled wine"
      Isaiah 65:11.

K. *Mezeg*
   1. "Mingled wine"
      Song of Solomon 7:2.

L. *Dam-anabim*
   1. "Blood of grapes"
      Genesis 49:11.

M. *Dam-enab*
   1. "Blood of the grapes"
      Deuteronomy 32:14.

N. *Mishrath-anabim*
   1. "Juice of grapes"
      Numbers 6:3.

O. *Ashishah*
   1. "Cake of raisins"
      2 Samuel 6:19; 1 Chronicles 16:3.

   2. "Cakes of raisins"
      Hosea 3:1.

   3. "Raisins"
      Song of Solomon 2:5.

P. *Anabim*
   1. "Cakes of raisins"
      Hosea 3:1.

Q. *Chomets*
   1. "Vinegar"
      Numbers 6:3, 3; Ruth 2:14; Psalm 69:21; Proverbs 10:26;
      25:20.

R. *Yekeb*

    1. "Winepress"

    Numbers 18:27, 30; Deuteronomy 15:14; 16:13; Judges 7:25; 2 Kings 6:27; Isaiah 5:2; Hosea 9:2.

    2. "Winepresses"

    Job 24:11; Jeremiah 48:33; Zechariah 14:10.

S. *Mamtaqqim*

    1. "Sweet"

    Nehemiah 8:10.

    2. "Most sweet"

    Song of Solomon 5:16.

II. Greek Terms

A. *Oinos*

    1. "Wine"

    Matthew 9:17, 17, 17; 27:34; Mark 2:22, 22, 22, 22; 15:23; Luke 1:15; 5:37, 37, 38; 7:33; 10:34; John 2:3, 3, 9, 10, 10; 4:46; Romans 14:21; Ephesians 5:18; 1 Timothy 3:8; 5:23; Titus 2:3; Revelation 6:6; 14:8, 10; 16:19; 17:2; 18:3, 13; 19:15.

B. *Gleukos*

    1. "New wine"

    Acts 2:13.

C. *Sikera*

    1. "Strong drink"

    Luke 1:15.

D. *Oxos*

    1. "Vinegar"

    Matthew 27:48; Mark 15:36; Luke 23:36; John 19:29, 29, 30.

E. *Gennema tas ampelou*

    1. "Fruit of the vine"

    Matthew 26:29; Mark 14:25; Luke 22:18.

TABLE TWO

Various Renderings of Methusthosin *in John 2:10*

1. "Drunk freely"
   English Revised Version, 1885
   American Standard Version, 1901
   Moffatt's Translation
   Weymouth's Translation
   Confraternity Revision (Roman Catholic)
   American Bible Union Version
   Young's Translation
   Centenary Translation
   Roman Catholic Version
   Amplified Bible
   Riverside New Testament
   Twentieth Century New Testament
   Revised Standard Version, 1946
   The Bible Reader
   New English Bible
   New American Standard Version
   New Berkeley Version
   Modern Reader's Bible

2. "Well drunk"
   Geneva Bible, 1560
   Bishop's Bible, 1568
   Rheims Bible, 1610 (Roman Catholic)

King James Version
Polyglot Bible
Holy Bible (Robert Aitken)
A New Translation

3. "Drunk deep"
   Williams Translation
   Knox Translation (Roman Catholic)

4. "Had plenty to drink"
   Phillips Translation
   Jerusalem Bible

5. "Ben fullid"
   Wycliffe's Bible, 1380

6. "Drunk largely"
   Living Oracles

7. "Drunk deeply"
   Goodspeed's Translation

8. "Well drank"
   Catholic Family Bible

9. Well supplied
   The New Testament (Rotherham)

10. "Everyone is full"
    The Living Bible

11. "Drunk more than enough"
    Berkeley Version

12. "Drunk a lot"
    Today's English Version

13. "Had enough"
    The Bible in Basic English

14. "Had too much"
    New International Version

15. "Tasted"
    The Holy Bible in Modern English (Fenton)

16. "Have been drinking awhile"
    The New American Bible

17. "Drunk much"
    The New Testament in the language of Today (Beck)

18. "Had their fill"
    New Testament (Kleist and Lilly)

APPENDIX B

TABLE THREE

Change in Alcohol Consumption in Seventeen Countries from Late 1950s to Early 1970s

Country	Dates of Data	Percentage Increase (+) or Decrease (-) in Consumption of:			
		Spirits	Wine	Beer	Total
France	1955–1968	+ 20%	- 18%	+ 3%*	- 9%
Italy	1957–1969	+ 80	- 8	+ 149	+ 1
West Germany	1957–1970	+ 66	+ 85	+ 54	+ 61
Switzerland	1950/55–1966/69	+ 38	+ 11	+ 6*	+ 13
Australia	1955/56–1969	+ 25	+ 45	+ 8	+ 15
Belgium	1956–1967	+ 42	+ 3681	+ 12*	+ 33
New Zealand	1956–1967	- 11	+ 158	+ 13	+ 13

Country	Dates of Data	Percentage Increase (+) or Decrease (-) in Consumption of:			
		Spirits	Wine	Beer	Total
U.S.A.	1958–1971	+42	+45	+20	+32%
Denmark	1956–1969	+115	+49	+44	+54
Canada	1956–1969	-27	+79	+101	+17
United Kingdom	1957–1970	+35	+89	+9	+20
Sweden	1957–1970	-5	+71	+93	+26
Ireland	1955–1970	+65	+103	+29	+41
Netherlands	1956–1969	+31	+186	+137	+83
Finland	1955–1969	-2	+37	+357	+50
Norway	1957–1970	+23	+64	+52	+42
Iceland	1952–1971	+31	+102	+21	+33[1]

* Includes Cider.

1. *Second Special Report*, p. 5, quoting V. Efron, M. Keller, and C. Gurioli, Statistics on Consumption of Alcohol and on Alcoholism, n.p.

TABLE FOUR

Renderings from Various Versions of
Oinon and *Oxos* in
Matthew 27:34, 48; Mark 15:23, 36; and John 19:30

Note: Each rendering is given in the same order as the passages in the heading.

1. English Revised Version
    "wine"
    "vinegar"
    "wine"
    "vinegar"
    "vinegar"

2. American Standard Version
    "wine"
    "vinegar"
    "wine"
    "vinegar"
    "vinegar"

3. King James Version
    "vinegar"
    "vinegar"
    "wine"
    "vinegar"
    "vinegar"

4. Revised Standard Version
    "wine"
    "vinegar"
    "wine"
    "vinegar"
    "vinegar"

5. Moffatt's Translation
   "wine"
   "vinegar"
   "wine"
   "vinegar"
   "vinegar"

6. Concordant Translation
   "wine"
   "vinegar"
   "wine"
   "vinegar"
   "vinegar"

7. Emphatic Diaglott
   "wine"
   "vinegar"
   "wine"
   "vinegar"
   "vinegar"

8. Centenary Translation
   "wine"
   "vinegar"
   "wine"
   "sour wine"
   "vinegar"

9. Berkeley Version
   "wine"
   "vinegar"
   "wine"
   "vinegar"
   "vinegar"

10. Williams Translation
    "wine"
    "vinegar"
    "wine"
    "vinegar"
    "sour wine"

11. Jerusalem Bible
    "wine"
    "vinegar"

"wine"
"vinegar"
"vinegar"

12. Riverside New Testament
"wine"
"sour wine"
"wine"
"sour wine"
"sour wine"

13. Living Bible Paraphrased
"drugged wine"
"sour wine"
"wine"
"sour wine"
"sour wine" (verse 29)

14. New International Version
"wine"
"wine vinegar"
"wine"
"wine vinegar"
"drink" ("wine vinegar" verse 29)

15. New American Standard Bible
"wine"
"sour wine"
"wine"
"sour wine"
"sour wine"

16. Amplified New Testament
"wine"
"vinegar (a sour wine)"
"wine"
"vinegar (a mixture of sour wine and water)"
"vinegar"

17. Phillips Translation
"wine"
"vinegar"
"drugged wine"
"vinegar"
"sour wine"

APPENDIX C

NUMBER ONE

Additional Arguments

The following deductive arguments apply to the material on pages 99–115. The first syllogism is stated as follows:

(1) If drunkenness implies the amount of ethyl alcohol which is consumed in "social" drinking, then persons who are engaged in "social" drinking are drunk.

(2) Drunkenness implies the amount of ethyl alcohol which is consumed in "social" drinking.

(3) Therefore, persons who are engaged in "social" drinking are drunk.

The proof for both propositions (1) and (2) is established in Chapter 3, pages 99–115. Since the argument is stated in valid form and both propositions are true the conclusion (3) irresistibly follows.

Pertaining to the same principle, an additional argument is advanced.

(1) If it is sinful to be drunk, and if persons who are engaged in "social" drinking are drunk, then it is sinful to engage in "social" drinking.

(2) It is sinful to be drunk and persons who are engaged in "social" drinking are drunk.

(3) Therefore, it is sinful to engage in "social" drinking.

In reference to both propositions (1) and (2), it should be observed that there are numerous passages in the Bible which condemn drunkenness, including Habakkuk 2:15, Luke 21:34, Romans 13:13, 1 Corinthians 6:9–10, Galatians 5:19–21, and Ephesians 5:18.

Passages which indicate various evils that are attached to strong drink include Proverbs 20:1; 23:20–21, 29–32, Isaiah 28:1–8, Nahum 1:10, and 1 Corinthians 5:11.

Abundant evidence is given in Chapter 3, pages 99–115, which proves that persons who are engaged in "social" drinking are drunk.

This argument is also stated in valid form and both propositions (1) and (2) are true. Since this is the case, it follows without the possibility of successful refutation that the conclusion (3) is true.

NUMBER TWO

Questions for Consideration

Note: These questions are designed to be asked by those who oppose so-called social drinking to those who consider the action to be acceptable to God.

(1) Do you hold the view that Jesus made alcoholic wine out of water at Cana of Galilee? (cf. John 2:1–11). If so, on what grounds do you free the Lord from violating Proverbs 23:31–32? Did the Lord obey the requirements of this text (Proverbs) at the wedding feast, or did He disregard the teaching of this powerful passage?

(2) Do you consider intoxicating wines of the first century to be as potent as the highly fortified wines of the present day?

(3) Medical scientific experiments have revealed that persons must imbibe larger amounts of ethyl alcohol over a period of time to produce changes in feelings and behavior which they had previously attained with smaller amounts. If you believe that drunkenness is sinful and that such changes in feelings and behavior constitute a stage of drunkenness, do you affirm that such imbibers can now imbibe greater quantities than they formerly could without sinning? If not, for what reason?

(4) If you engage in the imbibing of alcoholic beverages, do you affirm that your marriage has been more wholesome and spiritual-minded since ethyl alcohol has entered your home? If so, how is this the case?

(5) If it is permissible (approved of God) to engage in "social" drinking in various nations *because* such is a custom there, would it not be permissible to engage in such activities as polygamy or canni-

balism in areas where they are customarily practiced? If not, for what reason?

(6) Is it not true that persons sin when they willfully, for no justifiable reason (medicinal, etc.), dull or sedate their intellects, wills, and consciences, thus causing losses of the powers of inhibition?

(7) Do you affirm, since medical science has determined that even an imbiber's weight has something to do with his level of alcohol concentration (the level is greater for lighter persons than it is for heavier persons), that heavier persons may consume more ethyl alcohol before they can be considered as drunk? If not, why not?

(8) If you imbibe ethyl alcohol as a beverage, do you believe that you have lost absolutely no fervor for spiritual activities since you began imbibing? If not, upon what basis do you make this claim?

(9) Upon what basis would you determine intoxication or drunkenness? Do you deny that persons do not know their personal limit of resistance until they imbibe?

(10) If you sanction the imbibing of ethyl alcohol as a *beverage* to *any* degree or under *any* circumstance, in private *isolation* or *otherwise,* do you consider yourself a partaker of the divine nature of God? (2 Peter 1:4). If so, upon what basis do you make the claim?

(11) Can a person who is drunk, become more drunk? If you answer no, how do you explain that which happens to a person who is obviously drunk, and upon additional consumption, loses complete motor control and, perhaps, even falls into a stupor? If you answer yes, and thus admit that a person can become more drunk, how do you conclude that drunkenness is not but a matter of degree?

(12) If persons cannot feel the effect of ethyl alcohol, there is no point in imbibing. If they can, they are mentally impaired to that degree. If this is not the case, why is it not?

(13) Is it permissible (approved of God), if one's influence upon others is the only basis upon which the imbibing of light quantities of alcoholic beverages is to be considered as sinful to so imbibe in an isolated setting? If not, upon what grounds?

(14) Do you affirm that persons can willfully impair their minds for non-medicinal reasons and please God?

(15) Do you affirm that it is permissible (approved of God) for persons to consume poisonous substances or agents for purposes other than medicinal? If so, why?

(16) Do you think that persons can display a better influence upon their children with an alcoholic beverage in their hand? If so, how?

(17) How much ethyl alcohol does it take to create intoxication? If you state that you do *not* know and yet agree that intoxication is sinful, are you not making yourself liable to sin if you imbibe? If you state that you *do* know how much it takes to become intoxicated, but do not hold the view that intoxication is a matter of degree, how did you determine the amount without becoming intoxicated and, thus, committing sin?

(18) If God would not allow Aaronic priests to imbibe intoxicating beverages while serving (Leviticus 10:8–10; cf. Ezekiel 22:26), do you think that He will allow persons of the Christian priesthood (1 Peter 2:9), members of the church, to serve under such conditions? If so, on what basis do you make such a determination?

(19) Is it true that if the intake of intoxicating beverages to the degree which they are imbibed in "social" drinking are harmful to the body, then such intake is sinful? If not, why is this not the case?

(20) Do you affirm that persons can successfully teach others about the Lord and His church while under the influence of alcoholic beverages? If so, how?

(21) Do you sanction the imbibing of beer, whiskey, vodka, tequila, brandy, or any alcoholic beverage other than wine, in so-called moderation? If so, on what grounds?

(22) What, if anything, is worthwhile and edifying about "social" drinking?

(23) Habakkuk pronounced woe upon a person who does the following things: (a) He "giveth his neighbor drink;" (b) he "puttest thy bottle to him;" and (c) he "makest him drunken also" (Habakkuk 2:15). "Social" drinking involves the first two of these and, in the writer's judgment, the third. Do you deny that it involves the first two? If so, on what basis?

(24) Can you sanction the imbibing of ethyl alcohol which has deceived so many persons when the Bible repeatedly warns persons about

the dangers of being deceived? If you can, upon what basis do you so affirm?

(25) Do you advocate the social—the writer does not mean medicinal—usage of other forms of drugs such as codeine, morphine, cocaine, and others? If so, by what reasoning do you establish your view?

(26) Do you affirm that it is permissible (approved of God) for persons to be under the *influence* of ethyl alcohol as a beverage? If so, by what reasoning?

(27) Can persons, while under the influence of ethyl alcohol, bring "into captivity every thought," in order to be obedient to Christ? (2 Corinthians 10:5). If so, how?

(28) Do you think that Christians can imbibe ethyl alcohol as a beverage in so-called moderation without any harm to either their physical, mental, or spiritual selves? If so, how do you condone such based on the grounds of their influence upon those who cannot?

(29) At what degree of consumption of ethyl alcohol as a beverage do persons sin? At what point does drunkenness occur?

(30) Do you think that persons under the influence of intoxicating beverages render themselves incapable of rational thinking? If you do not, why?

(31) When the Son of God comes at the end of time, would you be perfectly willing to meet Him with an alcoholic beverage in your hand and alcohol on your breath? Do you comprehend the significance of this question? Are you prepared to answer it correctly? No *thinking* person would desire to meet the Lord while under the influence of an intoxicating beverage! If you view the matter otherwise, for the sake of your soul and the souls of those whom you will influence, and are now influencing, you should *stop* what you are doing *right now* and begin studying the Bible in regard to alcoholic beverages!

NUMBER THREE

Viticultural History

Grapes

The grapevine has been known from antiquity. It was common among the Canaanites from whom the Israelites borrowed the process of viticulture, the cultivation of grapes. Its home is thought to be the hills of Armenia and around the Caspian Sea. The first biblical reference to the production of grapes may be found in the story of Noah[1] who planted a vineyard on his return from Mount Ararat, where the ark rested.

Grape kernels have been discovered in mummy cases in Egypt, dating from about 2000 B.C. Murals from Egyptian tombs dating even centuries before that time depict the harvesting and pressing of grapes. In antiquity a special variety of dark red grapes with small kernels was referred to as *sorek.*[2] Reference is also made to *gephen sadeh,* a vine of the fields.[3] A wild vine, bearing worthless grapes, was referred to as *gephen nokri.*[4] The ripening grapes, which are called *boser* in some passages and nearly the same term in others,[5] were sour and set the teeth on edge.[6] Because of blight, unhealthy vines often dropped their grapes in this stage.[7]

The time when grapes were ripe varied with local conditions. In the valley of the Jordan and in the district of Tiberius various kinds were

---

1. Gen. 9:20ff.
2. Gen. 49:11; Is. 5:2; Jer. 2:21.
3. 2 Kings 4:39.
4. Jer. 2:21.
5. Is. 18:5; cf. Job 15:33.
6. Ezek. 18:2.
7. Job 15:33.

ripe in June. In the coast plain, the vintage season occurred about the middle of August, while in the mountains it occurred in September. It is mentioned in connection with the feast of tabernacles which took place at that general time.[1]

Palestine, particularly in its hill section, was well suited for the growing of grapes. The valley of Eshcol, named from its bunches of grapes, which often weighed from 10 to15 pounds, produced the large cluster which the two spies carried home between them on a staff.[2] The hills near Jezreel, where Naboth's vineyard was situated, were famous for their vines, as was the area about Ephraim.[3] The Moabite hills of Sibmah,[4] along with those of Heshbon and Elealeh, and Engedi in Judah, were renowned. The *sorek* grew in the hills of Judah,[5] and the valleys of Sorek and Eshcol received their names from these, along with Beth-haccherem, "the house of vines," near Tekoa.[6] The wines of Lebanon[7] and of Helbon, one of the exports from Syria to Tyre,[8] were also well known in antiquity.

Vineyards

Vineyards were often put on very fertile hills or areas which could be reached by the sun from all sides. Some vineyards, however, were in the valleys, such as the valley of Sharon.

Two or three times annually vineyards needed to be cultivated or plowed in order that the top soil might remain loose,[9] and free from weeds or other vegetation. As the vines grew, they were either allowed to run along the ground[10] or were placed on stakes over which the branches were trained.[11] Since much of the area was quite rocky, in

---

1. Deut. 16:13.
2. Num. 13:21–27.
3. Judg. 8:2.
4. Is. 16:8–9; Jer. 48:32.
5. Gen. 49:11.
6. Jer. 6:1.
7. Hos. 14:7.
8. Ezek. 27:18.
9 Is. 5:2, 6; 7:25.
10. Is. 16:8; Ezek. 17:6.
11. Ezek. 19:10–12.

preparing a vineyard, stones both large and small often had to be removed from the soil.[1] To protect the vineyard from wild animals, such as boars and foxes, along with thieves,[2] the area was often fenced with a stone wall, hedge, or a ditch.[3] Hillsides were the most desirable locations.[4] A large vineyard usually had a tower or *purgos* in which those who watched the vineyard stayed,[5] while booths served the same purpose in smaller vineyards.[6]

Winepresses

Winepresses of antiquity usually consisted of two receptacles or vats, set one above the other, each hewn out of a piece of solid rock.[7] The fresh grapes were dumped into the upper vat. A certain amount of juice usually dripped into the lower vat as a natural result of the weight of the grapes upon each other. This was the juice of the ripest and softest of the grapes, which was carefully gathered and kept separate from the juice later pressed out. It was the "sweet wine" *(asis),*[8] or "new wine" *(tirosh).*[9] After this had been gathered, the pressing of the grapes began through the ancient process of treading. Depending upon the size of the vat, one or more men would tramp on the grapes with their bare feet. In this process their feet, legs, and clothing became red with the juice.[10] The juice thus expressed, flowed freely into the lower vat where it was collected in various vessels. Sometimes this juice was preserved in the unfermented state and consumed as *must* or, as would be stated today, grapejuice. Such unfermented wine or *must* was often preserved in jars or bottles.[11]

---

1. Is. 5:2.
2. Ps. 80:13; Ezek. 13:4; Jer. 49:9.
3. Num. 22:24; Mt. 21:33.
4. Is. 5:1; Jer. 31:5; Amos 9:13.
5. Mt. 21:33.
6. Is. 1:8.
7. Joel 3:13; Is. 5:2.
8. Amos 9:13.
9. Prov. 3:10.
10. Gen. 49:11; Is. 63:2–3.
11. Harold N. Moldenke and Alma L. Moldenke, *Plants of the Bible* (Waltham, Mass.: Chronica Botanica Co., 1952), p. 214.

In antiquity, winepresses were usually either in the vineyard or nearby. Most of the harvested grapes which were cut with a *mazmerah*, or pruning hook,[1] were taken to the presses in baskets by girls or children. There they were either spread out for several days for the purpose of increasing the amount of sugar and decreasing the amount of water in the grapes, or they were immediately deposited into the presses. The juice which flowed at the beginning of the process, especially that produced solely by the weight of the grapes when piled up, was kept separated from that which was thoroughly trodden with the bare feet. Such juice was of much better quality or grade than the latter. The Hebrew term employed to indicate the treading process was the ordinary word for "walk."[2] Often the treaders, both men and women, would hold to cords attached to a roof over the upper portion of the press. Their clothing and feet were dyed with the "blood of the grape."[3] As they worked they shouted and sang vintage songs, fragments of which are thought to be preserved.[4] The shout was referred to as the *hedad*. After the treading, the husks and stalks were piled in the middle of the vat and pressed by means of a wooden beam, one end of which was attached to a wall of the vat.

In regard to Hebrew winepresses, it is evident from archaeological specimens and from detailed references in the Mishna that there might be as many as four vats or as few as one. The purpose of a third vat was to allow the *must* to settle and clarify in the second before allowing it to pass into the third. When only one vat was used, it may have served either as a press vat, in which case the *must* was at once transferred to earthen jars, or as a wine vat to receive the *must* after the grapes had been pressed in a wooden trough. The two-part press, which seems to have been in general use, consisted of the upper vat or *purah*, referred to in the Septuagint as *prolenion*, or winepress proper.[5] From the bottom of the upper section a pipe or *zinnor* led to the lower receptacle or *yekeb*, referred to in the Septuagint as *hupolenion*.[6] In area, the upper vat was

---

1. Is. 2:4.
2. Neh. 13:15; Job 24:11; Is. 16:10.
3. Is. 63:3; Jer. 25:30; 48:33; Lam. 1:15.
4. Is. 16:10; Jer. 25:30; 48:33; cf. Is. 27:2; 65:8.
5. Is. 63:3; 5:2.
6. Is. 16:10; Hag. 2:17; Zech. 14:10; Mk. 12:1.

usually about twice as large as the lower, while the latter portion was much deeper.

The presses were cavities either hollowed out of rock or built on the ground and lined with masonry and cement.[1] They were referred to as *gath*[2] or, in the Septuagint, *lenos,* which is also used to represent *yekeb* in some passages, the root meaning of which is "to excavate." The distinction between the *gath* and the *yekeb* is not always observed by Old Testament writers, *yekeb* being occasionally used to denote the press vat[3] while either may be used by metonymy for the entire winepress. The term *purah,* which may be rendered "winetrough," is used as a synonym both of *gath*[4] and *of yekeb.*[5] The two vats, *gath* and *yekeb,* are mentioned together only in ". . . the winepress *(gath)* is full, the vats *(yekeb)* overflow . . .,"[6] thus indicating that the upper vat is full of grapes and the lower vat is overflowing with *must.*

By New Testament times, *yekeb* as the name of the wine vat had become almost, if not entirely, obsolete, its place being supplied by *bor* or, according to the Mishna, *passim.* The term *gath,* however, continued to be employed for the press vat.[7] It is interesting to note that the winepress is often referred to by the prophets as a figure typifying the judgment of God on sin.[8]

Commerce

Although a large part of the grape harvest was used in making wine, a considerable portion was used in making a kind of honey or *dibs* by the expressed juice which was boiled into a syrup. The *dibs* or *debash,* as it was called in Hebrew, was a commercial article of export from

---

1. Mt. 21:33.
2. Judg. 6:11.
3. Is. 16:10; Job 24:11.
4. Is. 63:3.
5. Hag. 2:16. See Appendix A, Table One, pp. 196–199.
6. Joel 3:13.
7. Neh. 13:15; Lam. 1:15; Is. 63:2.
8. Is. 63:3; Lam. 1:15; Rev. 14:20.

Palestine to Tyre, and sent by Jacob to Egypt.[1] It was also used as food in Palestine, as well as for a common sweetener of pies and cakes.[2]

From the best grapes, which were dried in the sun into raisins, cakes or *zimmuk* were compressed. The Old Testament refers to Abigail who brought a hundred such cakes to David, who refreshed the fainting Egyptian with two cakes. Reference is also made to Ziba, who brought similar cakes to David.[3]

Multiple documents reveal that viticulture developed into an important agricultural activity in antiquity, with the export and trade of grape products becoming a commercial enterprise of considerable size.

1. Ezek. 27:17; Gen. 43:11.
2. Lev. 2:11.
3. 1 Sam. 25:18; 30:12; 2 Sam. 16:1; 1 Chron. 12:40.

INDEX

Index of Scripture Citations

Note: (1) Verses followed by numbers enclosed in brackets, indicate two or more usages on a particular page. (2) Verses in Appendices A and B are not recorded in the index.

16. Psalms

1:1–3	140
19:7	140
22:5	54
23:5	54
36:8	54
40:8	140
60:3	28
69:21	78
75:5	54
75:8	36
75:10	54
78:1	140
80:13	218
94:20	177
102:9	35
104:15	28, 133
119	140

17. Proverbs

3:1–6	140
3:5–6	163
3:10	30, 32, 218
4:17	28
4:23	114
5:19	54
9:2	35
9:2–5	29
9:5	35
14:34	176
20:1	12, 28, 133, 193, 211
22:6	137
23:20	68
23:20–21	91, 134, 211
23:21	133
23:29	36
23:29–32	28, 211

II. The Septuagint Translation

A. Genesis

| 42:34 | 54 |

B. Job

| 32:19 | 66 |

C. Psalms

22:5	54
36:8	54
75:5	54
75:10	54

D. Proverbs

| 5:19 | 54 |
| 23:20 | 68 |

E. Isaiah

| 49:26 | 66 |

F. Jeremiah

| 38:14 | 54 |

BIBLIOGRAPHY

Abbot, Lyman. *A Life of Christ.* 2nd ed. New York: Harper and Brothers, 1882.

Abbott-Smith, G. *A Manual Greek Lexicon of the New Testament.* New York: Charles Scribner's Sons, 1921.

"Alcohol Affects Unborn Babies." Cookeville, Tennessee: *The Herald-Citizen,* 26 September 1979, p. 7.

"Alcohol Danger for Youths Told." Memphis: *The Commercial Appeal,* 25 April 1977, p. 3.

Alcohol: Some Questions and Answers. Washington, D.C.: Government Printing Office, 1981.

Alcohol: Its Action on the Human Organism. London: His Majesty's Stationery Office, n.d.

"Alcoholism: Another Problem for Aging Americans." Nashville: *The Tennessean,* 9 November 1980, p. 6A.

Alford, Henry. *The Greek Testament.* vol. 1. London: Rivingtons, 1861.

Anstadt, P. "Communion Wine." *The Quarterly Review of the Evangelical Lutheran Church* 16 (January 1886):1–42.

"Are You Fit to Drive?" Journal of the American Medical Association. np.: n.p., 1960.

Aristotle. *Meteorologica.* Translated by H. D. P. Lee. Loeb Classical Library. Cambridge: Harvard University Press, 1952.

Arndt, William Frederick, and Gingrich, Felix Wilbur. *A Greek-English Lexicon of the New Testament.* 4th ed. Chicago: University of Chicago Press, 957.

Athenaeus. *The Deipnosophists.* Translated by Charles Burton Gulick. Loeb Classical Library. Cambridge: Harvard University Press, 1951.

Bacon, Margaret, and Jones, Mary Brush. *Teenage Drinking.* New York: Crowell, 1968.

Bailey, D. "Some Undesirable Drug-Alcohol Interaction." *Journal on Alcoholism* 9 (1974):62–68.

Barnes, Albert. *Matthew and Mark.* Notes on the New Testament. vol. 1. London: Blackie and Son, n.d.

————. *Isaiah.* Notes on the Old Testament. vol. 1. Edinburgh: Gall and Englis, 1845; reprinted. Grand Rapids: Baker Book House, 1950.

————. *Thessalonians, Timothy, Titus, and Philemon.* Notes on the New Testament. vol. 8. London: Blackie and Son, n.d.

Bennett, Ivan L., Jr. "Disorders Caused by Venoms, Bites, and Stings." In *Harrison's Principles of Internal Medicine.* Edited by Maxwell M. Wintrobe et al. New York: McGraw-Hill Book Co., 1970.

Benzinger, Immanuel. "Wine, Hebrew." In *New Schaff-Herzog Encyclopedia of Religious Knowledge,* 12:382–83. Edited by Samuel Macauley Jackson. Grand Rapids: Baker Book House, 1957.

Berry, George Ricker. *Classic Greek Dictionary.* Chicago: Follett Publishing Co., 1962.

Berry, R. E., Jr.; Boland, J. P.; Smart, C. N.; and Kanak, J. R. *The Economic Costs of Alcohol Abuse / 1975.* Draft Report Prepared for National Institute on Alcohol Abuse and Alcoholism, 1977.

Bevan, William Latham. "Wine." In *Smith's Dictionary of the Bible,* 4:3541–45. Edited by Horatio Balch Hackett. Boston: Houghton, Mifflin, and Co., 1890.

Beverage Alcohol: What Does It Do to You? Nashville: United Tennessee League, n.d.

Bjerver, K., and Goldberg, L. "Effects of Alcohol Ingestion on Driving Ability." *Quarterly Journal of Studies on Alcohol* 11 (1950):1–30.

Blees, Robert A. *Counseling with Teen-Agers.* Successful Pastoral Counseling Series. Englewood Cliffs, New Jersey: Prentice-Hall, 1965.

Block, Marvin A. *Alcohol and Alcoholism.* Belmont, Calif.: Wadsworth, 1970.

Bloomfield, Samuel Thomas. *Greek New Testament with English Notes.* 2 vols. London: Longman, Brown, Green, and Longmans, 1855.

Boak, E. R. *A History of Rome to 565 A.D.* New York: Macmillan Co., 1955.

Bogan, J., and Smith, H. "Analytical Investigation of Barbiturate Poisoning— Description of Methods and a Survey of Results." *Journal of Forensic Science* 7 (1967):37–45.

Bogen, Emil, and Hisey, Lehmann. *What about Alcohol?* Los Angeles: Angelus Press, n.d.

Boles, Henry Leo. *A Commentary on the Gospel According to Matthew.* Nashville: Gospel Advocate Co., 1952.

————. "The Kind of Wine in the Lord's Supper." *Gospel Advocate* 110 (17 October 1968):664.

————. "The Wines of the Bible." *Gospel Advocate* 75 (23 February 1933): 178.

Bozeman, Estelle. *Scientific Answers.* New York: Signal Press, 1947.

Braucht, G. Nicholas; Follingstad, Diane; Brakarsh, Daniel; and Berry, K. L. "Drug Education: A Review of Goals, Approaches and Effectiveness, and a Paradigm for Evaluation." *Quarterly Journal of Studies on Alcohol* 34 (December 1973):1279–92.

Brecher, Edward M. *Licit and Illicit Drugs.* Boston: Little, Brown and Co., 1972.

Broadus, John A. *Commentary on the Gospel of Matthew.* Philadelphia: American Baptist Publication Society, 1886.

Brown, Francis; Driver, Samuel Rolles; and Briggs, Charles. *A Hebrew and English Lexicon of the Old Testament.* 8th ed. Oxford: Clarendon Press, 1976.

Bruce, Alexander Balmain. "The Synoptic Gospels." In *Expositors Greek Testament,* 1:328. Edited by W. Robertson Nicoll. Grand Rapids: Wm. B. Eerdmans Publishing Co., 1976.

Bullinger, William Ethelbert. *A Critical Lexicon and Concordance to the English and Greek New Testament.* London: Samuel Bagster and Sons, Limited, 1969.

Bumstead, Horace. "The Biblical Sanction for Wine." *Bibliotheca Sacra* 38 (January 1881):47–116.

Burford, R.; French, I. W.; and Leblanc, A. E. "The Combined Effects of Alcohol and Common Psychoactive Drugs I. Studies on Human Pursuit Tracking Capability." In *Alcohol, Drugs and Traffic Safety.* Edited by S. Israelstam and S. Lambert. Toronto: Addiction Research Foundation of Ontario, 1975.

Cahalan, D.; Cisin, I. H.; and Crossley, H. M. *American Drinking Practices: A National Study of Drinking Behavior and Attitudes.* New Brunswick, New Jersey: Rutgers Centers of Alcohol Studies, 1969.

Cato, *De Re Rustica.* Translated by William Davis Hooper. Loeb Classical Library. Cambridge: Harvard University Press, 1960.

Clarke, Adam. *Genesis to Deuteronomy.* A Commentary and Critical Notes. vol. 1. New York: T. Mason and G. Lane, 1837; reprint ed. New York: Abingdon Press, nd.

———. *Matthew to Acts.* A Commentary and Critical Notes. vol. 5. New York: T. Mason and G. Lane, 1838; reprint ed. New York: Abingdon Press, n.d.

———. *Romans to Revelation.* A Commentary and Critical Notes. vol. 6. T. Mason and G. Lane, 1837; reprint ed. New York: Abingdon Press, n.d.

Clinebell, Howard J., Jr. *Understanding and Counseling the Alcoholic.* Revised and enlarged ed. Nashville: Abingdon Press, 1968.

Coffman, James Burton. *Commentary on John.* Austin: Firm Foundation Publishing House, 1974.

Cohen, Peter J., and Dripps, Robert D. "Signs and Stages of Anesthesia." In *The Pharmacological Basis of Therapeutics*. Edited by Louis S. Goodman and Alfred Gilman. London: Collier-Macmillan, Limited, 1970.

Columella. *De Re Rustica*. Translated by E. S. Forster and Edward H. Heffner. Loeb Classical Library. Cambridge: Harvard University Press, 1955.

Come, Arnold Bruce. *Drinking, A Christian Position*. Philadelphia: Westminster Press, 1964.

Copi, Irving Marmer. *Introduction to Logic*. 4th ed. New York: Macmillan Co., 1972.

Creighton, James Edwin. *An Introductory Logic*. 5th ed. New York: Macmillan Co., 1926.

Cremer, Hermann. *Biblio-Theological Lexicon of New Testament Greek*. Edinburgh: T. and T. Clark, 1872.

Davis, H. S.; Collins, W. F.; Randt, C. T.; and Dillon, W. H. "Effects of Anesthetic Agents on Evoked Central Nervous System Responses: Gaseous Agents." *Anesthesiology* 18 (1957):634–42.

Dayton, P. G., and Perel, J. M. "Physiological and Physicochemical Bases of Drug Interaction in Man." *Annual of New York Academy of Science* 179 (1972):67–87.

Deaver, Roy Clifton. "Establishing Bible Authority." *Harding Graduate School of Religion Lectures*. Nashville: Gospel Advocate Co., 1971.

De Kruif, Paul, *Microbe Hunters*. New York: Harcourt, Brace and Co., n.d.

Delling, Gerhard. "Teleios." In *Theological Dictionary of the New Testament*, 8:74. Edited by Gerhard Friedrich. Grand Rapids: Wm. B. Eerdmans Publishing Co., 1972.

Dixon, W. E. *Pharmacology*. 6th ed. n.p.: n.p., 1935.

"Doctors Debunk Liquor as an Rx." Nashville, *The Tennessean,* 16 November 1979, n.p.

Douglas, Roy. Surgeon gynecologist in Jackson-Madison General Hospital, Jackson, Tennessee. Interview, 31 January 1978.

Drew, C. G.; Colquhoun, W. P.; and Long, Hazel A. "The Effects of Small Doses of Alcohol on a Skill Resembling Driving." *Traffic Safety Review* 3 (1959):1–11.

Driver, Samuel Rolles. *The Books of Joel and Amos*. Cambridge Bible for Schools and Colleges. Cambridge: University Press, 1898.

"Drug." In *Webster's New Collegiate Dictionary,* p. 350. Edited by Henry Bosley Woolf. Springfield, Mass.: G. and C. Merriam Co., 1973.

Dunning, George Thomas. *Alcohol and the Christian Ethic*. Wallington, Great Britain: Religious Education Press, Ltd., 1958.

Easton, Burton Scott. "Wine." In *International Standard Bible Encyclopedia,* 5:3086–88. Edited by James Orr. Grand Rapids: Wm. B. Eerdmans Publishing Co., 1939.

Edersheim, Alfred. *The Life and Times of Jesus the Messiah.* 2 vols. Grand Rapids: Wm. B. Eerdmans Publishing Co., 1962.

Efron, V.; Keller, M.; and Gurioli, C. *Statistics on Consumption of Alcohol and on Alcoholism.* New Brunswick, New Jersey: Rutgers Center of Alcohol Studies, 1974.

Elliott, C. J. *Numbers.* A Bible Commentary for English Readers. Edited by Charles John Ellicott. New York: Cassell and Co., n.d.

Emerson, Haven. *Alcohol: A Food, a Drug, a Poison.* Newark, New Jersey: Foundation for Narcotic Research and Information, Inc., n.d.

――――. *Alcohol and Man.* New York: Macmillan Co., n.d.

――――. *Alcohol: Its Effects on Man.* New York: Appleton-Century Co., nd.

Encyclopaedia Britannica, 1959 ed. s.v. "Drunkenness," by Clarence Weinert Muehlberger, p. 683.

Encyclopaedia Britannica, 1959 ed. s.v. "Fusel Oil," by Donald Guyer Zink, pp. 952–53.

Encyclopaedia Britannica, 1959 ed. s.v. "Hemp," by A. H. Wright, pp. 421–22.

Encyclopaedia Britannica, 1959 ed. s.v. "Hop," by Frank Rabak, pp. 734–36.

Encyclopaedia Britannica, 1959 ed. s.v. "Methyl Alcohol," by Donald Guyer Zink, p. 362.

Encyclopaedia Britannica, 1959 ed. s.v. "Papaya," by Wilson Popenoe, p. 229.

Encyclopaedia Britannica, 1959 ed. s.v. "Perfumes," by William A. Poucher, pp. 505–507.

Encyclopaedia Britannica, 1959 ed. s.v. "Poison," by William Henry Willcox and John Glaister, pp. 117–23.

Encyclopaedia Britannica, 1959 ed. s.v. "Propyl Alcohols," p. 591.

Encyclopaedia Britannica, 1959 ed. s.v. "Psychosis," by Henry W. Broslin, pp. 721–23.

Encyclopaedia Britannica, 1959 ed. s.v. "Resins," by Edward L. Kropa, pp. 210–12.

Encyclopaedia Britannica, 1959 ed. s.v. "Rum," by John George Noel Gaskin, p. 635.

Encyclopaedia Britannica, 1959 ed. s.v. "Whiskey," by Francis G. H. Tate, pp. 569–70.

Epstein, Isidore, ed. *The Babylonian Talmud.* London: Soncino Press, 1948.

Family Health Guide and Medical Encyclopedia, 1970 ed. s.v. "Alcohol," p. 21.

Family Health Guide and Medical Encyclopedia, 1970 ed. s.v. "Narcotic," p. 742.

Family Health Guide and Medical Encyclopedia, 1970 ed. s.v. "Why You Need a Balanced Diet," pp. 34–36.

Fenton, Ferrar. "The Bible and Wine." In *Paul's Letters to Timothy and Titus,* pp. 301–31. Edited by Don De Welt. Joplin, Missouri: College Press, 1961.

Ferguson, Everett. "Wine as a Table-Drink in the Ancient World." *Restoration Quarterly* 13 (1970):141–53.

Field, Leon C. *Oinos: A Discussion of the Bible Wine Question.* New York: Phillips and Hunt, 1883.

First Special Report to the U.S. Congress on Alcohol and Health. By Elliott L. Richardson, Chairman. Washington, D.C.: Government Printing Office, 1971.

Fisher, Irving. *Prohibition at Its Worst.* New York: Macmillan Co., n.d.

Fleming, Robert E. "On Certain Medical Aspects of Alcoholism." *Bulletin of the Academy of Medicine of New Jersey* 1 (15 June 1956):14–15.

Forbes, R. J. *Studies in Ancient Technology.* 3 vols. Leiden: E. J. Brill, 1955.

Forney, R. B., and Hughes, F. W. "Effects of Caffeine and Alcohol on Performance under Stress of Audio-Feedback." *Quarterly Journal of Studies on Alcohol* 26 (1965):206–12.

Fort, Joel. *Alcohol: Our Biggest Drug Problem.* New York: McGraw-Hill Book Co., 1973.

Foster, R. C. *Studies in the Life of Christ.* vol. 1. Cincinnati: F. L. Rowe, Publisher, n.d.

Fourth Special Report to the U.S. Congress on Alcohol and Health. By Ernest P. Noble, ed. Washington, D.C.: Government Printing Office, 1981.

French, J. D. "The Reticular Formation." In *Handbook of Physiology.* vol. 2. Edited by H. W. Magoun. Washington, D.C.: American Physiological Society, 1960.

Gantry, Susan Nadler. "Gettin' Drunk on Saturday Night." Nashville 6 (November 1978):46.

"Geraniol." In *Webster's New Collegiate Dictionary,* p. 482. Edited by Henry Bosley Woolf. Springfield, Mass.: G. and C. Merriam Co., 1973.

Gerard, Donald L. "Intoxication and Addiction." In *Drinking and Intoxication,* pp. 27–34. Edited by Raymond Gerald McCarthy. Glencoe, Illinois: Free Press, 1959.

Gesenius, Friedrich Heinrich Wilhelm. *Hebrew and Chaldee Lexicon to the Old Testament Scriptures.* Translated by Samuel Prideaux Tregelles. n.p., 1857; reprint ed. Grand Rapids: Wm. B. Eerdmans Publishing Co., 1957.

Gibbon, Edward. *The History of the Decline and Fall of the Roman Empire.* 8 vols. Philadelphia: Porter and Coates, n.d.

Globetti, G. "A Survey of Teenage Drinking in Two Mississippi Communities." *Preliminary Report* 3 (1964):3.

Goldberg, L. "Effects of Ethanol in the Central Nervous System." In *Alcohol and Alcoholism.* Edited by R. E. Popham. Toronto: University Press, 1970.

Greenberg, Leon A. "Alcohol in the Body." In *Drinking and Intoxication,* pp. 7–13. Edited by Raymond Gerald McCarthy. Glencoe, Illinois: Free Press, 1959.

————. "The Concentration of Alcohol in the Blood and Its Significance." *Alcohol, Science and Society: Twenty-Nine Lectures with Discussions as Given at the Yale Summer School of Alcoholic Studies.* Westport, Conn.: n.p., 1945.

Guthrie, Donald. *The Pastoral Epistles.* Grand Rapids: Wm. B. Eerdmans Publishing Co., 1957.

Hanlon, John J., and McHose, Elizabeth. *Design for Health.* 2nd ed. Philadelphia: Lea and Febiger, 1971.

Harger, Rolla N. "The Response of the Body to Different Concentrations of Alcohol: Chemical Tests for Intoxication." In *Alcohol Education for Classroom and Community,* pp. 90–103. Edited by Raymond Gerald McCarthy. New York: McGraw-Hill Book Co., 1964.

————. "The Sojourn of Alcohol in the Body." In *Alcohol Education for Classroom and Community,* pp. 77–89. Edited by Raymond Gerald McCarthy. New York: McGraw-Hill Book Co., 1964.

Hatch, Edwin, and Redpath, Henry A. *A Concordance to the Septuagint and Other Greek Versions of the Old Testament.* 2 vols. Graz: Akademische Druck-u Verlagsanstalt, 1954.

Haynes, Wilson Albinus. *Beautiful Word Pictures of the Epistle to the Ephesians.* Caney, Kansas: Busy Man's Bible Co., 1911.

Heidland, Hans Wolfgang. "Oxos." In *Theological Dictionary of the New Testament,* 5:288–89. Edited by Gerhard Kittel and Gerhard Friedrich. Grand Rapids: Wm. B. Eerdmans Publishing Co., 1967.

Henry, Matthew. *Genesis to Joshua.* Commentary on the Whole Bible. vol. 1. New York: Fleming H. Revell Co., n.d. Hericourt, J. *The Social Diseases.* London: Routledge, 1920.

Herndon, E. W. "Wine in the Lord's Supper." *Christian Quarterly Review* 5 (July 1886):329.

Hill, Albert. "Moderate Drinking." *Gospel Defender* 8 (March 1967):1.

————. "Moderate Drinking (No. 2)." *Gospel Defender* 8 (April 1967):1.

Hobbs, Herschel H. *An Exposition of the Gospel of John.* Grand Rapids: Baker Book House, 1968.

Holman, Mrs. T. P. "Communion Wine." *Gospel Advocate* 31 (24 July 1889):473.

———. "Wines of the Ancients and of the Bible." *Gospel Advocate* 27 (3 June 1885):342.

———. "Wines of the Bible and of the Ancients." *Gospel Advocate* 27 (27 May 1885):326.

The Holy Bible; American Standard Version. New York: Thomas Nelson and Sons, 1901.

The Holy Bible; King James Version. New York: Oxford University Press, 1919.

The Holy Bible; New Berkeley Version in Modern English. Grand Rapids: Zondervan Publishing House, 1959.

The Holy Bible; New English Bible. New York: Oxford University Press, 1961.

The Holy Bible; Phillips Translation. New York: Macmillan Co., 1964.

The Holy Bible; Septuagint Version. Grand Rapids: Zondervan Publishing House, 1970.

The Holy Bible; Williams Translation. Chicago: Moody Press, 1963.

Homer. *Odyssey.* Translated by Samuel Butler. Roslyn, New York: Walter J. Black, Inc., 1944.

Horton, David. "Alcohol, Science, and Society." *Quarterly Journal of Studies on Alcohol 15* (1954):158.

Hovey, Alvah. "Shekar and Leaven in Mosaic Offerings." *The Old Testament Student* 6 (September 1886):16.

How to Talk to Your Teenager about Drinking and Driving. Washington, D.C.: Government Printing Office, 1981.

Hughes, F. W. and Forney, R. B. "Dextro-Amphetamines, Ethanol and Dextro-Amphetamine-Ethanol Combinations of Performance of Human Subjects Stressed with Delayed Auditory Feedback (DAF)." *Psychopharmacologia* 6 (1964):234–38.

Humphrey, A. E. *The Epistles to Timothy and Titus.* Cambridge: University Press, 1901.

Ivy, A. C. "Alcohol as a Depressant." *Twentieth Century Christian* 18 (January 1956):20–21.

Jackson, Douglas. *Stumbling Block.* Nashville: Parthenon Press, 1960.

Jaffe, Jerome H. "Drug Addiction and Drug Abuse." In *The Pharmacological Basis of Therapeutics.* Edited by Louis S. Goodman and Alfred Gilman. London: Collier-Macmillan, Limited, 1970.

Jeffcoat, William Dawson. "Christian, Abstain from Social Drinking!" *The Spiritual Sword* 4 (January 1973):20–23.

———. "The Case against Social Drinking." *Gospel Advocate* 119 (3 February 1977):65, 71–72.

Jellinek, E. M. *The Disease Concept of Alcoholism*. New Haven, Conn.: Hillhouse Press, 1960.

Jellinek, E. M., and McFarland, R. A. "Analysis of Psychological Experiments on the Effects of Alcohol." *Quarterly Journal of Studies on Alcohol* 1 (1940):361.

Jenkins, Dan. "Small Matters." *The Shell Street Sower* 1(26 October 1980):2.

Jessor, R.; Graves, T. D.; Hanson, R. C.; and Jessor, S. L. *Society, Personality, and Deviant Behavior: A Study of a Tri-Ethnic Community*. New York: Holt, Rinehart, and Winston, 1968.

Jessor, R., and Jessor, S. L. *Problem Drinking in Youth: Personality, Social, and Behavioral Antecedents and Correlates*. Boulder, Colorado: Institute of Behavioral Science, 1973.

Johnson, L. *Drugs and American Youth*. Ann Arbor: University of Michigan Institute for Social Research, 1973.

"John the Baptist." In *The New Schaff-Herzog Encyclopedia of Religious Knowledge,* 6:207–208. Edited by Samuel Macauley Jackson. Grand Rapids: Baker Book House, 1953.

Jones, Kenneth L.; Shainberg, Louis W.; and Byer, Curtis O. *Drugs and Alcohol*. 2nd ed. New York: Harper and Row, Publishers, 1969.

Jones, R. W, and Helrich. A. R. "Treatment of Alcoholism by Physicians in Private Practice: A National Survey." *Quarterly Journal of Studies on Alcohol* 33 (1972):117–31.

Josephus, Flavius. *Antiquities.* Loeb Classical Library. Cambridge: Harvard University Press, 1965.

Journal of American Medical Association. n.p.: n.p., 11 July 1908.

Joyce, C. R. B.; Edgecombe, P. C.; Kennard, D. A.; Weatherall, M.; and Woods, D. P. "Potentiation of Phenobarbitone of Effects of Ethyl Alcohol on Human Behavior." *Journal of Mental Science* 105 (1959):51–60.

Kalant, H. "Some Recent Physiological and Biochemical Investigations on Alcohol and Alcoholism." *Quarterly Journal of Studies on Alcohol* 23 (1962):52–93.

Keller, John E. *Ministering to Alcoholics*. Minneapolis: Augsburg Publishing House, 1966.

Keller, M., and Gurioli, C. *Statistics on Consumption of Alcohol and on Alcoholism*. New Brunswick, New Jersey: Rutgers Center of Alcohol Studies, 1976.

Keller, Mark, and McCormick, Mairi. *A Dictionary of Words about Alcohol*. New Brunswick, New Jersey: Publications Division, Rutgers Center of Alcohol Studies. 1968.

Kennedy, Archibald Robert Stirling. "Wine and Strong Drink." In *Encyclopaedia Biblica,* 4:5306–22. Edited by Thomas Kelly Cheyne and John Sutherland Black. London: Adam and Charles Black, 1903.

Kent, Homer Austin, Jr. *The Pastoral Epistles.* Chicago: Moody Press, 1958.

King, Albion Roy. *Basic Information on Alcohol.* Washington, D.C.: Narcotics Education, Inc., 1964.

Kissin, B. "Interactions of Ethyl Alcohol and Others Drugs." In *The Biology of Alcoholism.* vol. 3. *Clinical Pathology.* Edited by B. Kissin and H. Begleiter. New York: Plenum Press, 1974.

Lange, John Peter. *Commentary on the Holy Scriptures: Matthew.* Grand Rapids: Zondervan Publishing House, n.d.

Lees, Frederick R., and Burns, Dawson. *Temperance Bible Commentary.* London: n.p., 1870.

Lees, Frederick R. "Wine." In *A Cyclopaedia of Biblical Literature,* 2:950–56. Edited by John Kitto. Edinburgh: Adam and Charles Black, n.d.

————. "Wine." In *Popular and Critical Bible Encyclopedia and Scriptural Dictionary,* 3:1724–26. Edited by Samuel Fallows. Chicago: Howard Severance Co., 1914.

Lenski, Richard C. H. *The Interpretation of St. Matthew's Gospel.* Minneapolis: Augsburg Publishing House, 1943.

Liddell, Henry George, and Scott, Robert. *A Greek-English Lexicon.* New York: Harper and Brothers, Publishers, 1896; reprint ed. Oxford: Clarendon Press, 1940.

Lipscomb, David. "Bible Wines." *Gospel Advocate* 27 (24 June 1885):386.

Lisansky, Edith S. "Psychological Effects." In *Drinking and Intoxication,* pp. 18–25. Edited by Raymond Gerald McCarthy. Glencoe, Illinois: Free Press, 1959.

————. "The Psychological Effects of Alcohol." In *Alcohol Education for Classroom and Community,* pp. 104–21. Edited by Raymond Gerald McCarthy. New York: McGraw-Hill Book Co., 1964.

Lloyd-Jones, David Martyn. *Life in the Spirit.* Grand Rapids: Baker Book House, 1974.

Lockyer, Herbert. *All the Men of the Bible.* Grand Rapids: Zondervan Publishing House, 1958.

Lolli, G.; Serianni, E.; Golder, G. M.; and Luzzatto-Fegiz, P. *Alcohol in Italian Culture: Food and Wine in Relation to Sobriety Among Italians and Italian-Americans.* New Brunswick, New Jersey: Rutgers Center of Alcohol Studies, 1958.

Lucia, Salvatore Pablo, ed. *Alcohol and Civilization.* New York: McGraw-Hill Book Co., 1963.

Luck, G. Coleman. "Wine." In *Wycliffe Bible Dictionary,* 2:1812–13. Edited by Charles F. Pfeiffer, Howard Frederic Vos, and John Rea. Chicago: Moody Press, 1975.

"Lupulin." In *Oxford Universal Dictionary on Historical Principles,* p. 1178. 3rd ed. Edited by C. T. Onions. Oxford: Clarendon Press, 1944.

Lythgoe, Herman D. *New England Journal of Medicine.* n.p.: np., n.d.

McCarthy, Raymond Gerald, and Douglass, Edgar M. *Alcohol and Social Responsibility: A New Educational Approach.* New York: Thomas Y. Crowell Co., 1949.

McCarthy, Raymond Gerald, ed. *Drinking and Intoxication.* Glencoe, Illinois: Free Press, 1959.

McCluggage, Martson M.; Baur, E. Jackson; Warrier, Charles K.; and Clark, Carrell D. "Summary of Essential Findings in the Kansas Study." In *Drinking and Intoxication,* pp. 211–18. Edited by Raymond Gerald McCarthy. New Haven, Conn.: College and University Press, 1959.

McGarvey, John William. *Matthew and Mark.* The New Testament Commentary. vol. 1. Delight, Arkansas: Gospel Light Publishing Co., nd.

McGarvey, John William, and Pendleton, Philip Y. *The Fourfold Gospel.* Cincinnati: Standard Publishing Foundation, n.d.

Maddox, G. L., and McCall, B. C. *Drinking Among Teenagers: A Sociological Interpretation of Alcohol Use by High School Students.* New Brunswick, New Jersey: Rutgers Center of Alcohol Studies, 1964.

Maisel, Albert Q. "Alcohol and Your Brain." *Reader's Digest* 96 (June 1970):65–69.

Malanga, Sandra C. *The Illness Called Alcoholism.* Monroe, Wisconsin: American Medical Association, 1973.

Marshall, Alfred. *The Interlinear Greek-English New Testament: Nestle Greek Text with a Literal English Translation.* London: Samuel Bagster and Sons, Limited, 1958.

"Medical Experts Back Alcohol Warning." Memphis, *The Commercial Appeal,* 1 February 1978, p. 20.

Menue, F. R. "Acute Methyl Alcohol Poisoning." *Archives of Pathology* 26 (1938):79–92.

Meyer, Heinrich August Wilhelm. *The Epistles to the Corinthians.* Meyer's Commentary on the New Testament. New York: Funk and Wagnalls, Publishers, 1884.

———. *The Epistle to the Romans.* Meyer's Commentary on the New Testament. New York: Funk and Wagnalls, Publishers, 1884.

Michelmore, Peter. "Could They Forgive Their Son's Killer?" *Reader's Digest* 128 (May 1986):136–40.

Milgram, Gail Gleason. "A Descriptive Analysis of Alcohol Education Materials." *Journal of Studies on Alcohol* 36 (March 1975):416–21.

Mill, John Stuart. *System of Logic.* n.p.: np., n.d.

Miller, Derek. *Adolescence: Psychology, Psychopathology, and Psychotherapy.* New York: Jason Aronson, Publisher, 1974.

Miller, T. Rothrock. Donahue Television Program, 24 November, 1980.

Milligan, Robert. *Scheme of Redemption.* St. Louis: Bethany Press. reprint ed. 1962.

Mills, Dorothy. *The Book of the Ancient Romans.* New York: G. P. Putnam's Sons, 1937.

Moldenke, Harold N., and Moldenke, Alma L. *Plants of the Bible.* Waltham, Mass.: Chronica Botanica Co., Publishers, 1952.

Moore, Dunlop. "The Bible Wine Question." *Presbyterian Review* 2 (January 1881):80–113.

"Mother's Alcohol Use Linked to Brain Damage in Infants." Nashville, *The Tennessean,* 1 March 1981, p. 17A.

Myerson, A. "Alcoholism: The Role of Social Ambivalence." In *Drinking and Intoxication,* pp. 306–12. Edited by Raymond Gerald McCarthy. Glencoe, Illinois: Free Press, 1959.

"Narcosis." In *Oxford Universal Dictionary on Historical Principles,* p. 1309. 3rd ed. Edited by C. T. Onions. Oxford: Clarendon Press, 1944.

"Narcotic," In *Oxford Universal Dictionary on Historical Principles,* p. 1309. 3rd ed. Edited by C. T. Onions. Oxford: Clarendon Press, 1944.

Newman, H. W., and Newman, E. J. "Failure of Dexedrine and Caffeine as Practical Antagonists of the Depressant Effect of Ethyl Alcohol in Man." *Quarterly Journal of Studies on Alcohol* 17 (1956):406–10.

Nowlis, Helen H. *Drugs on the College Campus.* Garden City, New York: Anchor Books, 1969.

Oates, Wayne E. *Alcohol In and Out of the Church.* Nashville: Broadman Press, 1966.

"Official Warning: Pregnant Women Shouldn't Drink." Cookeville, Tennessee, *The Herald-Citizen,* 19 July 1981, p. 9.

Orford, Jim; Walker, Seta; and Peto, Julian. "Drinking Behavior and Attitudes and Their Correlates Among University Students." *Quarterly Journal of Studies on Alcohol* 35 (December 1974):1316–74.

Overton, Frank. *Applied Physiology Including the Effects of Alcohol and Narcotics.* New York: American Book Co., n.d.

Pace, Nello. "Planning for Alcohol Education." *Proceedings of a Conference Jointly Sponsored by the Departments of Public Health, Education, and*

Mental Hygiene, Division of Alcohol Rehabilitation. Berkeley: Department of Public Health, 1960.

Packard, Vance. *The Status Seekers.* New York: David McKay Co., 1959.

"Parade." Nashville, *The Tennessean,* 11 October 1981, p. 7.

Parkhurst, John. *A Greek and English Lexicon of the New Testament.* London: William Baynes and Son, 1826.

"Patterns of College Drinking Linked to High School Habit." Memphis, *The Commercial Appeal,* 16 March 1978, p. 12.

Pattison, E. Mansell, and Kaufman, Edward. "Alcohol and Drug Dependence." In *Psychiatry in General Medical Practice.* Edited by Gene Usdin and Jerry M. Lewis. New York: McGraw-Hill Book Co., 1979.

Patton, William. *Bible Wines: The Laws of Fermentation and Wines of the Ancients.* New York: New York Temperance Association, 1874; reprint ed. Fort Worth: Star Bible and Tract Corporation, 1976.

Payne, Clifford. "Drinking: Can It Be Arrested?" *Firm Foundation* 78 (28 March 1961):196.

Plaut, T. F. A. *Alcohol Problems: A Report to the Nation By the Cooperative Commission on the Study of Alcoholism.* New York: Oxford University Press, 1967.

Pliny. *Natural History.* Translated by W. H. S. Jones. Loeb Classical Library. Cambridge: Harvard University Press, 1951.

Plumptre, E. H. *St. Matthew, St. Mark, and St. Luke.* A Bible Commentary for English Readers. Edited by Charles John Ellicott. New York: Cassell and Co., nd.

"Poison." In *Webster's New Collegiate Dictionary,* p. 888. Edited by Henry Bosley Woolf. Springfield, Mass.: G. and C. Merriam Co., 1973.

Poznanski, Andrew. "Our Drinking Heritage." *McGill Medical Journal* (1956):35–41.

Rachal, J. Valley; Williams, Jay R.; Brehm, Mary L.; Cavanaugh, Betty; Moore, R. Paul; and Eckerman, William C. *A National Study of Adolescent Drinking Behavior, Attitudes and Correlates.* Research Triangle Park, North Carolina: Research Triangle Institute, Center for the Study of Social Behavior, 1975.

Rackham, Richard Belward. *The Acts of the Apostles.* London: Methuen and Co., 1901.

Ramsey, William. "Vinum." In *Smith's Dictionary of Greek and Roman Antiquities,* pp. 1201–9. Edited by William Smith. London: Walton and Maberly, 1849.

Rich, A. B. "Do the Scriptures Prohibit the Use of Alcoholic Beverages?" *Bibliotheca Sacra* 37 (July 1880):401–18.

Ritchie, J. Murdoch. "The Aliphatic Alcohols." In *The Pharmacological Basis of Therapeutics*. Edited by Louis S. Goodman and Alfred Gilman. London: Collier-Macmillan, Limited, 1970.

Roberts, J. W. "What Kind of Element in the Cup on the Lord's Day, Fermented or Unfermented?" *Firm Foundation* 81 (18 August 1964):524, 532.

Robertson, Archibald Thomas. *Word Pictures of the New Testament*. 6 vols. Nashville: Broadman Press, 1932.

Robinson, Edward. *Greek and English Lexicon of the New Testament*. New York: Harper and Brothers, Publishers, 1877.

Rolston, Holmes, *Timothy and Titus*. Layman's Bible Commentary. vol. 23. Richmond: John Knox Press, 1963.

Room, R., and Roizen, R. *Drinking and Drug Practice Surveyor*. Berkeley, Calif.: n.p., 1973.

Ross, J. F. "Wine." In *Interpreter's Dictionary of the Bible,* 4:849–52. Edited by George Arthur Buttrick. New York: Abingdon Press, 1962.

Roueche, Berton. *Alcohol, Its History, Folklore, and Its Effect on the Human Body*. New York: Grove Press, Inc., 1960.

Russell, Emmet. "Wine." In *Zondervan Pictorial Bible Dictionary,* pp. 894–95. Edited by Merrill C. Tenney. Grand Rapids: Zondervan Publishing House, 1963.

Russell, Robert D. "Alcohol and Other Mood-Modifying Substances in Ecological Perspective: A Framework for Communicating and Educating." *Quarterly Journal of Studies on Alcohol* 35 (June 1974):606–19.

Sandmaier, Marian. *Alcohol and Your Unborn Baby*. Washington, D.C.: Government Printing Office, 1981.

Schilder, P. *Psychoanalysis, Man and Society*. New York: Norton, 1951. Schmidt, Wolfgang, and Smart, Reginald G. "Drinking-Driving Mortality and Morbidity Statistics." *Alcohol and Traffic Safety*. Washington, D.C.: Government Printing Office, 1963.

Second Special Report to the U.S. Congress on Alcohol and Health. By Morris E. Chafetz, Chairman. Washington, D.C.: Government Printing Office, 1974.

Seevers, M. H. "Psychopharmacological Elements of Drug Dependence." *Journal of American Medical Association* 206 (1968): 1263–66.

Seixas, F. A. "Alcohol and Its Drug Interactions." *Annual on Internal Medicine* 83 (1975):86–92.

Seneca. Epistle LXXXIII: On Drunkenness. Classics of the Alcohol Literature. *Quarterly Journal of Studies on Alcohol* 3 (1942):302–306.

Shore, T. Teignmouth. *The First Epistle to the Corinthians.* A Bible Commentary for English Readers. Edited by Charles John Ellicott. New York: Cassell and Co., n.d.

Shull, W. Russell, ed. *The Alcohol Problem Visualized.* Chicago: National Forum, Inc., 1950.

Sinacore, John S. *Health, a Quality of Life.* 2nd ed. New York: Macmillan Co., 1974.

Skidmore, Marguerite, and Brooks, Carolyne LaGrange. *Boys and Girls Learning about Alcohol.* Nashville: Abingdon-Cokesbury Press, n.d.

Small, Samuel W. *The White Angel of the World.* Philadelphia: Peerless Publishing Co., n.d.

Smiley, A.; Leblanc, A. E.; French, I. W.; and Burford, R. "The Combined Effects of Alcohol and Common Psychoactive Drugs. II. Field Studies with an Instrumented Automobile." In *Alcohol, Drugs, and Traffic Safety.* Edited by S. Israelstam and S. Lambert. Toronto: Addiction Research Foundation of Ontario, 1975.

Smith, David. "Vinegar." In *Dictionary of Christ and the Gospels,* 2:803. Edited by James Hastings. Grand Rapids: Baker Book House, 1973.

Smith, William. "Wine." In *A Dictionary of the Bible,* pp. 746–47. Edited by Francis Nathan and M. A. Peloubet. Chicago: John C. Winston Co., 1884.

Starling, Ernest Henry. *The Action of Alcohol on Man.* London: Longmans, Green and Co., n.d.

Straus, Robert, and Bacon, Seldon D. *Drinking in College.* New Haven, Conn.: Yale University Press, 1953; reprint ed., Westport, Conn.: Greenwood Press, 1971.

Strong, James. *Dictionary of the Greek New Testament.* np.: np., nd.

. Sulkunen, P. "Changes in the Consumption of Alcoholic Beverages in the 1960's." *Alkoholipolitiikka* 38 (1973):147–54.

———. "The Production and Consumption of Alcoholic Beverages." *Alkoholipolitiikka* 38 (1973):111–17.

Summers, Thomas Osmond. *Commentary on the Gospels.* vol. 1 Nashville: A. H. Redford, 1872.

Tatum, Sam Davis. *Words of Wisdom for Parents and Teenagers.* Nashville: n.p., 1965.

"Ten to Twelve Million Americans Said Alcoholics; Numbers Rising." Nashville, *The Tennessean,* 6 December 1979, n.p.

Thayer, Joseph Henry. *Greek-English Lexicon of the New Testament.* New York: American Book Co., 1889; reprint ed. Grand Rapids: Zondervan Publishing House, 1962.

"The Rising Number of Drinkers." *Washington Post,* 10 June 1974, p. B2.

Third Special Report to the U.S. Congress on Alcohol and Health. By Ernest P. Noble, ed. Washington, D.C.: Government Printing Office, 1978.

Thompson, Phil. "Social Drinking: Right or Wrong?" Term Paper, Presented to Professor Thomas Bratton Warren, Harding Graduate School of Religion, 1977.

Tilson, Everett. *Should Christians Drink?* New York: Abingdon Press, 1957.

"Tirosh." *Gospel Advocate* 31 (24 July 1889):472–73.

Todd, Frances. *Teaching about Alcohol.* New York: McGraw-Hill Book Co., 1964.

Toman, James E. P., and Davis, Jean P. "The Effects of Drugs upon the Electrical Activity of the Brain." *Pharmacological Review* 1 (1949):452–92.

Transeau, Emma L. Benedict. *Effects of Alcoholic Drinks.* Scientific Temperance Federation, 1938.

Trench, Richard Chenevix. *Notes on the Miracles of Our Lord.* 15th ed. London: Kegan Paul, Trench, Trubner and Co., 1895.

———. *Synonyms of the New Testament.* Grand Rapids: Associated Publishers and Authors, Inc. reprint ed. n.d.

Turner, George Allen. *The Gospel According to John.* Grand Rapids: Wm. B. Eerdmans Publishing Co., n.d.

Varro. *De Re Rustica.* Translated by William Davis Hooper. Loeb Classical Library. Cambridge: Harvard University Press, 1960.

Victor, Maurice, and Adams, Raymond D. "Alcohol." In *Harrison's Principles of Internal Medicine.* Edited by Maxwell M. Wintrobe et al. New York: McGraw-Hill Book Co., 1970.

Vine, William Edwyn, ed. *An Expository Dictionary of New Testament Words.* 4 vols, Old Tappan, New Jersey: Fleming H. Revell Co., 1940.

"Vines." In *A Dictionary of the Bible,* 2:31–34. Edited by James Hastings. Edinburgh: T. and T. Clark, 1889.

Weeks, Courtenay C. *Alcohol and Human Life.* 2nd ed. London: H. K. Lewis and Co., 1938.

Westcott, Brooke Foss, and Hort, Fenton John Anthony. *The New Testament in the Original Greek.* New York: Macmillan Co., 1949.

Weymouth, Richard Francis. *The Resultant Greek Testament.* London: James Clarke and Co., 1905.

Wiley, Harvey W. "Legislative Hearing." *Scientific Temperance Journal* 3 (May 1920):1–12.

Wiltenburg, W. J. "The Bible and the Attitudes of Ministers on Drinking." *Pastoral Psychology* 9 (April 1958):36–41.

Winchester, James H. "The Social Problem of Women Alcoholics." *Reader's Digest* 112 (March 1978):207–12.

"Wine." In *Cyclopaedia of Biblical, Theological, and Ecclesiastical Literature*, 10:1010–17. Edited by John McClintock and James Strong. New York: Harper and Brothers, Publishers, 1894.

"Wine." In *Fausset's Bible Dictionary*, pp. 722–23. Edited by Andrew Robert Faussett. Grand Rapids: Zondervan Publishing House, 1975.

"Wine." In *People's Bible Encyclopedia*, pp. 1176–77. By Charles Randall Barnes. New York: Eaton and Maine, 1900.

"Wine." In *The Oxford Universal Dictionary on Historical Principles*, p. 2433. 3rd ed. Edited by C. T. Onions. Oxford: Clarendon Press, 1944.

"Wine." In *Unger's Bible Dictionary*, pp. 1167–69. Edited by Merrill Frederick Unger. Chicago: Moody Press, 1957.

"Wine-bibber." In *The Winston Dictionary*, p. 1143. Philadelphia: John C. Winston Co., 1945.

Woods, Guy N. "Elders and Deacons in the Church." *Adult Gospel Quarterly* 83 (9 October 1977):27–32.

———. *Questions and Answers Open Forum Freed-Hardeman College Lectures*. Nashville: Williams Printing Co., 1976.

Young, Robert. *Analytical Concordance to the Bible*. New York: Funk and Wagnalls Co., n.d.

"Youth and Alcohol." In *Alcohol Topics in Brief* vol. 1. np.: National Institute on Alcohol Abuse and Alcoholism, nd.

Zirkle, G. A.; King, P. D.; McAtee, O. B.; and Van Dyke, R. "Effects of Chlorpromazine and Alcohol on Coordination and Judgment." *Journal of American Medical Association* 171 (1959):1496–99.

———. "Meprobamate and Small Amounts of Alcohol: Effects on Human Ability, Coordination, and Judgment." *Journal of American Medical Association* 173 (1960):1823–25.